CATHOLIC THEOLOGICAL FORM

General Editor: Kevin Zilverberg

The Catholic Theological Formation Series is sponsored by The Saint Paul Seminary School of Divinity, the graduate school of theological formation for Roman Catholic seminarians and laity enrolled at the University of Saint Thomas in Saint Paul, Minnesota. As a premier institution of theological formation for the region and beyond, The Saint Paul Seminary School of Divinity seeks to form men and women for the task of fulfilling the specific call God has for them, a call grounded in their common baptismal vocation to serve one another in Christ.

As an institution of the Archdiocese of Saint Paul and Minneapolis, the school is intentional in its commitment to priestly formation for the archdiocese and the broader region. As an institution of graduate theological education, the school prepares the laity for the equally compelling task of making Christ known and loved in the world. Though distinct in their various ministries, the common goal of intense theological formation is shared across the curriculum.

It is this challenge of theological formation—the challenge to faithfully inform one's understanding—that serves as the focus of this series, with special attention given to the task of preparing priests, teachers, and leaders within the Roman Catholic tradition. Although the series is academic in tenor, it aims beyond mere academics in its intellectual approach. We seek to promote a form of discourse that is professional in its conduct and spiritual in its outcomes, for theological formation is more than an exercise in academic technique. It is rather about the perfecting of a spiritual capacity: the capacity on the part of the human person to discern what is true and good.

This series, then, aims to develop the habits of mind required of a sound intellect—a spiritual aptitude for the truth of God's living Word and his Church. Most often, it will draw from the more traditional specializations of historical, systematic, moral, and biblical scholarship. Homiletics and pastoral ministry are anticipated venues as well. There will be occasions, however, when a theme is examined across disciplines and periods, for the purposes of bringing to our common consideration a thesis yet undeveloped.

Despite the variety of methodologies and topics explored, the series' aim remains constant: to provide a sustained reflection upon the mission and ministry of Catholic theological formation of both priests and laity alike.

The general editor of the Catholic Theological Formation Series, Fr. Kevin Zilverberg, serves as assistant professor of sacred Scripture and the founding director of Saint Paul Seminary Press at The Saint Paul Seminary School of Divinity.

The Revelation of Your Words

*The New Evangelization and the Role
of the Seminary Professor of Sacred Scripture*

Edited by

Kevin Zilverberg and Scott Carl

**SAINT PAUL
SEMINARY PRESS**

SAINT PAUL, MINNESOTA • 2021

Cover image by user Jorisvo on iStock (by Getty Images);
    taken in the cathedral of Brussels, Belgium; purchased
Cover design by Willem Mineur

Published 2021 by
Saint Paul Seminary Press
2260 Summit Ave., Saint Paul, Minnesota 55105

LC record available at https://lccn.loc.gov/2021931884

Catholic Theological Formation Series

ISSN 2765-9283
ISBN 978-1-953936-03-5 (paperback)
ISBN 978-1-953936-53-0 (e-book)

www.spspress.com

Contents

Abbreviations

ACCSOT	Ancient Commentary on Christian Scripture, Old Testament
ACW	Ancient Christian Writers
AMar	Anecdota Maredsolana
AnBib	Analecta Biblica
AncB	Anchor Bible
BTCB	Brazos Theological Commentary on the Bible
BJSt	Brown Judaic Studies
BZAW	Beihefte zur Zeitschrift für die alttestamentliche Wissenschaft
CCSSc	Catholic Commentary on Sacred Scripture
CTFS	Catholic Theological Formation Series
CCC	*Catechism of the Catholic Church*
CWS	Classics of Western Spirituality
DS	*Enchiridion symbolorum*, ed. Heinrich Denzinger and Adolf Schönmetzer
DCLS	Deuterocanonical and Cognate Literature Studies
ECF	Early Church Fathers
FaCh	Fathers of the Church
IBT	Interpreting Biblical Texts
ICC	International Critical Commentary
NAB	New American Bible
NABRE	New American Bible, revised edition
NCoBC	The New Collegeville Bible Commentary
NRSV	New Revised Standard Version
OTL	Old Testament Library
PCNT	Paideia Commentaries on the New Testament
PL	Patrologia Latina
RSVCE	Revised Standard Version, Catholic edition
RSV2CE	Revised Standard Version, 2nd Catholic edition
SaPaSe	Sacra Pagina Series
SBEC	Studies in the Bible and Early Christianity
THOT	Two Horizons Old Testament Commentary
USCCB	United States Conference of Catholic Bishops
WBC	Word Biblical Commentary
WOSA	Works of Saint Augustine
WUNT	Wissenschaftliche Untersuchungen zum Neuen Testament

Introduction

The student of sacred Scripture can prayerfully proclaim, "The revelation of your words sheds light, gives understanding to the simple" (Ps 119:130 NABRE). God's written word does not reveal itself; it awaits the attentive reader, docile to the promptings of the Holy Spirit. The sacred page then comes to life and from mere words becomes "revelation" for the reader as it sheds light and gives understanding.

Some students seek a deeper encounter with God's written word, a deeper experience of revelation. Candidates for ministry surely must experience this deep encounter before going forth to preach. Here enters the professor of sacred Scripture, who accompanies the student seeking the revelation of God's written word. This is no small task: a seminary charges its Scripture professors to impart knowledge about the Bible and to foster a love of it. The first aspect of this twofold mandate can be quantified through ordinary classroom examination. The second aspect, however, eludes quantification. The professor of the Bible can foster a love of it by his or her enthusiasm in and out of the classroom, by speaking reverently about the truths of the faith, and by helping the students understand the necessity of serious biblical study for authentic preaching and mission. Perhaps most of all, the professor's living witness according to the biblical message draws students to fall more in love with the Bible. Nevertheless, the professor cannot force the student into that deep encounter with the written word. Once the professor has facilitated the encounter, he or she must trust that the Holy Spirit can accomplish the rest in due time.

This collection of essays treats the role of the seminary professor of sacred Scripture within the context of the New Evangelization. Some of them concern principally the imparting of knowledge and best practices to accomplish this; others concern the fostering of delight in the sacred page and spiritual encounter with God. Although these essays are Catholic, written within a Catholic theological framework and with Catholic seminaries in mind, many of their insights can be transferred to non-Catholic seminary environments. I hope that, even beyond the seminary, teachers of the Bible will benefit from this book, regardless of their denomination and level of instruction.

Although the term "New Evangelization" has much to do with evangelization in general, it properly pertains to the heirs of Christian lands and cultures where belief and religious practice have given way to secularization. This situation has challenged the Church to develop new ways to call people to belief, since many of the baptized do not pass on the faith to the next generation. Readers unfamiliar with the term "New Evangelization" may wish to read the first section of Peter S. Williamson's essay in the present volume.[1] Each chapter of this book concerns the New Evangelization, whether directly or indirectly. If this collection of essays helps professors and teachers of sacred Scripture to contribute more fruitfully to evangelization, it will have succeeded.

The two parts of this book correspond to two conferences sponsored by the Msgr. Jerome D. Quinn Institute for Biblical Studies, at the Saint Paul Seminary (University of Saint Thomas in Saint Paul, Minnesota). The appendix, though not presented at a Quinn conference, was composed by a scholar present at both conferences. Fr. Scott Carl directed the institute until I took over in the summer of 2019, and he oversaw these conferences, the first in 2013 and the second in 2015.[2] He invited the conference presenters and, from their written submissions, selected those essays fit for publication in this book. As the initial editor for this book, he contacted some of the authors to request revisions. However, because of his increased administrative duties at the seminary, Carl was unable to bring this project to completion.

When I was named director of the institute, Carl entrusted me with the completion of this work. I reviewed all of the essays and requested revisions from the authors. Although these essays have not been subjected to double-blind

---

1. See the subheading "The Urgency of the New Evangelization," in "Implications of the New Evangelization for Priestly Ministry and for Teaching Scripture to Seminarians," 11–15.

2. He also edited select essays from the first two conferences, held in 2009 and 2011: Scott Carl, ed., *Verbum Domini and the Complementarity of Exegesis and Theology*, CTFS (Grand Rapids, MI: Eerdmans, 2015).

peer reviews, it is fair to say that they have undergone a quality-control process. We hope that our colleagues would agree that they surpass the threshold for scholarly publication. Future Quinn conference essays will be peer reviewed before publication; this has already been done for those presented in 2017.

Part One of this book corresponds to a conference held on June 12–14, 2013: "The New Evangelization for the Transmission of the Catholic Faith: The Role of the Seminary Professor of Sacred Scripture."

Williamson begins this first half of the present volume with "Implications of the New Evangelization for Priestly Ministry and for Teaching Scripture to Seminarians." In it, he draws attention to the urgency for the New Evangelization in the face of secularization and abandonment of the Catholic Church, especially by the young. Although he provides a biblical context for evangelization by priests, he helpfully situates the proclamation of the written word of God within the broader evangelical enterprise. For example, in his section on implications of the New Evangelization for priestly ministry, Williamson not only challenges the clergy to prioritize the ministry of the word but also calls them to move beyond mere maintenance of the parochial status quo and to nourish the sort of priestly fraternity that will help to sustain them over a lifetime. Finally, he devotes considerable attention to implications of the New Evangelization for teaching Scripture to seminarians. Here the professor, lay or ordained, must lead by example, appropriating the biblical message into his or her own life. Effective seminary teaching requires much more than a graduate degree in biblical studies could ever certify, and it requires a markedly different approach to the biblical text than that taken by a graduate-school professor training his students to carry out research. For seminarians, it is essential to develop a personal relationship with Scripture, learning to be attentive to charisms of the Holy Spirit. Our future priests need to be convinced of the inspiration and truth of Scripture, have an integrated command of the whole of salvation history related in Scripture, and have an ability to articulate the *kerygma* for leading others to be intentional disciples. Moreover, it is crucial to teach seminarians about controversial aspects and themes of Scripture such as the "dark" passages, sexuality, and Christology. Williamson draws on his own experience to recommend helpful literature treating these issues. Seminary scriptural formation for the sake of the New Evangelization should also involve a deep study and engagement of the figure of St. Paul as an example of virtue and pastoral zeal for future priests.

In "Stand and Deliver: Scripture and the Role of the Seminary Professor in Forming Priests for the New Evangelization," Steven C. Smith examines the role of the seminary professor in preparing future priests for the New

Evangelization. In the first half of his essay he asks open-ended questions of Scripture professors, concerning the priority that they give to the New Evangelization in the classroom. He recognizes that they already feel pressure to cover a vast amount of material in the classroom, so the mandate to prepare students for the New Evangelization may be experienced as a burdensome additional requirement. Nevertheless, he challenges the professor to adapt to this priority. Smith then devotes the second half of the essay to three practical suggestions for doing so, taking inspiration from three common NT words in Greek. He calls on professors to lead seminarians to give witness (*martureo*) to their faith, especially in their field assignments. The professors can teach seminarians to proclaim (*kerusso*) the Good News, especially in biblically grounded homilies. This chapter culminates with a call to initiate seminarians in apologetics (*apologia*), for which the author proposes a classroom exercise. The activity, known as "Stand and Deliver," features both written preparatory work on a biblical question, along with a set of pastoral guidelines in order to yield a clear, balanced and attractive response to that question in the course of a real conversation.

Michael Magee builds upon advances in Johannine studies of recent decades in "Looking but Not Always Seeing: The Relevance of Johannine Irony to the New Evangelization." In particular, he traces the growing scholarly appreciation for the Fourth Gospel's rich use of irony, a technique that today's readers can learn to appreciate much in the same way as early readers would have done. Magee shows how this literary aspect of the Gospel can be harnessed for the New Evangelization addressed to a post-Christian society, especially those who possess a superficial knowledge of Jesus and his teachings; superficial knowledge conceals him and impedes the revelation of who he really is. John's irony consists in a higher perspective that the Evangelist shares with his readers, enabling them (1) to see beyond the surface to the deeper truths being conveyed, (2) to recognize the short-sightedness and prejudiced judgments of the characters, and (3) to take delight in their own sense of belonging to the community of those who see Jesus as he truly is. The modern addressee of the New Evangelization is invited to a similar privilege and a similar voyage of discovery.

Stephen Ryan, OP, argues that Old Testament Wisdom literature can be taught in seminary contexts in such a way as to demonstrate its relevance to the New Evangelization, in "Old Testament Wisdom literature and Formation for a New Evangelization." These books teach us in attractive and accessible ways, a pedagogy to be imitated by professors and priests. Ryan expands upon Williamson's insights from the previous Quinn Institute volume concerning the cultivation of a love for and knowledge of Scripture in the seminary.[3] He applies particular verses to the preparation of preachers and confessors, and advocates an approach that draws out theological implications of the texts within the broad Catholic theological tradition. Finally, Ryan connects teaching on friendship within the Wisdom literature to the New Evangelization: this teaching is relevant to all, for we are called to the blessed life of friendship with God.

Juana L. Manzo presents a pedagogical strategy to teach the theme of the hardening of pharaoh's heart (Exod 4–14) in "Free Will and the Hardening of Pharaoh's Heart: Integrating Modern and Ancient Interpretations into the Seminary Classroom." She anticipates her students' struggles to reconcile God's hardening of Pharaoh's heart with their prior theological commitment to the endowment of all human beings with free will. Her pedagogical strategy is based on the interpretations of one modern scholar, Brevard Childs, and two church Fathers, Gregory of Nyssa and Augustine of Hippo. Childs studies the variance of linguistic sources, and the stages of literary composition, to interpret the motif of the hardening within the function of divine signs, whose purpose is to reveal God's knowledge and judgment. For Gregory of Nyssa, free will is an essential anthropological element for the understanding of the motif of the hardening of Pharaoh's heart. Augustine attributes the hardening of the heart to the monarch's refusal to accept God's grace. By exposing students to ancient and modern attempts to reconcile the tension between God's hardening of heart and Pharaoh's free will, Manzo teaches her students to seek the aid of interpreters both ancient and modern to work through a difficult passage.

Part Two of this book corresponds to a conference held June 10–12, 2015: "The Joy of the Gospel, the New Evangelization, and the Role of the Seminary Professor of Sacred Scripture." The presenters looked to Pope Francis's Apostolic Exhortation *Evangelii gaudium*[4] for inspiration.

Kelly Anderson proposes a model of biblical fatherhood in "The Father of Proverbs 1–9: A Spiritual Father for Seminary Professors." The father of Proverbs 1–9 has so thoroughly assimilated wisdom, beginning with the Decalogue, into his existence, that as he teaches it he gives of his very being. In doing so he imitates God the Father, who gives his substance to his Son from all eternity. The father of Proverbs also imitates the Father by "creating" through his life-giving words. Moreover, the father of Proverbs models a teaching method both gentle and strong. The father attends especially to his son's desires, guiding him toward lasting fulfillment. He presents difficult moral truths to his son

---

3. P. 66.

4. *Evangelii gaudium* (November 24, 2013) (Washington, DC: USCCB, 2013).

in a non-confrontational way, so that the son can more readily accept them. Even so, he does not spare the son the truth about the deadly wages of sin. Anderson goes on to describe how she has observed a colleague exemplify fatherly virtues in a seminary setting. Indeed, it is possible to imitate the father of Proverbs 1–9, taking him as a biblical model of paternal virtue for the particular vocation of seminary professor.

Carl proposes principles for a spiritual reading of Scripture that builds upon the literal sense of the text, in his essay "Honey in the Comb: Toward a Spiritual Reading of Sacred Scripture in the Twenty-First Century." He first draws attention to the need for the spiritual reading of sacred Scripture by quoting key magisterial passages and the works of certain theologians. Carl then lays down the principles for "extracting the honey," that is for drawing from a biblical text a spiritual meaning that delights and nourishes the soul. First of all, the Old Testament must be read in light of Jesus Christ. The rule of faith sets interpretive boundaries and opens interpretive horizons for the one who recognizes the same divine author for all of Scripture. Furthermore, given the analogy of faith, the biblical interpreter reads diverse biblical texts in light of one another and finds in certain passages a "fuller sense" not directly intended by the human author. The interpreter cannot expect to understand the Scriptures and extract their honey without living in accord with them; his conduct affects his interpretation. Finally, Carl demonstrates the application of his principles, in a two-step process, to Psalm 87: First he summarizes a historical/literary commentary of Gianni Barbiero, and then he points out scriptural parallels and suggests ways to read the psalm in light of the Paschal Mystery and the new life that comes from it.

Magee contributed a second essay to this volume: "'We have found him!': The Joy of Discovery in the Fourth Gospel." He examines a selection of passages from the Gospel of John in which the words and gestures of a given witness are indicative not only of his or her dawning awareness of Jesus's identity but of the palpable joy of discovery. Magee proposes a careful analysis of details, including (1) the immediate context of the biblical passage, (2) the demonstrative words employed, (3) the specific doubts being overcome and hopes being fulfilled, (4) the exhilaration of coming to know and of being known, and (5) the bodily gestures bespeaking interior transformation of the persons involved. The careful analysis of these details allows insights into the way in which the reader or hearer of the Gospel message is privileged to experience, together with the Gospel characters, the joy of discovering Jesus. At the same time, the reader or hearer is being offered the opportunity to become Jesus's witness, so that others may come to know the same joy.

The final chapter of Part Two, "The Exegete as Seminary Formator," constitutes James Keating's response to the other essays. He builds upon them and highlights key points from them that support his own vision of a sustained, fruitful encounter with sacred Scripture in the seminary. To be reasonable, he argues, is to allow oneself to be affected by the supernatural, which has profound implications for the seminary Scripture professor. By letting his or her prayer and spirituality impact his discipline, the Scripture scholar does not enter the "undisciplined" world of affect, image, and poetry, but rather is brought into a sharper clarity about the need for intellectual distinctions, sound logic, and deliberate and critical thought.

Keating writes, "We have chased prayer out of Scripture study in the name of objectivity, but I truly believe that it is in the service of fear."[5] Although some secular biblical scholars may consider exegesis done in the seminary's milieu of faith and prayer to be substandard, the opposite is true: the seminary is the freest academic space on earth since it welcomes Truth at the source. This does not mean that the seminary is a place where critical reading is dispensed with in order simply to deepen devotion. Rather, the seminary is Scripture's home, the place where critical reasoning comes to its fullest powers in a matrix of one's own and the Church's loving response to the Paschal Mystery of Christ.

After Part Two, this book concludes with an appendix by André Villeneuve: "On the Importance of Biblical Hebrew in Catholic Seminaries and Academic Institutions." Under ten headings, Villeneuve makes the case for Catholic students to learn Biblical Hebrew. He begins by surveying pertinent church teaching and goes on to highlight Hebrew's status as a holy language, being the one in which most of the Bible was composed. Learning Hebrew helps us bridge the enormous cultural gap between ourselves and the ancient hagiographs. Indeed, it is essential in order to interpret the Old Testament well. If that were not enough, knowledge of Hebrew contributes significantly to the proper understanding of Jesus and the New Testament. Moreover, it leads to a better understanding of the Psalms, which are so prominent in the liturgical prayer of the Church.

The final four sections of Villeneuve's essay describe expected benefits that may be less obvious than the ones just outlined. He explains the great impoverishment caused by the Church's distancing itself from its Jewish roots, and the great advantage of reversing course. The student of Biblical Hebrew can participate in the revived language, Modern Hebrew, with relative ease; he or she gains access to "the rich world of modern Israeli literature, scholarship, arts, and

5. P. 151.

culture."[6] Indeed, the Catholic who learns Hebrew can participate in Hebrew Catholicism, part of a larger Christian movement to (re-)connect to our Jewish roots. Finally, Villeneuve urges readers to take part in the Hebrew "Renaissance," which many of our evangelical brothers and sisters have embraced. Catholics, he argues, need not lag behind. Moreover, "Hebraiophilia" can both revitalize the Church and help it to reject a newly resurgent anti-Semitism.

These ten contributions provide ample material for reflection on the role of the seminary professor of sacred Scripture, in the context of the New Evangelization. If they make their desired impact in the seminary classroom, they will help professors to make God's written word become revelation for students. These future ministers will in turn be able take the psalmist's words as their own, as they profess to the divine author of Scripture, "The revelation of your words sheds light, gives understanding to the simple" (Ps 119:130 NABRE).

I would like to thank people who have contributed to this volume in various ways. Fr. Scott Carl and I thank the benefactors of the Monsignor Jerome D. Quinn Institute for Biblical Studies, which has underwritten the conferences and book production. This institute has recently been renamed as an endowment, while keeping the same purpose as before. The Quinn Endowment will continue to fund Quinn biblical conferences under the auspices of The Saint Paul Seminary's Institute for Catholic Theological Formation. I also thank my editing and production team for their work: Dawn Eden Goldstein, copy editor; David McEachron, proofreader; Erika Zabinski, indexer; and Judy Gilats, typesetter. Your skills and diligence are appreciated.

FR. KEVIN ZILVERBERG
February 22, 2020

---

6. P. 187.

PART ONE

Implications of the New Evangelization for Priestly Ministry and for Teaching Scripture to Seminarians

Peter S. Williamson

The Urgency of the New Evangelization

Origins

Although the New Evangelization has its roots in Vatican II's aim to proclaim the gospel to the modern world, and in Paul VI's *Evangelii nuntiandi*, it really began in 1983, when Pope John Paul II started calling for a "new evangelization," new not in content, but in ardor, methods, and expression.[1] His intention became clearer in *Redemptoris missio* (1990):

> I sense that the moment has come to commit all of the Church's energies to a new evangelization and to the mission *ad gentes*. No believer in Christ, no institution of the Church can avoid this supreme duty: to proclaim Christ to all peoples.[2]

That encyclical made some helpful distinctions, which Ralph Martin summarizes:

> [Pope John Paul II] distinguished "primary evangelization" directed toward those who have never heard the Gospel before, "pastoral care" directed toward those who were living as believers, and "new evangelization or re-evangelization" directed toward those from traditionally Christian

---

1. Pope John Paul II, "March 9, [1983]: At the 'CELAM' Meeting in Port-au-Prince Cathedral," *L'Osservatore Romano*, April 18, 1983, p. 9.

2. Pope John Paul II, *Redemptoris missio* (December 7, 1990) (Washington, DC: United States Catholic Conference, n.d.), §3.

cultures or backgrounds "where entire groups of the baptized have lost a living sense of the faith, or even no longer consider themselves members of the Church, and live a life far removed from Christ and his Gospel" (*RM*, §33).[3]

Thus, the New Evangelization arises both from a renewal of the Church's mission to evangelize and as a pastoral response to a serious challenge to Christian faith, namely the problem of secularization.

Saint John Paul states the unvarnished facts in *Novo millennio ineunte* (2001): "Even in countries evangelized many centuries ago, the reality of a 'Christian society' which . . . measured itself explicitly on Gospel values, is now gone."[4] The remedy that the pope proposes bears a direct relationship to sacred Scripture: "to nourish ourselves with the Word in order to be 'servants of the Word' in the work of evangelization."[5]

Subsequent Developments

Since the pope wrote these words at the turn of the millennium, the situation in Western society has deteriorated. Because society's secularization has been gradual, it has been easy for Catholics to grow accustomed to it and to fail to respond decisively, like the proverbial frog in a pot that never jumps as the water is gradually brought to a boil. The situation has reached a tipping point in North America, whereas in Europe it appears to have gone past the point of no return.

Indications of the secularization of American society are not hard to find. The general acceptance of sex before marriage and of homosexual acts, along with the dramatic change in attitudes toward gay marriage (especially among young people) are perhaps the most obvious signs. But it is not just about sex: the prevailing attitudes in society toward authority, religion, violence, alcohol, drugs, and money are equally contrary to the teaching of Christ and his Church on these topics.

Sobering statistics reveal the losses among American Catholics. "Only 30 percent of Americans who were raised Catholic are still 'practicing,'"

---

3. Ralph Martin, *The Urgency of the New Evangelization: Answering the Call* (Huntington, IN: Our Sunday Visitor, 2013), 14.

4. Pope John Paul II, *Novo millennio ineunte* (January 6, 2001) (Boston: Pauline Books and Media, 2001), §40.

5. Pope John Paul II, *Novo millennio ineunte*, §40. Pope Benedict proposes the same remedy in his proclamation of 2012–2013 as "the year of faith": "We cannot accept that salt should become tasteless or the light be kept hidden (cf. Mt 5:13–16). . . . We must *rediscover a taste for feeding ourselves on the word of God*, faithfully handed down by the Church." Pope Benedict XVI, *Porta fidei* (October 11, 2011), www.vatican.va/content/benedict-xvi/en/motu _proprio/documents/hf_ben-xvi_motu-proprio_20111011_porta-fidei.html, §3, emphasis added.

generously defined as attending Mass at least once a month.[6] Nearly four times as many adults have left the Church in the United States as have entered. Comparative statistics between 2000 and 2010 in a typical large midwestern diocese show a decrease of 40–50 percent in the number of baptisms, Catholic marriages, and people being received into the Church. These trends are clearly unsustainable.[7] Significantly, those who are leaving the Catholic Church are young people. More than 70 percent of those who have left have done so by the age of twenty-three.[8]

The Church's losses in Europe and Canada are greater and the dechristianization of society is more advanced. The same processes are underway in Latin America, although secularization there is slowed by the growth of evangelical Protestantism. Meanwhile, the attitude of these post-Christian societies has become increasingly unfriendly toward the Church and especially toward her moral teaching on sexuality and human life. No one knows where this wind will take us, but it does not look positive, at least in the short run. Speaking in 2010 of the changing attitudes in society, Cardinal Francis George famously said, "I expect to die in bed, my successor will die in prison and his successor will die a martyr in the public square."[9]

What is going on? The West is witnessing a large-scale falling away from Christian faith that, in its scale and rapidity, is historically unprecedented. When before, except in response to coercion, have so many in predominantly Christian societies turned away from Christian faith and practice? Without jumping to apocalyptic conclusions, it is possible to see that our historical period is not unlike the period of apostasy and of loss of faith foretold by our Lord and the Apostle Paul (Luke 18:8; 2 Thess 2:3; 2 Tim 3:1–5). Seen in this light, the New Evangelization is not simply a pastoral program of renewal that merits our support. It is the Church's response to a grave threat to the salvation of the human race and her members.

6. Sherry Weddell, *Forming Intentional Disciples: The Path to Knowing and Following Jesus* (Huntington, IN: Our Sunday Visitor, 2012), 24–26. The first chapter of Weddell's book is full of illuminating statistics and analysis.

7. For the statistics and for more evidence about the losses among Catholic youth, see Ralph Martin, *The Urgency of the New Evangelization* (Huntington, IN: Our Sunday Visitor, 2013), 16–18.

8. Weddell, *Forming Intentional Disciples*, 33–34.

9. Cardinal Francis George, quoted in Tim Drake, "Cardinal George: The Myth and Reality of 'I'll Die in My Bed,'" *National Catholic Register Blogs*, April 17, 2015, www.ncregister.com /blog/tim-drake/the-myth-and-the-reality-of-ill-die-in-my-bed.

Signs of Hope

The challenges are serious enough that if our hope were grounded in human solutions and prospects, we would be a rather dispirited group. But our hope is in a God who raises the dead (2 Cor 1:9)! Although the situation is serious and requires an intelligent and vigorous pastoral and spiritual response, there are encouraging indications that the Holy Spirit has been at work "below the radar" to prepare the Church for this difficult period.

Few doubt that the Holy Spirit inspired Pope John XXIII to convene the Second Vatican Council, or that the Church has been blessed since then by a string of extraordinary popes, each of whom has made a distinctive contribution to equipping the Church for this hour. The post-conciliar period has also been a very fruitful time for the blossoming of ecclesial movements among the laity, as well as new religious communities and associations of apostolic life. These have brought a fresh impulse to evangelization, as well as new methods and ways of engaging the culture.

Under the long tenure, able leadership, and steady hand of Pope St. John Paul II, a new clarity of doctrine as well as a greater unity in the college of bishops has emerged. The *Catechism of the Catholic Church* was a signal achievement in this regard, especially in the wake of the doctrinal confusion that followed the Council. As a consequence, over the last twenty years there has been a steady improvement in many seminary programs, manifest in doctrinal faithfulness and unity of spirit among faculty members. My observation is that there has also been an improvement in the quality of seminarians, undoubtedly due both to improved criteria and discernment in admissions,[10] and to the Holy Spirit calling some fine men.

Among the Catholic faithful there has been a resurgence of healthy fervor, whether focused on rediscovery of the Bible, Eucharistic devotion, Catholic apologetics, Catholic radio and television, prolife activity, jail, prison and hospital ministry, Catholic action in the political arena, contemplative prayer, or new devotions, such as the Divine Mercy. Among a core of Catholic youth and young adults, there is also positive ferment linked to the foci mentioned above as well as to the theology of the body and evangelization. So far, these developments affect only a small minority, but there is vitality and growth among

---

10. In that regard, implementation of the Congregation of Catholic Education's "Criteria for the Discernment of Vocations with regard to Persons with Homosexual Tendencies" (2005) seems to have improved both the quality of candidates and the tone of seminary life.

those involved. George Weigel has given a name to some of these positive developments, speaking of "evangelical Catholicism."[11]

Implications of the New Evangelization for Priestly Ministry

As I reflect on the New Evangelization against the backdrop of an aggressively secular culture, three implications for priestly ministry stand out: the importance of the ministry of the Word; the need to emphasize mission over maintenance; and the urgency of strengthening mutual support among priests.

Priority of the Ministry of the Word

Pope Benedict XVI underscores the importance of the ministry of the word in *Verbum Domini*, recalling St. John Paul's teaching in *Pastores dabo vobis*: "The priest is first of all a *minister of the word of God*."[12] Why do both popes speak first of the priest's ministry of the Word before speaking of the priest's sacramental ministry? Because to be effective, sacraments depend on faith, and "faith comes from what is heard, and what is heard comes by the preaching of Christ" (Rom 10:17 RSV). The Word of God is the *seed* of the divine life that the sacraments are intended to nourish. Thus, in many of Jesus' parables about the kingdom of God, the seed that mysteriously grows and produces fruit is the word of God. Peter teaches that Christian life itself springs from this source: "you have been born again, not of perishable seed but of imperishable, through the living and abiding word of God" (1 Pet 1:23), and Paul speaks of "the word of the truth, the gospel which has come to you, as indeed in the whole world it is bearing fruit and growing" (Col 1:5–6).

Not only does the Word of God fulfill an essential role at the outset of Christian life, the word remains key to enabling the Christian people to attain their goal. Addressing bishops in *Verbum Domini*, Pope Benedict recalls the words of St. Paul to the elders of Ephesus: "Every Bishop must commend himself and feel himself commended 'to the Lord and to the word of his grace, which is able to build up and to give the inheritance among all those who are sanctified' (Acts 20:32)."[13] According to the Apostle there is a power resident in the gospel, "the word of his grace," that not only initiates life in Christ, but

---

11. George Weigel, *Evangelical Catholicism: Deep Reform in the 21st-Century Church* (New York: Basic, 2013).

12. Pope Benedict XVI, *Verbum Domini* (September 30, 2010) (Boston: Pauline Books and Media, 2010), §80, quoting Pope John Paul II, *Pastores dabo vobis* (March 25, 1992) (Boston: Saint Paul Books and Media, 1992), §26, emphasis in the original.

13. Pope Benedict XVI, *Verbum Domini*, §79.

"builds up" and is capable of bestowing an eternal inheritance on those sanctified by faith and baptism (Acts 20:32).

Returning to Pope Benedict's words about priesthood, "the priest is first of all a minister of the word of God, *consecrated and sent to announce the Good News* of the Kingdom to all, calling every person to the obedience of faith and leading believers to an ever increasing knowledge of and communion in the mystery of God."[14] The priest is set apart for a sacred task and sent to convey an invitation and knowledge of God's mystery. The vocation and identity of the priest is missionary and apostolic.

The priority of the ministry of the word has implications for the spirituality of the priest, beginning with seminary formation. "Those aspiring to the ministerial priesthood are called to a profound personal relationship with God's word, particularly in *lectio divina*, so that this relationship will in turn nurture their vocation."[15]

What Benedict means is that the seminarian's personal relationship to Christ is mediated in an important way through sacred Scripture. In his human nature, Jesus grew in intimacy with the Father and understanding of his vocation through reading and reflecting on the Torah and the Prophets (Luke 2:42–52; 4:16–21); the seminarian follows this pattern.

Speaking of the priest's relationship with Scripture, Benedict writes:

> Knowledge of its linguistic and exegetical aspects, though certainly necessary, is not enough. He needs to approach the word with a docile and prayerful heart so that it may deeply penetrate his thoughts and feelings and bring about a new outlook in him—'the mind of Christ' (1 Cor 2:16).[16]

In other words, the priest's way of looking at the world is shaped by his relationship with sacred Scripture. The pontiff adds, "Only if he 'abides' in the word will the priest become a perfect disciple of the Lord. Only then will he know the truth and be set truly free."[17]

The priority of the ministry of the word in the life of a priest has practical implications: "For this reason the priest himself ought first of all to develop a great personal *familiarity* with the word of God."[18] The way this familiarity is acquired is through regular prayerful reading, meditation, and study of

---

14. Pope Benedict XVI, *Verbum Domini*, §80, emphasis added.
15. Pope Benedict XVI, *Verbum Domini*, §82.
16. Pope Benedict XVI, *Verbum Domini*, §80.
17. Pope Benedict XVI, *Verbum Domini*, §80.
18. Pope Benedict XVI, *Verbum Domini*, §80, emphasis added.

Scripture.[19] My experience teaching Scripture to seminarians has demonstrated that the daily reading of the Lectionary and Liturgy of Hours alone does not lead to familiarity with the biblical books, since the selections are not read in their contexts.[20] Only a repeated *lectio continua* brings about the kind of familiarity that enables a pastoral minister to be fluent in preaching, teaching, or counseling from sacred Scripture.[21]

An Orientation to Mission Over Maintenance

The second implication of the New Evangelization for the priesthood is ministry that is vigorously oriented to mission and advancing the kingdom, rather than simply providing pastoral care to those who already come to church.

It must be acknowledged that after twenty centuries of Christianity, the culture and habits of the Church today are largely directed toward maintenance rather than mission, toward ministering to those inside the Church rather than seeking those outside it.[22] Especially when the Church is facing external pressures, the temptation is to circle the wagons and adopt a preservation model of ministry. However, the New Evangelization of recent popes summons the Church to take an opposite approach, to proclaim the gospel with new ardor, methods, and expression. Very often the best defense is a good offense.

Many of the fine young men coming forward to discern a priestly vocation come with a vision of priestly ministry suited to a more tranquil time. Once upon a time the role of the priest was to celebrate the sacraments, give homilies on Sundays, preside over an appreciative parish, and perhaps oversee a Catholic school. If they did those things well, they could count on a flourishing

19. Paragraphs 72–87 are particularly strong on the centrality of Scripture to ministry and on these three basic means of drawing nourishment from it.

20. Each year I begin my graduate Pauline Literature class with a pretest to ascertain my students' familiarity with Paul's letters. The pretest consists of sixteen well-known quotations or topics and the titles of the letters attributed to Paul, asking the students to indicate in which letter or letters the topic or quote is found. Taking a very generous view of what constitutes a correct answer, the seminarians have scored on average between 2.6 and 4.3 out of 16. These are bright, highly motivated second-year theologians who have completed college seminary or two years of pre-theology, during which they attended Mass and prayed the Office daily.

21. In the early 1990s Cardinal Ratzinger proposed a pattern of *lectio continua* that could help seminarians acquire the familiarity with the Bible that they will need. He recommended reading through the New Testament once every year and through the Old Testament once every two years. Practically speaking, this works out to about a chapter a day of the New Testament and about a chapter and a half of the Old Testament.

22. See Robert S. Rivers, *From Maintenance to Mission: Evangelization and the Revitalization of the Parish* (New York: Paulist, 2005).

parish and the esteem of the community. But times have changed. Today's seminarians must be prepared not just to provide sacraments and catechize but to evangelize, to find bold and creative ways of reaching out to the unchurched in their parish boundaries. Within the parish they also need to evangelize, to lead adults and children to conversion, to a personal relationship with Jesus Christ. If Catholics who attend Church are to withstand the winds of secularization, their priests will need to lead them further, to become intentional disciples,[23] centering their lives around the Lordship of Jesus Christ on a path to Christian maturity.

Today priests need to develop strategies to evangelize and form youth and young adults, and to help young families pass on the faith to their children. Rather than attempting to do all this ministry themselves, they need to see their role as equipping the people of God for ministry (Eph 4:11–12). They need to promote a variety of expressions of community life in the parish as a means of social support that will sustain Catholics who live in a culture that is often hostile to their values. They need to gather, lead, and encourage a Christian community that may face societal disapproval for its "intolerant" beliefs and mores. They need to be able to speak intelligently and clearly regarding the erroneous ideas circulating in the culture and often in the Church.

The kind of pastoral-evangelistic savvy that I have been describing is not something seminarians can learn in a classroom alone. Pastoral formation has to change to provide more front-line experience in these various aspects of ministry, as well as personal mentoring (discipling) by pastors who excel in these missionary skills.

A Priority on Mutual Support among Priests

As a married layman, I hesitate to speak about the needs of celibate priests. Nevertheless, it seems to me that the New Evangelization requires significant changes to strengthen the mutual support among diocesan priests. Three recent experiences confirm for me this impression. First, a bishop friend told me how much time and effort he and other bishops spend attending to priests in crisis and cleaning up the pastoral problems in parishes that result. Second, a foreign priest studying in the United States confided his disappointment at the discovery that the priests with whom he found lodging share no regular meals or prayers in common. Although they are good men, their lifestyle is completely individualistic and dominated by their work. Finally, a few months ago a fervent thirteen-year-old about to be confirmed told me he aspires to be a permanent

---

23. See Weddell, *Forming Intentional Disciples*, 64–67.

deacon, but not a priest. I asked if that was because he wants to be married. Not at all, he said. "I just don't want to be alone. I prefer living with people."

Our aggressively secular culture makes it difficult for priests to survive, but we need them to thrive if they are to fulfill the challenging mission of the New Evangelization. The number of diocesan priests who have major personal and spiritual crises that cause them to drop out of regular ministry is too high, perhaps at an unsustainable level. When God said, "It is not good for man to be alone," the comment applies also to celibate priests. Jesus sent out his disciples two-by-two, and the Church is not wiser than her Lord. Of course, it is not enough for two priests to inhabit the same rectory—they must have a brotherly relationship and a commitment to mutual support and to basic elements of life together.

Priests can derive a lot of support from relationships with staff, deacons, and mature lay parishioners. However, an essential element of the support they require comes from fellow priests. New structures that promote mutual support among priests need to be identified and promoted. These may include priestly fraternities and associations of diocesan priests, as well as less formal means of community. If the Latin-rite Catholic Church wants to preserve the ideal of celibacy for diocesan priests, ways must be found for priests to share life together in a way that nourishes them spiritually and as human beings, and that strengthens them in their priesthood.

For change to occur, it would require the commitment of the diocesan bishop to make the mutual support of priests a high priority in pastoral assignments. This would also require acceptance on the part of the Catholic faithful, who might need to sacrifice having a priest live in their parish rectory for the sake of priestly mutual support. However, I suspect a healthy team of two or three priests working with gifted lay co-workers can discover a way to evangelize and meet the needs of a number of parishes better than if those same people were deployed in a more isolated fashion. Apostolic teamwork was the method of Paul, Silvanus, Timothy, and their coworkers in Ephesus, and the result was that "that all the residents of Asia heard the word of the Lord" (Acts 19:10).

The contribution of seminary formation must be to place a high priority on fraternity and community—training seminarians not to be lone rangers, but men of communion.[24] Seminary must serve as a time to develop habits of communion as well as strong supportive relationships with fellow seminarians and with priests that will continue into their years of ministry.

24. See *Pastores dabo vobis*, §18 and §43.

Implications of the New Evangelization for Teaching Scripture to Seminarians

Given the importance of the New Evangelization and its implications for priestly ministry, what difference should this make for how Scripture professors teach seminarians? The New Evangelization has implications for both the manner and the content of our instruction.

Preparing ministers of the word in a seminary is not the same as teaching graduate students at a university. That is important to say, since the academic requirements for seminary Scripture professors are usually similar to those of university professors. However, the graduate formation in Scripture given in both secular and ecclesial universities prepares students for academic scholarship rather than for forming pastoral ministers. In order to teach Scripture to seminarians, we need to pass on to our students something different from what we received from our professors, and we need to learn different ways of doing it.[25] This has many ramifications, but space permits me to touch upon only a few.

Prayer, the Holy Spirit, and Charisms

To raise up ministers of the word entails being ministers of the word ourselves and not just teachers and scholars. When the apostles coined the phrase "ministry of the word," they combined it with prayer: "We will devote ourselves to prayer and to the ministry of the word" (Acts 6:4).

Pope Benedict spoke of the importance for seminarians' vocation of developing "a personal relationship with Scripture." In order to help the seminarians do this, we professors must enjoy a personal relationship with the Lord through Scripture that will manifest itself in our teaching. Love for Scripture, faith in it as God's word, and an instinct for how it applies to life is something that must be caught, not just taught. So it is important to tell stories, to speak about the role Scripture has in our lives, to draw attention to passages that have been important to us or people we know, and to share how we came to understand the relevance of these texts for our lives.

Besides having a personal relationship with the Lord through the mediation of Scripture, the minister of the word must learn how to let the Holy Spirit speak through him or her. Paul summons all Christians to do this: "Let the word of Christ dwell in you richly, teach and admonish one another in all wisdom" (Col 3:16). It is a matter of cooperating with the Holy Spirit, the

---

25. For more on this topic, see Peter S. Williamson, "Biblical Scholarship with a Pastoral Purpose," *Homiletic and Pastoral Review* 107, no. 2 (2006): 8–13.

indwelling Christ who wishes to speak through us.[26] In Paul's famous passage about charisms in 1 Corinthians 12, he mentions a few charisms of inspired speech. Two of them are particularly related to teaching. Paul writes,

> To each is given the manifestation of the Spirit for the common good. To one is given through the Spirit the utterance of wisdom [*logos sophias*], and to another the utterance of knowledge [*logos gnōseōs*] according to the same Spirit.[27]

These refer to the ability to express theological truth or practical insight for living with a particular effectiveness that comes from the Spirit.[28] Paul often speaks of the transforming power of knowledge.[29] The activity of the Spirit may be recognized by its effects. Many Catholics have experienced these gifts without realizing it, when teaching or conversing with someone and suddenly realizing one has said something much better than he or she planned or even knew. Or sometimes it happens when we say something fairly ordinary, but the effects on the hearers, or some of the hearers, is particularly strong. These charisms cannot be exercised simply at will but depend on the action of the Spirit. On the other hand, praying before we speak, and asking and trusting the Lord to speak through us, increases the frequency in which we will experience the Lord work through us this way. We can also aim to be sensitive to inspirations of the Spirit as we speak, something that gets easier as our familiarity with the material and confidence as teachers increase.

Another charism that priests and preachers need, and that professors should seek to exercise as well, is the charism of prophecy, the ability to speak to others on behalf of God (1 Cor 14:1). According to Paul, prophecy is Spirit-inspired speech that has a particular purpose and effect: "the one who prophesies speaks to people for their upbuilding and encouragement and consolation." (1 Cor 14:3). It can, though does not usually, entail prediction or supernatural

---

26. While some scholars interpret "the word of Christ" to mean "the message about Christ," I take it as a subjective genitive meaning the word of the indwelling Christ on the basis of a parallel with the preceding verse about Christ's peace and the parallel passage in Eph 5:18–20 which speaks of the Holy Spirit and offering worship "in the name of our Lord Jesus Christ."

27. 1 Cor 12:7–8.

28. Pentecostals and some in the Catholic charismatic renewal interpret "word of knowledge" as referring to supernatural knowledge of information not gained by natural means. However, both John 4:17–19 and 1 Cor 14:24–25 associate such knowledge with the gift of prophecy. I follow the interpretation of Albert Vanhoye, "Charisms," in *Dictionary of Fundamental Theology*, ed. René Latourelle and Rino Fisichella (New York: Crossroad, 1995), 103–108.

29. Rom 12:1–2; Eph 1:16–18; 4:22–24; Col 1:9–10; 3:9–10. Prescinding from questions of authorship, in this paper I refer to Paul as the New Testament presents him, the canonical Paul.

knowledge (1 Cor 13:2; 14:24–25). While this charism is sometimes expressed in oracles or visions, it can be expressed in preaching. It is often manifest by a power and penetration of the message. It puts people in contact with the Lord. It reflects an inspired spiritual understanding of the situation and needs of the community. It convicts of sin and strengthens faith, hope, and love (Acts 15:32).[30]

If we are called to raise up ministers of the word, we must seek to exercise these charisms as well. We must model them in the classroom and in our relationships with students. Granted, it is not only up to professors of Scripture. Other faculty members, mentors, and spiritual directors involved in preparing ministers of the word must do likewise. Each of us does so in accord with the graces and charisms given us, and the gift-mix of each individual is unique. While we should "earnestly desire the spiritual gifts" and pray for them (1 Cor 14:1), we should not worry about the gifts we lack. Paul's word about financial giving also applies to exercising charisms in teaching: "For if the eagerness is there, it is acceptable according to what one has, not according to what one does not have" (2 Cor 8:12). The primary way we bring the Holy Spirit into our teaching is to pray during our preparation, on our way to class, at the beginning of class, and afterwards.

Attention to Evangelization and Pastoral Praxis

The New Evangelization summons professors of Scripture to prepare ministers who are competent both to evangelize and to shepherd the flock, and that has important implications for the content of our courses. Again, it helps to remember that this is a different goal than that which determined the content of our own graduate Scripture study. The focus needs to be on the content of Scripture, the ways in which it reveals something about the Lord, the way God teaches us to believe or to act through his inspired word. That does not mean turning lectures into homilies or meditations, although expressing our passion about what Scripture says from time to time is a good thing. Scripture enlightens our minds and primarily affects the rest of our faculties through that point of access. In this section I will discuss some of the topics most important to treat in light of our cultural setting and the requirements of the New Evangelization.

Presenting the theology of sacred Scripture helps students to give proper respect to what it says, even if that entails wrestling with a text. While seminarians must understand the role of the human authors and the necessity of discovering what they meant, it is equally important to stress the role of the

---

30. On the charism of prophecy, see Bruce T. Yocum, *Prophecy: Exercising the Prophetic Gifts of the Spirit in the Church Today*, rev. ed. (Ann Arbor, MI: Servant, 1993).

divine Author, i.e., the *inspiration and truth of sacred Scripture*. It is not enough to go over *Dei verbum* and other magisterial writings on this subject. It is also important to unpack texts across the canon to draw out what Scripture says about itself.[31]

Alongside its inspiration and truth, it is important that our students grasp Scripture's unity, a unity manifest through the grand narrative of salvation history that Scripture relates. Many Catholics unconsciously practice a practical Marcionism marked by little regard for or familiarity with the Old Testament. But the teaching of both the New Testament (2 Tim 3:16 *et passim*) and of the Church is clear (*DV*, §§14–16): the books of the Old Testament are inspired and of lasting value. They are important both for what they tell us of God's teaching and activity in Israel's history and for the light they shed on the mystery of Christ. Our students should learn from us the main types and themes that link the testaments. We cannot study the Old Testament books only in their individual historical and literary contexts, as is common in the academy, but rather we must interpret them in their canonical context, in the light of Christ and in the light of Christian tradition and faith today. Likewise, we must explain New Testament texts in light of the Old Testament texts, teachings, and institutions they presuppose.

Clarity about the grand narrative of Scripture should lead to an ability to articulate the *kerygma*—the basic Christian message that was the preaching of the apostles in Acts, is embedded in the epistles, and that is summed up in the creeds. Seminarians need to be able to explain the gospel from the Scriptures in a few simple points.[32] Once clarity about the *kerygma* has been achieved, it is valuable to relate various aspects of it to accounts of conversion and healing in the gospels, so that seminarians may get an idea of how to preach the basic message of salvation from the readings. It is also worth highlighting texts that summon people beyond basic faith toward intentional discipleship and Christian maturity—for instance, the gospel texts that speak of the cost of discipleship.

31. I am referring to texts such as Deut 6; Neh 8:1–12; Pss 19B and 119; Matt 7:24–29; 28:20; John 10:35; 14:23–24; Rom 15:4; 1 Cor 10:11; 2 Cor 10:4–5; Eph 6:17; 2 Tim 3:14–16; Heb 6:5; 2 Pet 1:19–21; 3:15–16. Somewhere along the way seminarians will profit from reading Raniero Cantalamessa's brief book, *The Mystery of God's Word* (Collegeville, MN: Liturgical Press, 1994).

32. See Mary Healy and Peter Williamson, "Biblical Orientations to the New Evangelization," *Josephinum Journal of Theology* 19, no. 1 (2012): 54–57; the article also appears as an appendix to Ralph Martin, *The Urgency of the New Evangelization*, 106–110. In the same issue of *Josephinum*, see also Raniero Cantalamessa on the *kerygma* in "The Year of Faith and the Catechism," 42–44.

In teaching Scripture, we should know the most common pastoral issues our students are likely to encounter—gathering input from priests and other pastoral ministers as we have opportunity—and should relate our teaching to these issues. As we teach through various parts of the biblical literature, we can highlight texts in each body of literature that have particular usefulness for evangelization, preaching, catechesis, or counseling.

Space does not permit treatment of many other themes that deserve our attention in the classroom, but here are three that I try to highlight. First, many Catholics do not grasp what Scripture says about the effects of faith, baptism, and the gift of the Spirit on moral life, so I find it important to explain what Paul and John teach about moral transformation. Even many seminarians approach morality and virtue primarily as a matter of human effort, instead of appropriating and learning to cooperate with the grace of the new life in Christ and the Spirit that the epistles explain. Specifically, I recommend explaining the practical implications of Paul's teaching about overcoming the "flesh" by the power of the Spirit (Gal 5:16–23; Rom 8:1–14[33]) and living in the new self (Eph 4:17–24; Col 3:9–10) and of John's teaching about abiding in Christ (John 15:1–17) and the difference that being born of God makes (1 John 3:9). Second, contemporary culture is so confused about personal relationships that there is great value in pointing out biblical wisdom in this area. I particularly recommend commenting on passages about marriage and childrearing, emotions, forgiveness, speech, whether from the Torah (Deut 6), Wisdom literature of the Old (especially Proverbs and Sirach) or New Testament (James), or the letters of Paul (Eph 4–5; Col 3). Finally, it is important for seminarians to acquire a clear grasp of the biblical worldview and what it says about the spiritual challenges Christians face. Colossians teaches that God has "delivered us from the domain of darkness and transferred us to the kingdom of his beloved Son" (Col 1:13). Ephesians teaches the reality of our current spiritual warfare (Eph 6:10–20). Several texts teach about the obstacle to Christian life that "the world" presents (e.g., John, *passim*; 1 John 2:15; Eph 2:1–3; Jas 4:4). All Scripture teaches the transitory nature of life while the New Testament teaches about the need to turn to the Lord and accept God's gracious offer of forgiveness and life in Christ, as well as the terrible consequences of refusing this gift.[34]

---

33. There are important translation issues in both texts. The New American Bible is more precise than the Revised Standard Version on Gal 5:16 but translates *pneuma* as "spirit" and "Spirit" in Rom 8:1–13 in an idiosyncratic and problematic manner.

34. See Martin, *The Urgency of the New Evangelization*, 57–73.

Preparation for Contested Issues

The goal of equipping seminarians to evangelize and pastor people in the world today necessitates wading into topics where popular or academic culture challenges the faith. We need to do this humbly and wisely, but what we must *not* do is ignore the issues that the people in the pew are encountering.

Some of these challenges concern the trustworthiness of the Bible. Seminarians need to be equipped to offer an explanation of difficult texts in the Bible touching on violence, slavery, and the treatment of women in traditional cultures. Insofar as we do not have the answers ourselves, it is okay to admit that, so long as we then apply ourselves to filling the gaps in our knowledge or understanding. Pope Benedict also points to the need to address the "dark" passages in Scripture and offers helpful orientations.[35]

Another challenge arises from those who deny the trustworthiness of the gospel accounts of what Jesus did and said, sometimes on the basis of problematic methodologies for studying the historical Jesus. Pope Benedict does a good job in *Jesus of Nazareth* of engaging many of these issues in an open-minded and balanced way. At least an hour or two should be spent in every Gospels course discussing the quests of the historical Jesus along with other challenges to the reliability of the Gospels.[36] Analogous challenges to the historical value of the Old Testament by minimalists deserve attention so that seminarians know that reasonable answers exist and where to find them.[37]

In recent years the canon of Scripture has come under attack, especially by scholars who claim the canon is only the product of ecclesiastical politics and who frequently advocate the cause of gnostic gospels and alternative forms of

---

35. Pope Benedict XVI, *Verbum Domini*, §42. A useful work touching on many of these hard texts is Paul Copan's *Is God a Moral Monster?: Making Sense of the Old Testament God* (Grand Rapids, MI: Baker, 2011).

36. Some dated but still useful resources on these issues include the chapter devoted to the historical Jesus in Raymond E. Brown, *Introduction to the New Testament* (New York: Doubleday, 1997), and "Historical Reliability" in *Dictionary of Jesus and the Gospels*, ed. Joel B. Green, Scot McKnight, and I. Howard Marshall (Downers Grove, IL: InterVarsity, 1992). More substantial resources include Paul William Barnett, *Is the New Testament Reliable? A Look at the Historical Evidence* (Downers Grove, IL: InterVarsity, 1986, 1992) and Richard Bauckham, *Jesus and the Eyewitnesses: The Gospels as Eyewitness Testimony* (Grand Rapids, MI: Eerdmans, 2006).

37. I have found that the following texts provide helpful ballast against extreme minimalist positions: Kenneth A. Kitchener, *On the Reliability of the Old Testament* (Grand Rapids, MI: Eerdmans, 2003), and Iain Provan, V. Philips Long, and Tremper Longman III, *A Biblical History of Israel* (Louisville: Westminster John Knox, 2003).

Christianity.[38] It is not enough that ministers of the word simply refer people to the teaching of the Church. It is important that seminarians learn to give a reasoned explanation of why the Church accepts the canonical books and not the others.[39]

Beside challenges to the trustworthiness of Scripture, many other challenges have arisen to Church teaching about the content of faith and the moral life.

Certainly the area of sexuality is one where many challenges to biblical and Catholic teaching arise. Most of these present themselves as the standard way our culture approaches relationships—sex as a normal aspect of dating, cohabitation before marriage, easy divorce, homosexual conduct, etc. So it is all the more necessary to prepare seminarians to teach what Scripture says about marriage, sexuality, holiness, and its implications for courtship. Seminarians should be familiar with and able to explain some of the key texts (e.g., 1 Thess 4:3–8; 1 Cor 6:12–20; Eph 5). As we teach through Scripture, we need to go over key texts that address homosexual acts, and respond to some of the arguments raised against Scripture as it has been interpreted by the Christian tradition. I have found it useful to point students toward Raymond Brown's discussion of the meaning of *arsenokoitai* and *malakoi* in 1 Cor 6:9–11.[40]

Christology and soteriology are often subject to attack in both academic and popular culture. As we teach future priests it is important to highlight the texts in every part of the New Testament that reveal the identity of Jesus and the way his Paschal Mystery brings about our salvation.[41] Secular academia

38. For example, see Elaine Pagels, *Beyond Belief: The Secret Gospel of Thomas* (New York: Random House, 2003) or Bart J. Ehrman, *Lost Christianities: The Battles for Scripture and the Faiths We Never Knew* (New York: Oxford University Press, 2003).

39. Any mainstream history of the canon shows the inadequacy of many of the challenges, e.g., Darrel Bock's critique of recent claims made about gnostic writings in *The Missing Gospels: Unearthing the Truth Behind Alternative Christianities* (Nashville: Nelson, 2006).

Another difficulty arises from scholars who exploit minor textual differences to undermine confidence in the reliability of the manuscripts on which our Bibles are based. Muslims claim, on the basis of statements in the Koran, that where their doctrine differs from ours, our texts have been changed by a (historically improbable) collaboration between Jews and Christians. When it comes to the trustworthiness of the manuscript tradition of the Bible, Christians stand on very firm ground, and it is helpful for seminarians to know something of the number and antiquity of biblical texts when compared to every other ancient writing.

40. *Introduction to the New Testament*, 528–530. Robert Gagnon's *The Bible and Homosexual Practice: Texts and Hermeneutics* (Nashville: Abingdon, 2002) provides a thorough and competent response to gay-advocacy interpretation.

41. For an accessible biblical theological overview, see Stephen B. Clark, *The Redeemer: Understanding the Meaning of the Life, Death, and Resurrection of Jesus Christ* (Ann Arbor,

often casts doubt on the historicity of miracles in the New Testament, so it is important to offer a robust defense, supported if possible by testimony to contemporary miracles.[42] Finally, the widespread notion in society and in the Church that everyone will be saved needs to be resisted by drawing attention to texts that emphasize the importance of the gospel, of faith, and of right conduct for eternal salvation.[43]

Of course, Scripture is not the only line of defense of Catholic teaching. *The Catechism of the Catholic Church* and other magisterial documents furnish valuable explanations and arguments; other disciplines such as philosophy, history, and fundamental theology also make important contributions. But Scripture is crucial, and that is the part that is our special responsibility.

St. Paul, a Model for Priests Today

Traditionally, one of the best means of forming people in a way of life is to present them with suitable models to imitate. I would like to propose that Scripture professors and formators point seminarians to St. Paul as a model for priesthood for the New Evangelization. It is true that the Curé of Ars, St. John Vianney, is a model and the patron for parish priests, and I am not denying that seminarians and priests can continue to learn a great deal from him. However, in the new missionary situation in which we find ourselves, the Church's first great missionary offers much for priests and seminarians to emulate—and not only for them. Scripture presents Paul as a model to all Christians. Paul frequently exhorts the members of his churches to imitate him, and the Holy Spirit has confirmed this teaching by including those exhortations in Scripture itself. After Jesus himself, there is no one about whom Scripture tells us more.

So what are the virtues of St. Paul that we can draw to the attention of seminarians when we teach Acts of the Apostles or Pauline Literature? Paul is

---

MI: Servant, 1992), available from Tabor House (www.sos-nar.com/tabor.htm). The New Age movement challenges traditional Christology and soteriology and has its proponents even among Catholics. Moira Noonan's *Ransomed from Darkness* (El Sobrante, CA: North Bay, 2005) recounts the author's experience in many aspects of New Age belief and practice and her conversion to Catholicism.

42. Craig Keener, a leading Scripture scholar, has written an authoritative two-volume work on biblical miracles, complete with numerous credible accounts of miracles in the early Church and today and a vigorous historical and philosophical defense: *Miracles: The Credibility of the New Testament Accounts* (Grand Rapids, MI: Baker, 2011).

43. See Ralph Martin, *Will Many Be Saved? What Vatican II Actually Teaches and Its Implications for the New Evangelization* (Grand Rapids, MI: Eerdmans, 2013), especially 57–92 on the Scriptural foundations of *Lumen gentium*, §16. See also, by the same author, *The Urgency of the New Evangelization*.

a chaste celibate with an undivided devotion to the Lord Jesus (1 Cor 7:35, 37) whom he loves above all else (Gal 2:20; Phil 3:7–14). He is a man of prayer, of faith, and of the Spirit. He is a servant of the word of God, deeply familiar with Scripture, a preacher and teacher in word and deed. Paul is a man who loves deeply, who draws strength and joy from relationships with the communities he pastors and from his many co-workers (Rom 16:1–16; Phil 4:1–2; 1 Thess 2:19).[44] He is a team leader who collaborates rather than a lone ranger, and he is a community builder and mentor who trains younger disciples to do what he does (Timothy, Titus). He is an encourager of charisms and ministries in the community (1 Cor 12:4–11; 14:1; Rom 12:4–8), viewing his role as "equipping the holy ones for the work of ministry" (Eph 4:12). As a pastor he is wise about relationships (1 Tim 5:1–2) and zealous for the unity of the local church, especially its leaders (Eph 4:1–6; Phil 1:27; 2:1–5; 4:1). He is a bold witness, ready to suffer for testimony to the truth (Phil 1:12–14; 2 Tim 1:8–12). He is a man of self-control and self-sacrifice, ready to adapt himself to win others rather than please himself (1 Cor 9:24–27). He does not shrink from hardship (2 Cor 6:3–10; 11:23–28) but welcomes it for the sake of the gospel and encourages his co-workers to do the same (2 Tim 2:3–10). Not content to remain where the gospel is known and accepted, Paul is zealous to bring the gospel to those who have not heard it (Rom 15:18–24).

Although the culture around us is growing darker by the day, we neither fear nor despair because the "God, who said, 'Let light shine out of darkness,' has shone in our hearts to give the light of the knowledge of the glory of God in the face of Jesus Christ" (2 Cor 4:6). The night is darkest immediately before the dawn. Whether that dawn brings a new springtime of faith or the return of the Lord, our hope burns bright.

The New Evangelization has so many implications for the priesthood and for teaching Scripture to seminarians that it would be easy for the professor to feel overwhelmed. Our part, however, is only to pray and to work patiently according to the light he gives us, trusting God to take care of the rest.

---

44. See E. Earle Ellis, "Paul and His Coworkers," in *Dictionary of Paul and His Letters*, ed. Gerald F. Hawthorne et al. (Downers Grove, IL: IVP Academic, 1993), 183–189.

CHAPTER 2

Stand and Deliver: Scripture and the Role of the Seminary Professor in Forming Priests for the New Evangelization

Steven C. Smith

> To reveal Jesus Christ and His Gospel to those who do not know them has been, ever since the morning of Pentecost, the fundamental program which the Church has taken on as received from her Founder. The whole of the New Testament, and in a special way the Acts of the Apostles, bears witness to a privileged and in a sense exemplary moment of this missionary effort which will subsequently leave its mark on the whole history of the Church.
>
> POPE ST. PAUL VI[1]

What is the role of the seminary professor—particularly the professor of sacred Scripture—in preparing Catholic priests for the New Evangelization today? How does it influence our theological pedagogy? In part one of this essay, I will examine seminary professors' own attitudes about the New Evangelization and consider tensions we may face with regard to our role in the seminary classroom. In part two, I turn to the urgent need to assist seminarians in preparing for the New Evangelization and offer three practical pathways for further reflection.

---

1. Pope St. Paul VI, Apostolic Exhortation *Evangelii nuntiandi* (December 8, 1975), www.vatican.va/holy_father/paul_vi/apost_exhortations/documents/hf_p-vi_exh_19751208 _evangelii-nuntiandi_en.html, §51.

To What Extent has the New Evangelization Escaped My Fullest Attention in the Classroom?

As formators in Scripture, we embrace our calling to equip seminarians to teach and preach the Word of God as ordained priests of Jesus Christ. We ourselves strive to model Christ to our seminarians and to assist them in a deep personal encounter with Christ in sacred Scripture. We labor to instruct them in the Church's principles for proper exegesis, and to understand the message of the Old and New Testaments. By their diaconal year, if not before, we strive to help them develop and nurture many skill sets that will together enable them to do excellent preaching for the sake of the people of God. Yet, despite the surety of our calling, and the goodness of our work, we each must put before ourself a basic and perhaps difficult question: To what extent has the New Evangelization escaped my fullest attention in the classroom?

If, as I suspect, some of us cringe just a bit at such questions, it may be because we ourselves are not doing all we know we should just yet. And if the question causes each of us a bit of discomfort, let us not despair of our failings, but rather "let us reason together" and strive to do better (Isa 1:18 RSVCE). I submit that if we are uninvolved or under-involved in the New Evangelization, it is not due to a lack of heightened awareness of its urgent need. Rather, I will stake out some ground here and suggest that if the New Evangelization has, to one degree or another, escaped the full attention of seminary professors today, it is not from a deficiency of Magisterial or episcopal emphasis upon it. Nor can even a casual gaze into the abyss of our darkened culture but enflame the need for us to do better in this regard. We are all well aware of the deep need for the New Evangelization in our time. We may have to look deeper and more personally for the reasons.

Let us face facts: all of us have over the past several decades become quite conversant with all the language and precepts of the New Evangelization, at least since St. John Paul II first introduced it into our collective vocabulary, if not well before his pontificate. As he expressed,

> The commemoration of this half of the millennium of evangelization will achieve its full meaning, if as bishops, with your priests and faithful, you accept it as your commitment; a commitment, not of re-evangelization, but rather of a new evangelization; new in its ardor, methods and expression.[2]

---

2. Pope St. John Paul II, Discourse to the XIX Assembly of CELAM (March 9, 1983), as cited in Synod of Bishops, XIII Ordinary General Assembly, *Instrumentum laboris* "The New Evangelization for the Transmission of the Christian Faith" (December 19, 2012), www

If we are honest, we must fully acknowledge that the New Evangelization is the work of the whole Church. It cannot, nor should it, be in any way diminished or sidelined as the "pet project" of a few well-intentioned "evangelistic types." And as Scripture professors, we must affirm that the New Evangelization is at the very bedrock of Christ's own mandate to His apostles: "Go therefore and make disciples of all nations, baptizing them in the name of the Father and of the Son and of the Holy Spirit, teaching them to observe all that I have commanded you; and lo, I am with you always, to the close of the age" (Matt 28:19–20).

As devoted disciples of Christ and as sons and daughters of the Church, we must re-calibrate ourselves upon Christ's missionary mandate—and do everything possible to help all of our future priests to do the same. To borrow the words from the Apostle himself, "Woe to me if I do not help seminarians to preach the Gospel!"[3]

With St. Pope Paul VI, we recognize that the entire Church is called to be evangelized and to evangelize. This primary task belongs to each member of the baptized. In embracing the Gospel, we are called to manifest it in our words and deeds. This is at the heart of the New Evangelization.[4]

Paul VI reminded us of the intrinsic connection between the new birth of baptism and the necessity of all to evangelize. We co-labor as members of the Church to bring the Good News to every human person, that each might encounter Christ and be transformed in the process, into someone new (per Rev 21:5). As Paul VI sketched out in *Evangelii nuntiandi*, it is this transformative renewal of the whole person that we strive after, with the love of Christ. The roots of the holistic re-application of the Gospel are laid out by the Apostle Paul across his epistles.[5]

As sons and daughters of the Church, who live and move in the shadow of the Second Vatican Council, we must also re-affirm that the biblical roots of the New Evangelization involve nothing less than the universal call to holiness. Jesus called each person to *zoe*—to eternal life, which is born in us at our baptism, and which continues to grow over our lives.[6] Jesus's words to us, "Be

---

.vatican.va/roman_curia/synod/documents/rc_synod_doc_20120619_instrumentum-xiii_en .html, §45.

3. Cf. 1 Cor 9:16.

4. See *Evangelii nuntiandi,* §13.

5. See Rom 1:16; 1 Cor 1:18, 2:4; 2 Cor 5:17.

6. See *Lumen gentium,* §39 in *Vatican Council II: The Conciliar and Post Conciliar Documents,* electronic edition of the new revised ed., vol. 1, Vatican Collection (Northport, NY: Costello, 1992).

perfect, as your Father in heaven is perfect" (Matt 5:48), are as much a vision for humanity as they are a stark command. All Christians have a role in the New Evangelization. The whole Church is summoned to go beyond our comfort zone. This will undoubtedly look different for each Christian.[7] Still, in teaching and forming our seminarians, we are mindful that all priests, by virtue of their being "united with the bishops in sacerdotal dignity"[8] bear a special responsibility in the New Evangelization.

Even so, the role of the priest is especially crucial in this mission. As seminary formators, we must come to grips with the responsibility given us by the Church to form holy priests who will boldly announce the Gospel of Jesus Christ and "proclaim the Gospel of God."[9] We must be vigilant of the need to help our future priests grow in holiness and as excellently trained heralds of the Gospel.

Let us return to our original question: To what extent has the New Evangelization escaped my fullest attention in the classroom? Our initial response was to assert the likelihood that, when it comes to the New Evangelization, we as seminary formators indeed fully affirm and support this mission.

We embrace the Great Commission of Christ; with St. Paul, we yearn for our seminarians to burn with greater and greater zeal to preach the Gospel. We know, perhaps by heart, the words of the Second Vatican Council on the topic of evangelization. We wholeheartedly agree with St. Paul VI and St. John Paul II,[10] and more recently Pope Francis, about preaching the Gospel in every street and from every rooftop.

Francis has spoken plainly about the need to be open to the Holy Spirit, to be present and ready to move:

> It is the Paraclete, Spirit, the Comforter, who grants us the courage to take to the streets of the world, bringing the Gospel! The Holy Spirit makes us look to the horizon and drive [sic] us to the very outskirts of existence in order to proclaim life in Jesus Christ. Let us ask ourselves: do we tend to stay closed in on ourselves, on our group, or do we let the Holy Spirit open us to mission? Today let us remember these three words: newness, harmony and mission.[11]

---

7. See *Evangelii nuntiandi, §66.*
8. *CCC,* §1595.
9. *Evangelii nuntiandi,* §68; see *Lumen gentium,* §28.
10. See Pope John Paul II, Homily at the Eighth World Youth Day (August 15, 1993), www .vatican.va/holy_father/john_paul_ii/homilies/1993/documents/hf_jp-ii_hom_19930815_gmg -denver_en.html.
11. Pope Francis, Homily, Solemnity of Pentecost (May 19, 2013), www.vatican.va/holy _father/francesco/homilies/2013/documents/papa-francesco_20130519_omelia-pentecoste _en.html.

Naturally, we desire our seminarians to understand and embrace these same truths concerning the New Evangelization as well. So, perhaps the question ought to be put another way: Is it possible to fully assent to the Church's mission of the New Evangelization and yet struggle to actually "respond" in meaningful and measurable ways in our seminary classrooms?

I suspect that for many seminary professors, it is not only possible but probable. For plentiful reasons, there exists, for the seminary professor, a kind of tension between (a) our heartfelt "convictions" about promoting and advancing the New Evangelization and (b) actually making inroads in regard to its implementation in our own classrooms. Assuming our personal, intellectual and spiritual commitment to the Gospel of Jesus Christ and the task of the New Evangelization, some soul-searching—yet very practical—questions must be asked of ourselves: To what extent have I allowed the New Evangelization to trickle down into my day-to-day teaching? What would it specifically look like if it did? What changes would be required, and am I committed to making them? Are there ways that I could measure my own efforts at the New Evangelization—and those of my seminarians? Do certain logistics (e.g., busyness, course structure) prevent me from opening up my seminarians to the task of the New Evangelization in tangible ways?

These are crucial questions, worthy of our meditation. Given the normal rigors of teaching, such as the demands of required course content, formation advising, spiritual direction, committee work, writing projects, and the like, it is important to set achievable goals when it comes to the New Evangelization.

Along these lines, we can ask ourselves periodically how we tend to measure success with regard to forming men in evangelization. A word of caution is in order. Pope Benedict XVI, in a speech given to catechists prior to his papacy, drew upon Jesus's Parable of the Mustard Seed to suggest that we not be so presumptuous as to think every sprinkling of seed will "immediately produce a large tree." As he stresses, "We either live too much in the security of the already existing large tree or in the impatience of having a greater, more vital tree." In place of such perceptions, he challenges us to embrace the mystery: "the Church is at the same time a large tree and a very small grain."[12] On all New Evangelization efforts, whether in the parish, the classroom, or the street corner, we must remind ourselves that "success" is not one of the Divine names. Such efforts will at times bring success, failure, and many places in between.

12. Joseph Cardinal Ratzinger, Address to Catechists and Religion Teachers, Jubilee of Catechists (December 12, 2000), d2y1pz2y630308.cloudfront.net/5032/documents/2014/0 /ADDRESS%20TO%20CATECHISTS%20AND%20RELIGION%20TEACHERS.pdf.

I suspect that if one or more of the above questions resonate with us, it is likely that we may be experiencing the kind of tension just mentioned. These are questions that the formator will have to sort through and decide what action, if any, is required. Such introspection will require work and a commitment to wisely introduce corrective adjustments. But it will be worth it in the long run.

I conclude the opening part of this essay with the following observations. First, over the past fifty years, our Church has rightly placed increasing emphasis on the great need for the New Evangelization. Second, as seminary formators, we agree with and embrace this missionary mandate. We want to help implement the New Evangelization as we form tomorrow's priests. Third, we may at times, if we are honest with ourselves, feel a bit *overwhelmed* or *powerless* in our daily circumstances to actually attempt any concrete efforts at the New Evangelization in own classrooms.

Have you ever felt the following way? "There is barely time in this semester as it is, to help these new seminarians learn how to read Scripture critically. I just don't have time to do anything else, no matter how noble the thing is;" or, "I'm pretty sure that ABC professor in my seminary addresses some aspects of the New Evangelization in XYZ class."

It is with a sense of optimism that we can and must move beyond the tension between what we believe about the New Evangelization and what we ourselves are committed to doing (or, at least, to attempting) in our own classrooms.

What Are Some Possible Ways I Might Take into Account the New Evangelization in My Own Classroom?

Here I would like to present three pathways for possibly helping our seminarians prepare for the New Evangelization. As I do so, I will rely on the words of Pope Benedict XVI, who reminds us that at the core of all evangelization is the renewal of human joy. It is true that there is a poverty of joy in our world today. In its absence, life feels like a great tedium. Our minds grow cynical, and our hearts become restless. As Benedict puts it,

> This poverty is widespread today, in very different forms in the materially rich as well as the poor countries. The inability of joy presupposes and produces the inability to love, produces jealousy, avarice—all defects that devastate the life of individuals and of the world. This is why we are in need of a new evangelization—if the art of living remains an unknown, nothing else works.[13]

13. Ratzinger, Address to Catechists and Religion Teachers.

With these wise words in mind, I would like to offer some practical suggestions. The following are humbly submitted as three possible ways of bringing the reality of the New Evangelization closer to our seminarians in order to encourage and challenge them to embrace this vocation of the whole Church to share Christ. Each of these pathways is represented by a key Greek word which reverberates across the pages of the New Testament. As we encounter the Good News in the four Gospels, Acts, Paul's epistles—and even in Revelation—we encounter these words over and over. They are: (1) *martureo* ("to witness"), (2) *kerusso* (to proclaim"), and (3) *apologia* ("defense").[14]

1. *Martureo* ("to witness"). "You are *witnesses* of these things" (Luke 24:48). The Council taught that the New Evangelization is a "rediscovery" of the Church's apostolic and missionary roots.[15] Certainly, there are many ways in which we might regularly challenge our seminarians to be a loving and truthful "witness" of Jesus Christ. In particular, I am thinking of the crucial ministry which they will be involved in with children, youth, and young adults. Our seminarians prepare to enter priestly ministry in an age of rampant secularism and the disintegration of the American family.

Many of the young people that they will minister to, even in their pastoral field education assignments, come from such "disintegrated" family backgrounds with divorced parents, single parent households, etc. For many such young adults, there is little or often no "witness" of Christ in their home or family. This is deeply sad and is one of the very situations that priests of the New Evangelization must reach into with Christ's love—as His witnesses.

In their book *American Grace*, authors Robert Putnam and David Campbell summarize the historical situation of religion and religious practice in the United States over the past four or five decades. It is sobering, to say the very least. In the book, the authors describe what they refer to as the rise of the "nones," i.e., those who grew up with really no religious affiliation.[16]

In light of such realities—and knowing that our seminarians are engaged in pastoral ministry in which, more and more, they minister to children of these nones—I now frame my debriefing questions accordingly. In the past, when discussing pastoral field education assignments with seminarians, my questions

---

14. On *martureo* in the NT, see Luke 24:48; Acts 1:22; 3:15; Rev 2:13. On *kerusso*, see Matt 9:35; 10:27; Mark 1:14; 1:35; 5:20; 10:27; 13:10; Luke 8:39; 12:3; Acts 20:25; 28:31; Rom 10:8; 1 Cor 9:27; 2 Cor 11:14; etc. On *apologia*, see 1 Pet 3:15; 1 Cor 9:3; Phil 1:7.

15. Synod of Bishops, *Instrumentum laboris*, §81.

16. See Robert D. Putnam and David E. Campbell, *American Grace: How Religion Divides Us and Unites Us* (New York: Simon & Schuster, 2010), 124–126.

for the seminarians ran along the lines of, "How is the teaching going with the sixth-grade class?" and "Are you able to organize the curriculum and accomplish what the site supervisor expects?" I still ask such questions, although now I try to spend as much time getting the seminarians to reflect on their presence with the children as a living gospel. If a future priest is able in some sense to reach children today with his witness and Christ's love, then this is a very positive development toward the New Evangelization.

Here, it is helpful to remember that the Gospel message is not merely data or information. Rather, it is "performative" and it "makes things happen."[17] Although there is a myriad of ways in which we can and should challenge our seminarians to preach the Gospel in our complex and darkened culture, a good place for them to begin is through simple actions: being on time; being patient; being forgiving; being a good listener; acting as a genuine friend; making another laugh or smile; being trustworthy; etc. With children and adult nones, such *martureo* is not just an important step to verbally sharing the Good News; it often *is* the Good News.

The Greek term *martureo* itself reminds us that it is in the giving of our ordinary lives for the sake of the Gospel that we ultimately witness the love of Christ to others. With respect to his own faith, Pope Benedict looks not only to the lives of great saints, whom he describes as "signposts," but also to more everyday, "simple saints," whether or not they are canonized:

> They are ordinary people, so to speak, without visible heroism but in their everyday goodness I see the truth of faith. This goodness, which they have developed in the faith of the Church, is for me the most reliable apology of Christianity and the sign of where the truth lies.
>
> In the Communion of Saints, canonized and not canonized, which the Church lives thanks to Christ in all her members, we enjoy their presence and their company and cultivate the firm hope that we shall be able to imitate their journey and share one day in the same blessed life, eternal life.[18]

---

17. Pope Benedict XVI, *Spe salvi* (*On Christian Hope*) (November 30, 2007), www.vatican.va/holy_father/benedict_xvi/encyclicals/documents/hf_ben-xvi_enc_20071130_spe-salvi_en.html, §2. He continues, "The dark door of time, of the future, has been thrown open. The one who has hope lives differently; the one who hopes has been granted the gift of a new life.... Is [the Gospel] 'performative' for us—is it a message which shapes our life in a new way, or is it just 'information' which, in the meantime, we have set aside and which now seems to us to have been superseded by more recent information?"

18. Pope Benedict XVI, General Audience (April 13, 2011), www.vatican.va/holy_father/benedict_xvi/audiences/2011/documents/hf_ben-xvi_aud_20110413_en.html.

2. *Kerusso* ("to proclaim"). "And [Paul] lived there two whole years at his own expense, and welcomed all who came to him, *preaching the kingdom of God* and teaching about the Lord Jesus Christ quite openly and unhindered" (Acts 28:30–31).

Moving to the second and third suggestions, I now turn from nonverbal evangelization (*martureo*) to verbal evangelization (*kerusso* and *apologia*). With regard to *kerusso*, I would like to consider the New Testament concept of "proclamation" of the Good News. Although there are many forms of "priestly proclamation" of the Good News, there is perhaps none as crucial as the Sunday homily. In *Verbum Domini*, Pope Benedict XVI devoted considerable space to a discussion of the homily and the crucial role of sacred Scripture.

Although I will not take up all of his timely considerations here, let me mention two that are particularly pertinent to the New Evangelization. The first is that the paramount task of the homilist is to make the Scriptures present and alive to the people of God, and to help them see the connections between the Gospels and their everyday lives.[19] We must help our seminarians, as they pray and study the Sacred Scriptures, to develop preaching skills toward that end: to enable listeners to encounter the living Christ in Scripture, and to see the connection between the Word of God and everyday life. On this point, Benedict stresses that abstractions and tangential remarks can become a detour away from the message of the Gospel. He cautions against speaking about "useless digressions" and other superfluous matters.[20] In preparing seminarians for the New Evangelization, do we, in Scripture classes and homiletics labs, help them strive toward such homiletic goals?

A second observation from *Verbum Domini* has to do with the homilist's own witness. The people of God can recognize when a homily that might be quite sophisticated is yet devoid of conviction. People must feel the priest's "compelling desire" to proclaim Christ, whom Benedict stresses must be at the very center of the homily.[21] This point recalls what was noted concerning *martureo*. In the age of the New Evangelization, what is urgently needed is a deeper sense of personal conviction about the truths which one is preaching. This urgency should not, however, result in the other extreme to be avoided—e.g., histrionics or dramatic presentations which only distract from the Gospel and

---

19. See Pope Benedict XVI, *Verbum Domini* (September 30, 2010) (Boston: Pauline Books and Media, 2010), §59.

20. See *Verbum Domini*, §59.

21. See *Verbum Domini*, §59.

Christ. Yet seminarians who simply read homilies as if they were tax records or the phone directory need to be challenged.

Accordingly, the priest needs to immerse himself in the Scriptures. This must be central to all preparation. *Verbum Domini* calls for "close and constant contact with the sacred text."[22] Study must be bathed in prayer, and prayer must be accompanied by rolling up one's sleeves—opening commentaries and other reliable resources. Benedict continues:

> The synodal assembly asked that the following questions be kept in mind: "What are the Scriptures being proclaimed saying? What do they say to me personally? What should I say to the community in the light of its concrete situation?" The preacher "should be the first to hear the word of God which he proclaims," since, as Saint Augustine says: "He is undoubtedly barren who preaches outwardly the word of God without hearing it inwardly."[23]

Again, in helping seminarians prepare for their pastoral ministry in the New Evangelization, do we, in every conceivable way, challenge them and encourage them to strive toward such goals in their practice homilies?

Finally, throughout all of our teaching outlines, discussions, exams, and papers, we are called to help our seminarians to preach the Kingdom of God in clear and compelling ways, as Pope Paul VI urges, "As an evangelizer, Christ first of all proclaims a kingdom, the Kingdom of God; and this is so important that, by comparison, everything else becomes 'the rest,' which is 'given in addition.'"[24]

3. *Apologia* ("defense").

> But in your hearts reverence Christ as Lord. Always be prepared *to make a defense* to anyone who calls you to account for the hope that is in you, yet do it with gentleness and reverence; and keep your conscience clear, so that, when you are abused, those who revile your good behavior in Christ may be put to shame. (1 Pet 3:15–16)

With this final suggestion, I turn to the New Testament concept of *apologia* "defense." Here, as I begin to consider the important role of "apologetics" in regard to Scripture and the New Evangelization, I am reminded of the above text from St. Peter's first epistle. Yet, what the Prince of the Apostles affirms at the end of the citation is as important as what he says at the beginning, that is "to make a defense . . . with gentleness and reverence."

---

22. *Verbum Domini*, §59.
23. *Verbum Domini*, §59; see Augustine, *Sermo* 179, caput 1 in PL 38, 966.
24. *Evangelii nuntiandi*, §8.

We should urge our seminarians to develop a greater sense of self-confidence and, yes, an appropriate amount of gravitas, in order to start friendly conversations with others about Christ. Unfortunately, some of our seminarians are in various stages of coming out of their shell. They want to be able to share Christ, but are terrified of failing or making a mistake, or they simply do not have enough self-confidence with regard to public speaking.

In recent years, my seminary has seen the growth of a New Evangelization Club. Twice a year, a group of approximately fifteen to thirty men travel to a prearranged site, for example, the university campus. They are given a fair amount of training prior to the trip from more experienced seminarians. Role-playing and other practical components are involved. Importantly, the goal is simply to draw people out in friendly conversation, typically around key evangelistic topics. (For example: Who are we? Is there such a thing as truth—and if so, how can we know? Is there life after death? Who was Jesus?) Seminarians who participate in this excursion are reminded of basic *kerygma*, not a script but guidelines in order to keep the conversation moving. Yet a key value is simply making real, human connections and not trying to force anything or anyone whatsoever.

By all accounts, these excursions have been very fruitful. They have facilitated many faith-filled encounters between Catholic seminarians and people from nearly every walk of life, including many nones. A related positive development that I have heard about firsthand is that many seminarians return with a renewed sense of clarity and confidence about sharing their faith. In a sense, such experiences demystify their concerns. Those who participate come to see that *apologia* does not have to be about "winning arguments" or getting into heated debates. Rather, it is, in a sense, a blend of *martureo* and *kerusso*, which is to say, an integration of "witness" and "proclamation" of Christ in natural, everyday ways.

One final suggestion comes from my own seminary classroom. Several years ago, our rector challenged all of the faculty to consider implementing some practical manner in the classroom to help them speak up and articulate the faith. "What good is it," I recall him saying, "if they know the 'goods of marriage' or Thomas [Aquinas]'s proofs of God's existence if they can't put that into everyday language that is clear and makes sense to the average adult?" Moreover, he added, every seminarian ought to be able to talk about God, Scripture, the Sacraments and the Creed, etc., in ways that are not only clear but also—and just as importantly—compelling and attractive to the average person. As he summed up, "We must help them to, at some point or another, 'Stand and Deliver' if their seminary education is to have been of any real use in the real world."

I decided to take him up on the challenge and began developing a Stand and Deliver component in each of my core classes. After some experimentation, I can affirm that most of my seminarians have come to enjoy the activity—even if it terrifies some!

Although individual professors' forays into such activities will certainly vary, the following are the basic elements of Stand and Deliver in my own classroom. First, seminarians are given a list of questions at the beginning of the term. The questions are posed from the vantage point of a parishioner: "Hi Father, I have a question for you. . . ." The question used varies but is tightly focused on scriptural themes. For example, who wrote the Gospels? Why would God harden Pharaoh's heart? What about all of the mistakes in Scripture? Can Catholics believe in evolution? Was the world really created in six literal days?

Each week, three seminarians are preselected and informed that they will Stand and Deliver on the appointed question. The day of the activity, I set up the scene as in a parish. One at a time, each seminarian has two minutes to answer the parishioner's question. I have found it helpful to have a seminarian role-play as the parishioner. The same question posed by the professor tends to yield a much more philosophical response, which is not the goal.

Related to the previous point, all seminarians are urged to think carefully about both the form and content of their response. For example, how would I succinctly address such a question in a clear, honest and winsome manner? For fairness, the rest of the seminarians vote for the winning response, and prizes are awarded. Although the atmosphere is kept light, seminarians are urged to play their part seriously. Some debriefing may follow depending upon time.

The entire activity takes about ten to twelve minutes of class time. Obviously, we cannot create real-world situations in the classroom and an actual conversation as this would have more give and take, transpiring over more than just a few minutes. Still, the activity affords seminarians an opportunity to try. It is a small demonstration of the fact that apologetics need not involve arm-wrestling or shouting, neither need it be about winning arguments. It may involve the winning of a friend or at least engaging another in a friendly and confident manner. Stand and Deliver is a work in progress, but I am gratified by how seriously the seminarians generally apply themselves and what it yields in the hearts and minds of our seminarians.

Conclusion

As seminary professors, and particularly as professors of sacred Scripture, we are in many ways preparing future priests for the front lines of the New Evangelization. This can be exciting and perhaps daunting work. It is hoped that this essay provides some measure of encouragement that the challenge is great but always worth whatever efforts we can make—for our students are the work of Christ. In the end, we seek to help our seminarians draw all people to the Living Word, to an encounter with Jesus Christ.

Moreover, as much as we are ourselves called to evangelize, we are reminded that first and foremost the most important task is being evangelized ourselves:

> The Church is an evangelizer, but she begins by being evangelized herself. She is the community of believers, the community of hope lived and communicated, the community of brotherly love, and she needs to listen unceasingly to what she must believe, to her reasons for hoping, to the new commandment of love. She is the People of God immersed in the world, and often tempted by idols, and she always needs to hear the proclamation of the 'mighty works of God' which converted her to the Lord; she always needs to be called together afresh by Him and reunited. In brief, this means that she has a constant need of being evangelized, if she wishes to retain freshness, vigor and strength in order to proclaim the Gospel.[25]

25. *Evangelii nuntiandi*, §15; see Acts 2:11; 1 Pet 2:9.

CHAPTER 3

Looking but Not Always Seeing: The Relevance of Johannine Irony to the New Evangelization

Michael Magee

At the close of the Thirteenth Ordinary General Assembly of the Synod of Bishops held in Rome in October 2012, the Synod Fathers' message to the People of God highlighted the beloved pericope of the Samaritan woman from the fourth chapter of John's Gospel as a paradigm for the longing for fulfillment experienced by every human heart:

> Let us draw light from a Gospel passage: Jesus' encounter with the Samaritan woman (cf. John 4:5–42). There is no man or woman who, in one's life, would not find oneself like the woman of Samaria beside a well with an empty bucket, with the hope of finding the fulfillment of the heart's most profound desire, that which alone could give full meaning to life. Today, many wells offer themselves up in order to quench humanity's thirst, but we must discern in order to avoid polluted waters. We must orient the search properly, so as not to fall prey to disappointment, which can be damaging.[1]

Certainly hidden beneath this insight is the realization of a similarity between the Samaritan woman's initial incomprehension and the incomprehension of the wider world to whom the Gospel must be addressed, between the stages by which the woman comes to know her interlocutor and the stages by which *any* and *all* unbelievers come to faith in Jesus Christ. First approached

---

1. Synod of Bishops, *Message to the People of God at the Conclusion of the 13th Ordinary General Assembly of the Synod of Bishops* (October 26, 2012), www.vatican.va/roman_curia/synod/documents/rc_synod_doc_20121026_message-synod_en.html, §1.

by a tired traveler who needs something from her ("Jesus said to her, 'Give me a drink'" [4:7 NABRE]), she quickly finds herself instead, by an unexpected reversal of roles, in the presence of One who has something valuable to give her ("If you knew the gift of God and who is saying to you, 'Give me a drink,' you would have asked him and he would have given you living water" [4:10]). This interchange thus opens up for the reader the two very distinct levels on which this conversation between Jesus and the Samaritan woman is simultaneously taking place.[2]

As the woman asks Jesus in puzzlement, "Are you greater than our father Jacob, who gave us this cistern and drank from it himself with his children and his flocks?" (4:12), the Greek text of her question (*mê sy meizôn ei . . .*) clearly assumes an answer in the negative. But the reader knows—and the course of the conversation nudges the woman toward the realization as well—that the correct answer is actually a resounding "Yes!" In fact, by the end of the Gospel, the reader will know from Jesus' own words his superiority even over Jacob's own forefather Abraham (8:53).[3]

The Samaritan woman quickly comes to understand that this mysterious visitor's offer of "living water" bespeaks the superhuman powers at his disposal, yet her concept of such "living water" (4:10) falls far short of what the reader will be able to deduce on the basis of clues given elsewhere in the text about this water (cf. 3:5, 7; 7:37–39; 19:34). She recognizes that he is *a prophet* but comes only by stages to recognize that he is in fact *the Messiah* of whom she speaks to him as someone absent (4:25). As the woman comes to accept, tentatively at first, the identification of Jesus as precisely this Messiah (4:29), the reader too has been prepared to accept his words by having gone through the whole revelatory process with the woman, experiencing with her the struggle to move from her own level of understanding to the true meaning of what Jesus is saying. In fact, the woman at each stage reveals a growing knowledge of the One with whom she is speaking, whereas as 4:26 makes clear, his own self-disclosure does not contradict what she knows, but rather transcends it.[4] Repeatedly (4:11, 15, 19) the woman addresses Jesus as *Kyrie*, which any translator correctly interprets as "Sir" according to her evident understanding, even while the reader is already prepared to hear in the same term a sense of which the woman herself is not yet aware, namely as "Lord"—indeed as the very word used throughout the Septuagint to stand for the unspoken divine name found

2. Gail R. O'Day, *Revelation in the Fourth Gospel* (Philadelphia: Fortress, 1986), 61.

3. O'Day, *Revelation in the Fourth Gospel*, 61.

4. O'Day, *Revelation in the Fourth Gospel*, 63–64, 73.

in the Hebrew text.[5] In the end, the woman's newly discovered insight results in a community of participants in the same vision that the reader will find resonates with his or her own experience of the relationship between evangelization, catechesis, and ecclesial communion (4:39–42).

In his 1929 commentary on the Gospel of John, John H. Bernard highlighted the "living water" of 4:10 among a series of "misunderstanding episodes" in chapters 3, 4, and 6, characterized by the pattern: 1) saying of Jesus; 2) misunderstanding; 3) repetitious expansion and explanation.[6] To the reader, the use of such double meanings might possibly appear to be merely a literary device in which the characters' misunderstanding then provides the occasion for a fuller explanation of the reality being highlighted. But Paul D. Duke's classic 1985 study characterizes such double meanings in the Gospel of John as only one element in a much more complex device, namely *irony*, yielding richer possibilities of interpretation here and throughout the Gospel.[7] John C. Fenton had earlier included 4:12 ("Are you greater than our father Jacob?") among a list of occurrences of irony in John's Gospel, meaning (in his estimation) that a character utters some truth even while being unaware of the truth—or at least the full truth regarding what is being said.[8] But Duke sees 4:10 within the con-

---

5. Gert J. Steyn, "Misunderstanding, Irony and Mistaken Identity in References to Jesus as Kyrios in John's Gospel," in *Miracles and Imagery in Luke and John*, BETL 218 (Dudley, MA: Peeters, 2008), 143, 148. Steyn notes similar examples in 9:35–38 and 20:14–16, in which someone unaware of Jesus' true identity addresses him as *Kyrie* while making reference to the Messiah/Son of Man/Jesus as if the latter were absent. Similarly, O'Day compares this double-meaning expression to the transition undergone in chapter 9 from v. 36, a *Kyrie* that the translator seems warranted in translating as "Sir," to a recurrence of the same word in v. 38 that the translator seems quite warranted in rendering as "Lord" because of the intervening revelation of Jesus' identity as the Son of Man in v. 37.

6. John H. Bernard, *A Critical and Exegetical Commentary on the Gospel According to John*, 2 vols., ICC 29 (New York: Scribner's Sons, 1929), pp. cxi–cxii. Cf. also Earl Richard, "Expressions of Double Meaning and their Function in the Gospel of John," in *New Testament Studies* 31, no. 1 (1985), 96. Bernard's other examples were: "born from above/again" in chapter 3; Jesus' "food" as doing the will of the Father in chapter 4; "food that lasts to eternal life" (6:27), thought by the hearers to be referring to manna; "Bread of Life," and the idea of Jesus' giving his flesh to eat, both also in chapter 6.

7. Paul D. Duke, *Irony in the Fourth Gospel* (Atlanta: John Knox, 1985), 101–103.

8. John C. Fenton, *The Gospel According to John in the Revised Standard Version* (Oxford: Clarendon, 1970), 21. The other examples given by him in the list are 2:9–10 ("You have kept the good wine until now"); 7:27 ("We know where this man comes from"); 7:42 ("The Christ is to come from Bethlehem"); 7:52 ("No prophet is to rise from Galilee"); 11:16 ("Let us also go, that we may die with him"); 11:36 ("See how he loved him!"); 12:19 ("Look, the world has gone after him!"); 13:37 ("I will lay down my life for you"); 18:31 ("It is not lawful for us to put

text of an extended irony in which the intended reader would have been conditioned by a series of Old Testament scenes at wells "to assume some context or overtone of impending marriage."[9] Thus the case of mistaken identity becomes all the more suspenseful as the reader, indeed already having seen Jesus characterized as the Bridegroom in the previous chapter, can see in him—albeit on a higher plane of interpretation—the very "Spouse" this unfortunate woman has been seeking in vain.

Duke masterfully shows the power of such a device, particularly in its manner of spurring the readers into active thought, refraining from dictating to them a specific meaning while leading them "to engage in an open search for solid ground that will make them grateful when they find it." "Inasmuch as irony does not coerce," he writes, "it has greater power among those who are at least somewhat open to its message."[10]

In Duke's analysis, the allure of irony may be traced as follows:

1) transfer of delight—i.e., the reader experiences pleasure in the experience of being led to reject a surface understanding while shifting to an alternate meaning and seeing the correctness of this shift confirmed;

2) an experience of community—i.e., such growth in insight creates a bond, first between the reader and the author, and then among readers, conveying a sense of a "privilege of election" in being part of a group who can now understand what is being said in the narrative from a privileged vantage point; and

3) the engagement of choice—i.e., the reader, because of having been actively involved in the process, experiences freedom of thought and the exhilaration of personal discovery.[11]

Duke convincingly characterizes this kind of presentation of truth as much more effective than simply presenting a logical case about the same truth: "Irony is precisely the appropriate instrument when reasoned argument has been set aside. It demands of its audience a choice, but its method is to win from *behind*—to launch an assault whose power is indirection, whose argument is a whisper."[12]

---

any man to death"); 18:38 ("I find no crime in him"); 19:5 ("Here is the man!"); 19:14 ("Here is your King!"); and 19:19–22 ("Jesus of Nazareth, the King of the Jews").

9. Duke, *Irony in the Fourth Gospel*, 101.

10. Duke, *Irony in the Fourth Gospel*, 37–38.

11. Duke, *Irony in the Fourth Gospel*, 154–155.

12. Duke, *Irony in the Fourth Gospel*, 153.

Even though the human author of the Gospel could not possibly have envisioned the audience referenced by the Synod of Bishops as calling for a "New Evangelization," it is truly striking how well some of the characteristics of its presentation, as described above, fit the needs of such an audience. Those who, "despite being baptized, live a life not in keeping with their Christian faith or express some kind of faith but have an imperfect knowledge of its basic tenets,"[13] would have some exposure to the Catholic Faith and probably think that they know more about it than they do, placing them in a situation not altogether unlike the characters of John's Gospel who look upon Jesus and only *think* that they understand him.

Similarly, the manner in which Johannine irony is used not simply to present a set of truths to readers, but actively to engage them in a process of coming to discover the full truth along with the characters, seems particularly illustrative of a method of evangelization suited to an age in which, as the *Instrumentum laboris* of the Synod explains, it is often "maintained that any attempt to convince others on religious matters is a limitation of their freedom."[14] In Johannine irony, on the contrary, the reader encounters something that is indeed an attempt to convince him of truths concerning Christ, but it *engages* rather than suppresses his freedom.

Additionally, in Johannine irony the reader experiences a privileged vantage point from which to apprehend the truth, and enjoys the possession of that truth as a function of becoming part of a privileged community who shares the same perspective. Such a process corresponds well to the ideal expressed by the Second Vatican Council's Declaration on Religious Freedom, *Dignitatis humanae*, §3, cited also in the Synod's *Instrumentum laboris*:

> Truth . . . is to be sought in a manner proper to the dignity of the human person and his social nature. The inquiry is to be free, carried on with the aid of teaching or instruction, communication and dialogue, in the course of which people explain to one another the truth they have discovered, or think they have discovered, in order thus to assist one another in the quest

13. Synod of Bishops, XIII Ordinary General Assembly, *Instrumentum laboris* "The New Evangelization for the Transmission of the Faith" (December 19, 2012), www.vatican.va /roman_curia/synod/documents/rc_synod_doc_20120619_instrumentum-xiii_en.html, §12. Cf. also Synod of Bishops, XIII Ordinary General Assembly, "Final List of Propositions" (October 27, 2012), www.vatican.va/news_services/press/sinodo/documents/bollettino_25 _xiii-ordinaria-2012/02_inglese/b33_02.html, Proposition 7, "New Evangelization as a Permanent Missionary Dimension of the Church."

14. Synod of Bishops, *Instrumentum laboris*, §35.

for truth. Moreover, as the truth is discovered, it is by a personal assent that people are to adhere to it.[15]

An observation of such vivid points of contact, even at a cursory examination, between the methodology of irony as used in the Gospel of John and the exigencies of the New Evangelization thus seems to invite a fuller study of irony as employed in the Gospel, followed by a concluding consideration of any insights that may be yielded thereby regarding the New Evangelization as such.

Studies of Irony in John

It seems clear that the technique of irony, similarly to most if not all techniques employed in art, emerged from the pens of literary artists long before it came to be analyzed and described as such. As Duke notes, the ancient Greeks "gave the name *eirôn* [to] that person who slyly pretended to be less than he really was," and cites as a prime example the great Socrates because of his "questioning his opponents with apparent innocence and admiration while ultimately intending to prove them fools."[16] The literary counterpart of such a figure was the *alazôn*, who contrarily exaggerated his importance and his knowledge.[17] The structure of dramatic or narrative irony is often such that either of these, the *eirôn* or the *alazôn*, might be cast in the role of the "victim," whose ignorance, dissimulation, or simulation is observed both by the ironist, who provides subtle clues on how to read the irony, and by the observer or reader, who is invited to read these clues and to view the action in the drama or the narrative from the privileged perspective constructed from these clues.[18]

The explicit observation of this technique in the Gospel of John became the object of sustained focus in the late twentieth century, primarily in English-language works focusing on the Gospel. The major works in question relied in turn on the findings of earlier studies. Already in 1919 H. A. A. Kennedy, while discussing the "symbolic element" in the Fourth Gospel in contrast to ancient Alexandrian allegorizing in his work *Philo's Contribution to Religion*, had noted John's "predilection for mysterious sayings which admit of divergent explanations," citing the allusiveness of passages such as 4:15–26 in the pericope of the

---

15. Synod of Bishops, *Instrumentum laboris*, §127.

16. Duke, *Irony in the Fourth Gospel*, 8.

17. Duke, *Irony in the Fourth Gospel*, 9.

18. R. Alan Culpepper, *Anatomy of the Fourth Gospel: A Study in Literary Design* (Philadelphia: Fortress, 1987), 177–179. The first edition of the work appeared in 1983.

Samaritan Woman.[19] In 1931, there followed W. F. Howard's "Symbolism and Allegory" in his edited work *The Fourth Gospel in Recent Criticism and Interpretation*.[20] Charles K. Barrett's 1955 commentary on the Gospel of John does make occasional reference to John's use of irony: for example, in reference to 7:42 regarding the misguided doubt on the part of some regarding Jesus' identification as the Messiah since the latter was supposed to come from Bethlehem rather than from Galilee, where they seem to think Jesus had been born.[21] And in mentioning Barrett's insights, Earl Richard observes that mention should also be made of Edwyn C. Hoskyns's *The Fourth Gospel*[22] and of C. H. Dodd's *The Interpretation of the Fourth Gospel*,[23] who consistently mention John's "expressions of double meaning" and who are acknowledged as Barrett's teachers.[24]

In 1973, George W. McRae published an article constituting a still more sustained focus on the theme, entitled "Theology and Irony in the Fourth Gospel."[25] The next year, there appeared Wayne C. Booth's work *A Rhetoric of Irony*, and all of the major works on irony in John's Gospel that appeared a decade later relied on the paradigm developed by Booth.[26] These works are principally three: Alan Culpepper's 1983 work *Anatomy of the Fourth Gospel*

19. Richard, "Expressions of Double Meaning," 96. Kennedy's work was published in London by Hodder & Stoughton.

20. Richard, "Expressions of Double Meaning," 96. Howard's work was republished in 1955.

21. Charles K. Barrett, *The Gospel according to St. John* (London: SPCK, 1955; Philadelphia: Westminster, 1978). Barrett's stated opinion ("We may feel confident that John was aware of the tradition that Jesus was born in Bethlehem. . . . [He] writes here in his customary ironical style," p. 330 of 1978 edition) seems far preferable to an interpretation that would miss the irony and suggest instead that that John was unaware of this tradition regarding the provenance of Jesus.

22. Edwyn C. Hoskyns, *The Fourth Gospel*, ed. Francis N. Davey (London: Faber & Faber, 1947).

23. C. H. Dodd, *The Interpretation of the Fourth Gospel* (Cambridge: Cambridge University Press, 1953).

24. Richard, "Expressions of Double Meaning," 108n7. These seem to be the works most prominently cited in the more recent literature, but it seems that very many other works could be cited at least as precursors to the study of irony in John: cf., Saeed Hamid-Khani, *Revelation and Concealment of Christ: the Theological Inquiry into the Elusive Language of the Fourth Gospel*, WUNT Reihe 2, 120 (Tübingen: Mohr Siebeck, 2000), 2n4.

25. George W. McRae, "Theology and Irony in the Fourth Gospel," in *The Word in the World: Essays in Honor of Frederick L. Moriarty, S.J.*, ed. Richard J. Clifford and George W. McRae (Cambridge, MA: Weston, 1973), 83–96.

26. Tom Thatcher, "The Sabbath Trick: Unstable Irony in the Fourth Gospel," in *Journal for the Study of the New Testament* 76 (1999): 54, in reference to Wayne C. Booth, *A Rhetoric of Irony* (Chicago: University of Chicago Press, 1974).

(already cited), opened up this specific forum of the discussion, and a much deeper inquiry into the theme occupies the entire volume published two years later by his student Paul D. Duke (also already cited), entitled *Irony in the Fourth Gospel*. The third work is Gail R. O'Day's *Revelation in the Fourth Gospel*.

O'Day published this book in 1986, one year after Duke's work, with the stated intention of mediating between and establishing a certain dialogue between the literary approaches of Culpepper and Duke on the one hand and the theological focus of McRae on the other. O'Day wished to provide "a more rigorous literary analysis than McRae does" at the same time placing "more emphasis on the integration of literary and theological dimensions than Duke and Culpepper do."[27] Tom Thatcher would comment in his 1999 article that these three books by Culpepper, Duke and O'Day "at once opened and seemingly closed the book on the subject."[28] At least up to the moment of publication of his own article—one which provided a very different perspective based on deconstructionist principles—Thatcher seems indeed to have been correct.

McRae borrowed his definition of irony from E. M. Good's study of irony in the Old Testament, locating its essence in the reader's perception of an incongruity—normally expressed in an understatement, double meanings, or the characters' saying the opposite of what is meant —and resting on the ironist's "claim to an insight into the truth of things that is not shared by everyone."[29] Duke's description is still more evocative when he refers to irony as

> a voice calling from great distance. It is an elevated perspective from which the initiated may view a world of rejected meanings and values far below. . . . So irony in the Fourth Gospel, with discourse splendidly extraordinary, invites the reader to abide with an ascended Christ and to see from that height what a world that loves darkness will not see.[30]

The Power of Irony in John

Herein lies a particular power pertaining to the use of irony in the proclamation of the Gospel message. Although all irony involves a distance shared between the reader and the ironist from the perspective of the victims of the irony in the drama or narrative, this distance in Greek irony exhibits a cathartic intention—e.g., in fearful situations "to bring about catharsis without actual terror."[31]

27. Cf. O'Day, *Revelation in the Fourth Gospel*, 6.
28. Thatcher, "The Sabbath Trick," 53.
29. McRae, "Theology and Irony in the Fourth Gospel," 84.
30. Duke, *Irony in the Fourth Gospel*, 1.
31. McRae, "Theology and Irony in the Fourth Gospel," 88.

In the Gospel, by contrast, this same distance rests on the reader's coming to share with the writer the perspective of *faith* in the one presented already in the Prologue as the preexistent *Logos*, whose identity and power have been vindicated by his dying and rising.[32]

A feature that Johannine irony shares with its Greek counterpart is the use of a prologue fulfilling the function of initiating the observers/readers to the privileged perspective from which they are empowered to interpret the events and the dialogue, and thus correctly to unmask the short-sightedness, the duplicity, and the misunderstandings.[33] The prologue thereby "provides firm footing for readers' reconstruction of hidden meanings and reception of suppressed signals behind the backs or 'over the heads' of its characters."[34]

Within the narrative, the reader is then able to see the misunderstandings that occur when characters fail to perceive the metaphors, double meanings, or other ambiguous expressions. In this way, the reader is trained to look for and to read such varying levels of meaning with a new sensitivity.[35] And as the narrative begins to present conflicts between Jesus and "the world," or between Jesus and "the Jews," both of which open up into the broader perspective of the conflicts "between the Christians contemporary with John and the Jewish communities that ostracized them, between the power of truth and error, between glory and suffering, between the divine and the human,"[36] the reader will already quite willingly have acquired a perspective that induces him freely to side with the perspective of the author. By the same token, the reader is led to side with the perspective of Jesus, who is sometimes the ironist in his own right, but never the victim of the irony in this narrative of his life and ministry (in fact, as Duke notes, Jesus is the *only* character in the Gospel who is never such).[37]

The use of irony also allows the Evangelist to present a message that not only stands in contrast to a popular misunderstanding but operates simultaneously on multiples levels. As Richard observes while discussing the multivalent term *anôthen* in Jesus' conversation with Nicodemus in chapter 3, "Many have suggested that John intends only one meaning . . . and uses the other as a literary ploy to allow Jesus to expound. . . . Instead, it is possible to conclude

---

32. McRae, "Theology and Irony in the Fourth Gospel," 88.

33. Thatcher, "The Sabbath Trick," 53.

34. Culpepper, *Anatomy of the Fourth Gospel*, 168.

35. Duke, *Irony in the Fourth Gospel*, 146.

36. McRae, "Theology and Irony in the Fourth Gospel," 88.

37. Duke, *Irony in the Fourth Gospel*, 45. On Jesus as the ironist, cf. Duke's discussion of "The Socratic Christ and his Little Children," and specifically of "The Irony of the Johannine Jesus," 43–53.

that John intended both." Although the word in question could mean "again" or "from above," or even "from the beginning," the author nowhere seems to choose between these meanings—provided that all of them are understood in a "heavenly" way—neither does he actively eliminate any one of them. Indeed, to Jesus as depicted by the Evangelist, being "born again" means precisely being "born from above."[38]

Examples of Johannine Themes Unveiled through Irony

Duke observes that not all themes in John are treated ironically, but that the focus in ironic passages is principally on the *origin* of Jesus (especially in contrast to certain expectations), the preeminence of Jesus in relation to the figures of Israel's past (namely the Patriarchs and Moses), and the meaning and effect of his death (particularly Israel's forfeiture of its prior status). In other words, Duke holds that the irony focuses principally on issues crucial to the debate between the Church and the synagogue at the time of the composition of the Gospel.[39] Besides the Gospel's Prologue, furthermore, he notes that the privileged perspective being shared with the reader rests on a firm knowledge of the Old Testament, albeit a knowledge that must be informed by the new perspectives being communicated.[40]

It is undoubtedly true that such debates as the one focusing on the origin of Jesus formed the crux of the conflict between the Church and the synagogue. But whereas this conflict provides the narrative setting for the irony constructed by the Evangelist, the same conflict of perspectives opens itself up to a plane of meaning that will be relevant to any reader, in any age. In the conflict over Jesus' provenance in chapter 7, for example, there does seem to be one level of irony present in 7:42, when some of the people doubt that Jesus could be the Christ/Messiah because he comes from Galilee rather than from Bethlehem. As Craig Keener argues, ancient sources indicate clearly that at least by the early second century, even non-Christian residents of Bethlehem recognized as longstanding a tradition locating the site of Jesus' birth in a specific cave there, so that it is highly unlikely that the Evangelist would have been unaware of this tradition. In this way, Keener supports the position of Barrett, already mentioned, that the idea of the non-provenance of Jesus from Bethlehem suggested by the characters contradicts a tradition of which the reader

---

38. Richard, "Expressions of Double Meaning," 103.
39. Duke, *Irony in the Fourth Gospel*, 93.
40. Duke, *Irony in the Fourth Gospel*, 141.

is assumed by the Evangelist to be aware.[41] Even so, this conflict of perspectives is not the only one constitutive of irony here; indeed, as Barrett notes, the question of Jesus' human birthplace pales in significance in relation to the far more profound perspective opened up to the reader not only by the Prologue, but even just a dozen verses earlier, in 7:28—Jesus' true "place of origin" is the Father.[42]

Particularly rich are the passages of the Gospel characterized by what Duke calls "sustained narrative irony," such as the stories of the man born blind in chapter 9 and the trial of Jesus in chapter 18. Here the reader is trained to perceive that it is not only individual words and expressions, but a whole picture of life that can be quite other than its surface appearance would indicate. There are many reasons to suppose that the "experts" appearing in the scene ought to have the correct answers and to judge things wisely, yet it is the physically blind man, enlightened by Jesus, who "sees with increasing clarity," whereas "the ones who claim sight plunge into progressively thickening night."[43]

In the trial scene, the reader is already in the thick of the principal irony concerning the destiny of Jesus, namely the characterization of his death as an exaltation.[44] Yet it is not merely words, either *of* Jesus or *about* Jesus, that prove to be susceptible of alternative interpretations on different levels; rather, it is the very appearance of the events themselves that may deceive an observer who fails to understand them from the vantage point to which the Evangelist invites the reader. As Richard puts it, "An important feature of this Johannine device is precisely that the reader can proceed through the trial narrative without being aware of the second meaning. Initiation to the Johannine perspective, however, offers insights into deeper meanings."[45] In this respect, much has been made of the ambiguity of possible meanings that characterizes the expression in 19:13, of which Pilate is the subject in either case: *ekathisen epi bêmatos.* The form of the verb here might be understood either as intransitive (meaning that Pilate himself sits on the judge's bench), or as transitive with Jesus as the object (meaning that Pilate causes Jesus to sit on the same bench).[46] Undoubtedly the former is more plausible in historical terms, but in the context of a Gospel so rich in irony, it is not unlikely that the Evangelist is inviting the insightful reader

41. Craig S. Keener, *The Gospel of John: A Commentary* (Peabody, MA: Hendrickson, 2003), 731.

42. Barrett, *The Gospel according to St. John,* 330–331.

43. Duke, *Irony in the Fourth Gospel,* 118.

44. Duke, *Irony in the Fourth Gospel,* 113.

45. Richard, "Expressions of Double Meaning," 104.

46. Barrett, *The Gospel according to St. John,* 544.

to realize that it is Jesus who is really in control here, as many surrounding clues regarding his royal status would suggest.[47] Indeed, one writer has provocatively encapsulated the irony of this trial scene by suggesting that it could be entitled "Pilate and the Jews before Jesus."[48]

In the realization of what is actually happening behind and even in contrast to the level of surface appearances, the reader comes to appreciate that in coming to see matters from the perspective of the Evangelist, one is not merely gaining a sane intellectual grasp of things but is moreover gaining a foothold from which to make practical and meaningful decisions as well. In fact, as one sees misguided characters pursuing courses of action that result in the very opposite of what they intended, one comes to appreciate the fact that living in the world of appearances will very likely degenerate into an exercise in futility on many levels. Here again, Duke's analysis is so well written that it cannot be paraphrased or abridged without significant loss:

> Had these patriots heard the double meaning in Jesus' early warning, they might not have fallen victim to their own zeal: "Destroy this temple," he had dared them (2:19). Accordingly, they did. They destroyed the temple of his body to save their own temple. But the temple rejected was in three days built again, and the temple "saved" was destroyed indeed.[49]

Such an interpretation rests on clues found elsewhere, both inside and outside of the Gospel. The intention of Jesus' enemies is understood in light of the statement of Caiaphas in 11:50 that "it is better for you that one man should die instead of the people, so that the whole nation may not perish."

Duke's reading of the irony seems also to presuppose a dating of the Gospel late enough so that the reader is aware of the actual destruction of the Temple in Jerusalem in AD 70. In fact, it is here in the passage concerning Caiaphas that the Evangelist does something that is generally alien to literary irony: he actually *tells* the reader why the situation is ironic (i.e., 11:51—"He did not say this on his own, but since he was high priest for that year, he prophesied"). Here, as Duke ascertains, "The author has broken the silence of irony to remind us that he himself is not the Ironist."[50] Ultimately it is God alone who provides the perspective from which the irony can be grasped.

---

47. Richard, "Expressions of Double Meaning," 103.

48. Duke, *Irony in the Fourth Gospel*, 127. Duke is referring to a suggestion of the German exegete Josef Blank.

49. Duke, *Irony in the Fourth Gospel*, 87.

50. Duke, *Irony in the Fourth Gospel*, 89.

Irony as Intrinsic to the Gospel Message

A sustained study of irony in the Gospel of John progressively seems to reveal that for the Evangelist, irony is not merely a preferred, clever tool for reaching an audience, but a methodology of presentation that corresponds profoundly to the reality of the Gospel message as such. The tension between the level of appearances and the level of meaning that is accessible only to the initiated is not only a tension that marks the real-life situation of the early Church whose message was so readily misunderstood by the world; this tension corresponds, in fact, to the logic of the Incarnation itself, and therefore to the manner in which God reveals himself in Christ as the *Logos*. Gail O'Day is referring to Bultmann's commentary but her insight seems valid in absolute terms when she observes that the Bultmann's exegetical "portrait of the *Logos* is actually more ironical than paradoxical," in the sense that "if a man wishes to see the *doxa* then it is on the *sarx* that he must concentrate his attention, without falling victim to appearances."[51]

Beyond the person of Jesus and in his light, John's irony therefore seems to constitute less a methodology than a worldview. McRae observes in this vein that Johannine irony rests on "the view that the world itself and the symbols it uses are *ambiguous*. These can be used as an avenue of access to the divine, but they can also lead only to themselves. . . . Indeed . . . in the Fourth Gospel theology *is* irony."[52] Symbolism, which all exegetes acknowledge to be so rich in the Gospel of John, is closely related to irony precisely because any symbols that are present there take on the quality of irony whenever one sees only the surface of things, and fails to apprehend the symbol precisely as such.[53] Thus, while it has sometimes been suggested that Johannine irony, as one of the literary features of the Gospel, suggests the characterization of the Gospel as a work of literary artifice *rather* than the account of an eyewitness,[54] such a false dichotomy is unnecessary, since irony actually seems to provide the key to the manner in which the Evangelist is understanding and depicting the profound truth embedded within the events themselves.

In the context of the Gospel's proclamation, by which a correct understanding of things is communicated to believers, the divergence of alternative visions constitutive of irony marks not only a metaphysical and epistemological divide, but a moral one as well. Jesus is "from above" (*anô*), whereas those who

51. O'Day, *Revelation in the Fourth Gospel*, 6.
52. McRae, "Theology and Irony in the Fourth Gospel," 88–89.
53. Richard, "Expressions of Double Meaning," 107.
54. E.g., Fenton, *The Gospel According to John*, 19–20.

oppose him are "from below" (*katô*, 8:23); he sees and communicates "heavenly matters" (*ta epourania*), whereas those who refuse to accept his message are confined to "earthly matters" (*ta epigeia*, 3:12), and therefore find themselves imprisoned in falsehood, deception and error.[55] As Culpepper affirms, "In a world in which people get what they want to avoid, lose what they want to protect, and cannot find what they are looking for, it is understandable that the Christ would not be recognized by those who were looking for him."[56]

Although it is true that irony depends upon a conflict between alternative meanings, O'Day insightfully emphasizes—even criticizing Culpepper and Duke for failing to note sufficiently—that the alternative meanings are not polar opposites. Rather, the reader, like the believer in Jesus, is being invited to see the real meaning not as independent or removed from the appearance, but as accessible by means of a correct grasp of the truth perceptible *in* and *through* the surface meaning.[57]

Meanwhile, the predicament of those who refuse to accept the privileged perspective offered by the Gospel message is actually exacerbated by their conviction of having grasped the totality when, in fact, they have only stopped at the threshold. Since the "signs" of Jesus are multivalent, they *can* be revelations of Jesus' glory to believers (2:11, at Cana), whereas in other cases they can become obstacles (4:48: "Unless you people see signs and wonders, you will not believe").[58] In this vein, Jesus shows (7:28) that those who profess to know his place of origin may in fact be touting a concrete truth, even as they fail to recognize his true origin from the Father, so that, as Bultmann states, "Their knowledge is unknowing, for they use their knowledge, which in itself is perfectly correct, to conceal the very thing which it is important to know."[59] Indeed, even the disciples themselves have fallen prey to similar misunderstandings and have had to move beyond them, as when Nathanael asks, "Can anything good come from Nazareth?" failing in that moment, at least, to recognize Jesus' true origin.[60]

Particularly interesting are the moments in which the "sign" to be grasped in its real depth—as is possible only from the standpoint provided by the Gospel message itself —is none other than the very Scriptures that Israel guards and cherishes as her own. Not infrequently, the enemies of Jesus demonstrate

---

55. Culpepper, *Anatomy of the Fourth Gospel*, 167.
56. Culpepper, *Anatomy of the Fourth Gospel*, 177.
57. O'Day, *Revelation in the Fourth Gospel*, 8.
58. McRae, "Theology and Irony in the Fourth Gospel," 93.
59. Duke, *Irony in the Fourth Gospel*, 48.
60. Duke, *Irony in the Fourth Gospel*, 54.

only a partial and fragmented grasp of their own Scriptures. For example, Jesus tells his listeners, "Moses wrote of me," in an apparent allusion to Deuteronomy 18:15–22. Ironically, however, some of these reject Jesus *precisely* on the basis of Deuteronomy 18:20, which condemns any prophet *presuming* to speak in God's name an oracle that he has not spoken.[61] It is because they see the Scriptures as a self-contained reality, complete in themselves, that they fail to see the truth beyond themselves to which the Scriptures point—namely Jesus.

Also figuring as interesting features of Johannine irony are the characters who embody the dynamic tension of irony either as paradigmatic of the journey of faith, as in the case of Peter, or as emblematic of the tragedy of loss owing to disbelief, as in the case of Judas. Duke encapsulates these features of the narrative by saying of Peter, "Ironically, it is the one who rushes to shout his early commitment first, the one who understands death least, who will come to himself only by miserable failure and will come to Jesus by freely chosen death." He observes conversely of Judas that "precisely at the moment of greatest grace from Jesus [i.e., having accepted the morsel from his hands] he wrenches himself from intimacy with the Light and plunges into outer darkness."[62]

The power of irony in the Gospel of John encompasses and yet transcends the features that render it effective in drama or literature elsewhere. Corresponding as it does to the stages by which the Incarnate Son invites disciples to pass through the appearances of his Person, his life and his works, and to proceed from there into the deeper truths and the invisible realities that he communicates, John uses the technique of irony precisely to enter into the very dynamism of this revelation itself. The engagement that this process demands of the reader creates a sense of involvement much greater than could possibly occur from reading a baldly straightforward text.[63] This quality of irony is expressed vividly in Duke's description of that dynamism in the story of Mary Magdalene's encounter with the risen Jesus in the garden:

> It is one thing to read an angel's announcement, "He has risen, he is not here."—to be *told* about the resurrection. But to watch tear-blinded Mary stumbling over angels and oblivious to the nearness of the one she mourns until she hears her name on his lips—that is to be *shown* resurrection, to savor it, and somehow to experience it.[64]

---

61. Paul N. Anderson, "The Not-having-sent-me Father: Aspects of Agency, Encounter, and Irony in the Johannine Father-Son Relationship," in *Semeia* 85 (1999): 49.

62. Duke, *Irony in the Fourth Gospel*, 99.

63. O'Day, *Revelation in the Fourth Gospel*, 30, 95.

64. Duke, *Irony in the Fourth Gospel*, 105.

On the one hand, the Gospel is ruthless in its depiction of the willful blindness of those who refuse to be open to the depths of its irony: they love darkness rather than light (3:19); they seek the glory of men rather than the glory of God (5:44); they see, but reject what they see (9:39–41). But at the same time, the Evangelist makes clear that the perspective from which to read the irony, and thus to arrive at the truth, belongs only to those who are given (6:37), drawn (6:44), or called (6:70; 10:3).[65] Thus, in the very proclamation of the Gospel, far more is happening than the transfer of information. A right comprehension of this Gospel not only requires but effects the extending of an invitation, the bestowal of a gift, and the creation of a community: "Irony involves not only position and values, but the interpretive act itself, which . . . draws the reader into an impression of belonging to a privileged minority who see the irony that uninitiated, ordinary eyes do not."[66]

Application to the Situation of the New Evangelization

Although the world of the original readers of the Gospel of John is quite different from the world of today, a number of the prejudices and predispositions of the characters that render the Gospel characters "victims" of Johannine irony seem to exhibit striking points of contact with those of the populations described at the outset of this study as the faithful to whom the "New Evangelization" is to be addressed.

Sometimes today, hearers of the divine word may tend to be over-confident of their certainty regarding the true nature of things but oblivious to the greater part of reality; apathetic in relation to any realities lying beyond the world of appearances; distrustful of claims of "truth" that they regard as threats to freedom of thought and action; and individualistic in their pursuits of solitary or at least self-serving satisfaction. These may find marked out in the Fourth Gospel a path not altogether unlike the one that they also would probably need to travel in order to grasp the same truths with true insight. Perhaps such points of contact, despite great differences in culture and technological development, help account for the perennial fascination that the Gospel of John holds for readers of every age. Even so, this Gospel derives much of its power and vitality from its proximity to the very events of Jesus' life and of the Paschal Mystery. In this regard, the written Gospel itself is utterly inimitable. It does not seem

65. Culpepper, *Anatomy of the Fourth Gospel*, 178–179.
66. Duke, *Irony in the Fourth Gospel*, 39.

possible to rewrite the same message, using the same kind of techniques, in a different way for the sake of the New Evangelization.

Even so, it seems that lessons for the New Evangelization can be learned not just from imitating the literary forms of the Gospel, but from paying close attention to the objectives that the Evangelist holds dear, and acknowledging that it is precisely his attention to these objectives —subordinate, of course, to the primary goal of introducing his readers to the Person of Jesus Christ—that renders the Evangelist so effective. Attention to the same objectives, again in subordination to the same supreme goal, seems to offer the promise of rendering the New Evangelization similarly vibrant and effective.

First, today's evangelist can learn from this Evangelist that he is most effective when he does more than present to his readers a straightforward enumeration of truths, whether of an historical or of a theoretical nature. To readers confident of their own grasp of reality, John shows characters who in many ways are similar to today's readers themselves. At the same time, he provides clues to help such readers perceive that their grasp of reality, although not incorrect, is only partial and—precisely in this sense—deceptive and unsatisfying. Like John the Evangelist, the New Evangelist must know his audience well, and must be conscious of having passed through the same antechamber of reality in which his audience still dwells. Having discovered a fuller truth, he must be able to beckon from his own gifted vantage point and to invite his hearers to recognize the signs that point beyond themselves to still greater realities. True stories of conversion and progressive enlightenment may serve to mark a path that others may follow.

Although homilies and other forms of proclamation certainly must incorporate good catechesis, they can never be limited to this if they are to be effective. Receptivity to catechesis presupposes an interest in learning the truths being conveyed. The homilist can learn much from John's way of coaxing the reader to become actively involved in his narrative. Only by means of such involvement does the reader come to a new awareness that is experienced as a personal discovery rather than merely an assimilated text or body of objective truth.

The hearer of the Gospel, while being evangelized, must be able to ascertain that he or she is not merely learning facts but moreover acquiring new eyes with which to see the same realities that he or she thought were already so familiar. It is not merely a self-contained list of realities but one's whole life— and indeed the world itself—that one will come to view differently from this new and privileged vantage point.

Just as integral to the methodology of the New Evangelist must be a respect for the freedom of the hearer similar to that which characterizes the

Johannine presentation of the Gospel message. The hearer of the word, having been induced to become involved and personally invested in the process of discovery by the way in which the message has been presented, experiences no limitation of his freedom in the presentation of the truths that now make a claim on him. Quite to the contrary, he experiences rather an *enhancement* of that freedom. One who has been effectively evangelized will spontaneously seek to share with others the same gift that he has received.

One crucial value upon which New Evangelization depends is the willingness to overcome individualistic tendencies and to participate in the shared perspectives of the faith community, something that is likewise essential to the presentation and apprehension of Johannine irony. Indeed, it is fascinating to imagine what would have been the result of the same text of John's Gospel if it had been discovered as an artifact in manuscript form, rather than as a treasured vehicle of a living community of believers. If such had been the case, it is difficult to imagine that the Gospel's message would ever have been heard in the same way as it has been, since the privileged vantage point from which the reader must discover the irony in the text is not completely encapsulated within the text but rests also on the Old Testament, on a knowledge of historical occurrences and cultural factors, and on the living memory of believers. Again, such a manner of coming to know the truth leaves the recipient of the message with the experience that ensures him that this community is no menace to his freedom but is in fact the milieu within which his own new and freely shared worldview has been nourished and strengthened.

Finally, the tension between appearance and reality found both in Johannine irony and in the Person of the Incarnate *Logos* manifests a tension that continues to challenge those who proclaim him as the Savior in any age. It will always be possible for one to stop at a partial, superficial or even distorted portrait of Jesus while presuming to have understood him fully and correctly. By contrast, it is precisely because Johannine irony leads to a deeper personal knowledge of Jesus that it not only titillates the mind but touches the heart as it does. Effective evangelization, accordingly, can never be assured by means of pedagogical method, canned programmatic presentations, or gnostic initiation into truths held collectively. John's dynamism of irony leads the attentive reader from surface appearances into deeper truths, and onward into infinity—and the knowledge to which it leads the attentive reader transcends even the most comprehensive catalogue of abstract truths. By its very nature, it aims ultimately at the revelation of the *personal* reality of the divine Word. The New Evangelist, just as all effective evangelists before him, will never be effective without realizing that one cannot grasp and master this reality but rather must *be grasped and mastered by it.* As John and his community know so well, in order to evangelize effectively one must be able to share the perspective that is articulated in the Gospel but continues to be passed on with undiminished vigor in the First Epistle of John, as exemplified by the latter's prologue:

> What was from the beginning, what we have heard, what we have seen with our eyes, what we looked upon and touched with our hands concerns the Word of life—for the life was made visible; we have seen it and testify to it and proclaim to you the eternal life that was with the Father and was made visible to us—what we have seen and heard we proclaim now to you, so that you too may have fellowship with us; for our fellowship is with the Father and with his Son, Jesus Christ (1 John 1:1–3).

CHAPTER 4

Old Testament Wisdom Literature and Formation for a New Evangelization

Stephen Ryan, OP

Assiduous reading of the Old Testament, love for learning, and pastoral charity are mentioned together in the Greek prologue to Sirach: "Now, those who read the scriptures must not only themselves understand them, but must also as lovers of learning be able through the spoken and written word to help the outsiders."[1] The topic addressed here is how these three elements can be highlighted in an introduction to Wisdom literature so as to better prepare seminarians for the new hearing of God's word and the New Evangelization being called for in recent decades.

The Wisdom books, especially the Psalms, play an indispensable role in both the initial and the ongoing formation of priests preparing for a New Evangelization. This essay suggests several ways to teach the Wisdom books (Job, Psalms, Proverbs, Ecclesiastes, Song of Songs, Wisdom of Solomon, and Sirach) with a view to preparing men to be more capable preachers and wiser confessors. The ministry of the Word exercised in preaching at Mass and in the sacrament of penance is a daily activity at the heart of priestly identity and ministry. The priest is sent to teach, to reconcile, to sanctify. In the ordination rite, the ordinandi are asked whether they are "resolved to exercise the ministry of the word worthily and wisely, preaching the gospel and explaining the Catholic faith." And in the Sacrament of Penance, priests are regularly afforded the opportunity to offer what John Paul II referred to as the vital core of the New Evangelization: "a clear and unequivocal proclamation of the person of Jesus Christ."[2]

---

1. Sirach, Prologue 5, NRSV. Biblical translations are taken from the NRSV or the NABRE unless otherwise noted.

2. Pope John Paul II, *Ecclesia in America* (January 22, 1999), www.vatican.va/content /john-paul-ii/en/apost_exhortations/documents/hf_jp-ii_exh_22011999_ecclesia-in-america .html, §66.

The task before us as educators and formators is daunting. We are asked to contribute to the forming of men docile to the Holy Spirit and to the grace of preaching, men who will be expected to be experts in the spiritual life, specialists in promoting the encounter between man and God.[3] *Lumen gentium* 37 puts it strongly: "The laity have the right [*ius habent*], as do all Christians, to receive in abundance from their spiritual shepherds the spiritual goods of the Church, especially the assistance of the word of God and of the sacraments."[4] With Paul we might ask, "Who is qualified for this?" (2 Cor 2:16). Benedict XVI cites Richard of Saint Victor's teaching "that we need 'the eyes of doves,' enlightened and taught by the Spirit, in order to understand the sacred text," (*Verbum Domini*, §16),[5] and, we could add, in order to teach it worthily.

Old Testament Wisdom and the New Evangelization

The term *wisdom* denotes a great number of realities, even within the Bible. On one level wisdom is an attribute of God, namely his truth ordering and governing all things.[6] Wisdom is also a gift of God, one of the seven gifts of the Holy Spirit and one that opens for the recipient a new way of seeing the world. "Wisdom," Joseph Ratzinger writes, "is a way of sharing in God's ability to see and judge things as they really are . . . a way of sharing in God's way of seeing reality."[7] Initially Scripture can help dispose us to receive and welcome the divine gift of wisdom. That divine gift can in turn lead to a more penetrating understanding of the biblical texts we have already encountered.

Scripture thus understood corrects and rightly orders our way of seeing, while vastly enlarging the scope of our vision, stretching it toward the divine,

3. These are the common expectations of priests as described by Benedict XVI, "Meeting with Clergy," Warsaw Cathedral, May 25, 2006, as cited in James Keating, "The Seminary and Western Culture: Relationships that Promote Recovery and Healing," *Nova et Vetera* 14 (2016): 1106.

4. Second Vatican Council, *Lumen gentium* (November 21, 1964), w2.vatican.va/archive /hist_councils/ii_vatican_council/documents/vat-ii_const_19641121_lumen-gentium_en .html, §37.

5. Pope Benedict XVI, *Verbum Domini* (September 30, 2010) (Boston: Pauline Books and Media, 2010), §16; cf. Richard of Saint Victor, *In Cantica Canticorum Explicatio*, caput 15 in PL 196, 450B and D.

6. *CCC*, §216: "God's truth is his wisdom, which commands the whole created order and governs the world."

7. Joseph Cardinal Ratzinger, *Principles of Catholic Theology* (San Francisco: Ignatius, 1987), 357. In *Verbum Domini* 87, in the context of a discussion of contemplation as the fourth stage of *lectio divina*, he refers similarly to "a gift from God, his own way of seeing and judging reality[,] . . . a truly wise and discerning vision of reality, as God sees it."

and opening the soul to divine grace. The Spirit's gifts of understanding and of wisdom are essential for readers to move from the words of the text to the realities they speak of. The gift of understanding, Aquinas teaches, "perfects faith by way of a certain penetrating vision" while the gift of wisdom "perfects charity by way of a certain experiential tasting."[8] As Mario Magrassi explains, wisdom "leads us to savor the divine Word, because it creates a kind of connaturality between the soul and Scripture. We read it under the guidance of the same Spirit who inspired it."[9]

In the Old Testament wisdom often denotes acquired wisdom, knowledge of the world gleaned from long experience. Most typically Wisdom literature deals with "daily human experience in the good world created by God."[10] To see order in the world and to perceive its intelligibility is already to know something of God the creator. The sage looks to the world, reflects on his own experience, and articulates the wisdom gained from experience in memorable, poetic form for the sake of the next generation. This kind of wisdom, although practical, is essentially concerned with the formation of character, not unlike the kind of human formation that is a focus of seminary education.

In addition to practical wisdom, the kind captured well in the French expressions *savoir faire* and *savoir vivre*, we also encounter what can be called theological, speculative, or theoretical wisdom. Examples are found in Proverbs 1–9, Wisdom of Solomon 7–9, and Sirach 24. Wisdom is described in many of these texts as coming from the Lord and as rightly orienting one toward God in a reverential fear that is said to be both the beginning (Prov 9:10) and the crown (Sir 1:18) of wisdom. Since personified wisdom in the Old Testament is one of the ways the New Testament lies hid in the Old (*in vetere novum latet*), careful study of these biblical texts in seminary contexts can aid especially the intellectual and spiritual formation of our students.

Wisdom thinking and wisdom genres such as proverbs and parables are not limited to the traditional Old Testament Wisdom books. Scholars note strong wisdom themes in Genesis, for example, especially Genesis 1–3 and 37–50, but also in a wide variety of biblical books. The practical instruction Tobit gives his son in Tobit 4, or the more speculative poem on wisdom in Baruch 3, are found in books categorized respectively as historical and prophetic. As Richard

---

8. Mario Magrassi, *Praying the Bible: An Introduction to* Lectio Divina (Collegeville, MN: Liturgical Press, 1998), 76. Here I rely on Magrassi's summary of Aquinas's commentary on the *Sententiae,* liber III, distinctio 34, quaestio 1, articulus 2.

9. Magrassi, *Praying the Bible,* 76.

10. Roland Murphy, *The Tree of Life,* 3rd ed. (Grand Rapids, MI: Eerdmans, 2002), 1.

Clifford has noted, "wisdom thinking was in the main stream of biblical literary production from whence its style and ideas radiated throughout biblical writings."[11] Wisdom teaching is also found in abundance in the New Testament, especially in the Sermon on the Mount and in the parables of Christ, in the paraenetic sections of Romans, and in the Letter of James.[12] All this is to say that biblical wisdom in its many facets is encountered throughout the Old and New Testaments, and awareness of this can help students to understand something of the unity of the Bible.[13]

There is a clear pedagogy in the Wisdom books. They teach in a manner that is attractive and accessible, giving understanding to the simple (Ps 119:130b) and strength even to the wise (Eccl 7:19). The Wisdom books contain divine teaching on fundamental areas of human experience, such as virtue, prayer, friendship, happiness, suffering, the nature of death, the immortality of the soul, the relationship of faith and reason, care for the poor, and the proper use and enjoyment of wealth. The transmission of Israelite wisdom is also depicted in these books, and it is often set in a familial context of a father instructing his sons (e.g., Prov 4:1; Sir 3:1). In Proverbs 1:8 we find a dual reference to a father's instruction and a mother's teaching: "Hear, my son, your father's instruction, and reject not your mother's teaching." These aspects of Old Testament wisdom can be connected to the pastoral formation of the students we teach, who will themselves teach and preach and who will be called to help mothers and fathers in their task of raising and educating children.

Old Testament Wisdom literature can be of particular relevance in the formation of priests prepared for the work of the New Evangelization. When one considers, for example, the work of human and intellectual formation, then the explicit focus on character formation and training in virtue found in books such as Proverbs and Sirach is seen to be directly relevant. Books such as Job

11. Richard Clifford, SJ, "Introduction to Wisdom Literature," in *The New Interpreter's Bible*, vol. 5 (Nashville: Abingdon, 1997), 1.

12. Jeremy Corley traces the influence of Sirach on all four Gospels in his article, "Tracing Wisdom from Sirach to the Gospels," in *Weisheit als Lebensgrundlage: Festschrift Friedrich Reiterer*, ed. Renate Egger-Wenzel, Karin Schöpflin, and Johannes F. Diehl, DCLS 15 (Berlin: de Gruyter, 2013), 27–46.

13. Edward Greenstein ("Wisdom in Ugaritic," in *Language and Nature: Papers Presented to John Huehnergard on the Occasion of His 60th Birthday*, ed. Rebecca Hasselbach and Na'ama Pat-El [Chicago: The Oriental Institute, 2012], 69) describes Wisdom literature as "an international literary category," noting that it is "much broader and vaguer than a genre." Wisdom themes, language, and teaching are found throughout the Bible. In teaching this material, I include a small sample of ancient Near Eastern texts, Baruch 3–4, Tobit 4, several Psalms, as well as passages from the New Testament and Pirqe Avot.

and Ecclesiastes address suffering and the ambiguities of the human experience in ways which broaden a student's experience and aid in his maturation. The spiritual formation of seminarians and priests, the forming of an ecclesial spirit, is closely associated with their daily and lifelong contact with the Book of Psalms. The Wisdom of Solomon can offer a powerful biblical model for the pastoral formation of seminarians preparing for the ministry of the Word in the New Evangelization. It is a beautiful and persuasive presentation and development of the truth of the biblical tradition for a minority community living in Alexandria, the heart of the intellectual marketplace of Hellenistic Egypt.[14] The Wisdom of Solomon's inspired use of earlier biblical texts exemplifies "a search for wisdom, a search for God's overarching, eternal plan, revealed by a careful, sagely reading of Scripture."[15] Reflection on the form and content of this book may well aid in finding new ways "to help the people of our time to hear the living and eternal Word of the Lord."[16]

Biblical Formation and Wisdom Literature

The Second Vatican Council addressed the biblical formation of seminarians in a number of places. Candidates for holy orders, *Optatum totius* 16 (1965) says, "are to be formed with particular care [*peculiari diligentia*] in the study of the Bible, which ought to be, as it were, the soul of all theology." Seminarians are to be instructed to learn how to pray with Scripture daily, so as "to receive from their daily reading of and meditating on the sacred books inspiration and nourishment." *Dei verbum* 25 instructs deacons and priests "to hold fast to the Sacred Scriptures through diligent sacred reading and careful study [*assidua lectione sacra atque exquisito studio*], especially the priests of Christ." Finally, *Presbyterorum ordinis* 19 (1965) speaks of the sacral character of a priest's ongoing intellectual formation: "The knowledge of the sacred minister ought to be sacred because it is

14. Richard J. Clifford, *The Wisdom Literature* (Nashville: Abingdon, 1998) 134, 136–137; see also Richard J. Clifford, *Wisdom*, NCoBC 20 (Collegeville, MN: Liturgical Press, 2013), 6. Clifford argues that the author of the Wisdom of Solomon seeks to demonstrate that Israel has in abundance everything an ancient philosophy needed to attract followers: miracles, an offer of immortality, and antiquity. For a more detailed discussion of the philosophical currents in Alexandria of the author's day see Otto Kaiser, *Die Weisheit Salomos* (Stuttgart: Radius, 2010), 77–89.

15. Peter Enns, "Pseudo-Solomon and His Scripture: Biblical Interpretation in the Wisdom of Solomon," in *A Companion to Biblical Interpretation in Early Judaism*, ed. Matthias Henze (Grand Rapids, MI: Eerdmans, 2012), 410.

16. Pope Benedict XVI, *Ubicumque et semper* (September 21, 2010), www.vatican.va /content/benedict-xvi/en/apost_letters/documents/hf_ben-xvi_apl_20100921_ubicumque -et-semper.html.

drawn from the sacred source[,] . . . drawn from reading and meditating [*lectione et meditatione*] on the Sacred Scriptures, and it is equally nourished by the study of the Holy Fathers and other Doctors and witnesses of the tradition."[17]

Peter Williamson has identified five points in *Verbum Domini* that have practical implications for preparing seminarians for the ministry of the Word.[18] The first is the exhortation's prioritizing of the ministry of the Word in the life of the priest. Citing the 1992 document *Pastores dabo vobis* of St. John Paul II, *Verbum Domini* 80 writes: "The priest is first of all a minister of the Word of God, consecrated and sent to announce the Good News of the Kingdom to all." Scripture is at the heart of seminary formation since it is at the heart of priestly ministry. "The word of God is indispensable in forming the heart of a good shepherd and minister of the word" (*Verbum Domini*, §78). The "Scripture Across the Curriculum" program at Sacred Heart Seminary in Detroit seeks to make that a reality.

The second point, found in *Verbum Domini* 82, is that seminarians "must learn to love the word of God" so that the divine Word can help them to discern, love, and follow their specific vocation. How might one do that in a course on Wisdom literature? Can love of the Word of God be taught in a class or only caught? It would be helpful to use several verses from Psalm 119, an integral part of midday prayers and so likely prayed by the students shortly before or after a weekday class, to indicate something of the depths of Old Testament spirituality and to join the classroom and the chapel.

Here are two brief examples: "I treasure your word in my heart, so that I may not sin against you" (Ps 119:11). The verb translated "treasure" (Hebrew צפן/*spn*) is rendered with verbs of hiding or concealing in the Greek (κρύπτω/ *kruptō*) and Latin (*abscondo*) translations. They suggest a deep interior assimilation of the words recited on the lips and recall the references to Mary "treasuring all these words and pondering them in her heart" in Luke 2:19. Augustine uses the psalm verse to speak of the fruit of any true reading of the Bible, *actio*. He describes the psalmist's desire to "learn [the ways of justice] as people

---

17. Second Vatican Council, *Optatam totius* (October 28, 1965), www.vatican.va/archive /hist_councils/ii_vatican_council/documents/vat-ii_decree_19651028_optatam-totius_en.html, §16; *Dei verbum* (November 18, 1965), www.vatican.va/archive/hist_councils/ii_vatican_council /documents/vat-ii_const_19651118_dei-verbum_en.html, §25; *Presbyterorum ordinis* (December 7, 1965), www.vatican.va/archive/hist_councils/ii_vatican_council/documents/vat-ii_decree _19651207_presbyterorum-ordinis_en.html, §19.

18. Peter Williamson, "Preparing Seminarians for the Ministry of the Word in Light of Verbum Domini," in *Verbum Domini and the Complementarity of Exegesis and Theology*, ed. Scott Carl, CTFS (Grand Rapids, MI: Eerdmans, 2015), 85–88.

who carry them out learn them, not as those who simply memorize them in order to have something to say . . . he wants to learn them by putting them into practice."[19] For preachers the *actio* born of love of the Word of God is preaching. To use Sirach's grandson's words, "it is the duty of those who read the scriptures not only to become knowledgeable themselves but also to use their love of learning in speech and in writing to help others less familiar."[20]

To move to a second example, Psalm 119:47–48 reads: "I find my delight in your commandments, because I love them. I revere your commandments, which I love, and I will meditate on your statutes." The Greek and Latin translations of the verb "I find my delight" in v. 47 substitute another image, replacing delighting in the commandments with meditating on them, using the verbs μελετάω (*meletaō*) and *meditor*. These translations thus indicate that the psalmist meditated or pondered because he loved. The psalmist was able to love God's commandments, Augustine comments,

> By the same power that enabled him to walk continually in wide freedom [v. 45 *ambulabam in latitudine*]: by the Holy Spirit through whom love itself is poured out, that love which enlarges the heart of the faithful . . . *Which I loved*, for the end of the commandment is charity springing from a pure heart (see 1 Tim 1:5) . . . for a person who loves God's commandments and keeps them delightedly in thought and deed is certainly happy in God's ways of justice and is even inclined to chatter about them.[21]

Including Wisdom 16:26 ("your word sustains those who trust in you") in the context of introducing the texts above could add another dimension to the love of the Word, that of the Word as food for the soul. This would help students to identify a similar spiritual depth even in books of such disparate origin and genre such as the Psalms and the Wisdom of Solomon. Integrating a reflective moment of silence during the presentation of these texts, or giving students some time to recall similar texts from the Bible could enrich the discussion.

The third aspect of *Verbum Domini* that has practical implications for seminarians has to do with the prominence given specifically to *lectio divina*, which is mentioned frequently and outlined in paragraphs 86–87. In recent decades the Church has been repeatedly renewing the call for all Catholics to appropriate aspects of this ancient way of Christian prayer. John Paul II refers to *lectio*

19. St. Augustine, "Exposition 5 of Psalm 118," in *Exposition of the Psalms 99–120*, ed. Boniface Ramsey, trans. Maria Boulding, OSB, WOSA 3/19 (Hyde Park, NY: New City, 2003), 361.

20. Unnumbered foreword to Sirach as translated in the NABRE.

21. St. Augustine, "Exposition 14 of Psalm 118," in *Exposition of the Psalms 99–120*, ed. Boniface Ramsey, trans. Maria Boulding, OSB, WOSA 3/19 (Hyde Park, NY: New City, 2003), 405–406.

divina as an "essential element of spiritual formation," and describes it as "a humble and loving listening of him who speaks" (*Pastores dabo vobis*, §47).[22]

The fourth point Williamson identifies, "the relationship between biblical studies and scriptural prayer" (*Verbum Domini*, §82), helps us to see the close connection between academic study and prayer. Prayer is a natural response to a growth in knowledge of God gained by study, and prayer can awaken a deeper desire to grow in knowledge of God through study. "Hence, great care should be taken to ensure that seminarians always cultivate this reciprocity between study and prayer in their lives" (*Verbum Domini*, §82). Drawing connections between the biblical texts of a given liturgical day or of the following Sunday and the subject matter being taught in class helps students to cultivate this reciprocity and become men of the Church, formed by the liturgical use of Scripture. The introduction of moments of reflective silence into the classroom is another way to help students to see the organic and reciprocal relationship *Verbum Domini* speaks of.

The fifth point is the exhortation's teaching about three aspects of the ministry of the Word: preaching better homilies (§59), developing more biblically inspired catechesis, (§74) and the centrality of the word of God in all of the pastoral work of the Church, "making the Bible the inspiration of every ordinary and extraordinary pastoral outreach" (§73). With regard to preaching, the continuity here with *Pastores dabo vobis* 47 is worth noting. Speaking of forming priests for the New Evangelization, John Paul II taught that "loving knowledge of the word of God and a prayerful familiarity with it are specifically important for the prophetic ministry of the priest. They are a fundamental condition for such a ministry to be carried out suitably, especially if we bear in mind the "new evangelization" which the Church today is called to undertake." If in the end preaching is a grace that has to be given, and even if the sacrament of ordination itself powerfully disposes a man to become an instrument of Christ who speaks through him, nonetheless the "fundamental condition" John Paul II describes is obtained by the hard work of study and daily fidelity to prayer.

Study and Wisdom Literature

Referring to the ancient practices of memorization and meditation on Scripture, John Cassian writes: "As our mind is increasingly renewed by this study, Scripture begins to take on a new face. A mysteriously deeper sense of it comes to us and somehow the beauty of it stands out more and more as we get farther

---

22. Pope John Paul II, *Pastores dabo vobis* (March 25, 1992), www.vatican.va/content /john-paul-ii/en/apost_exhortations/documents/hf_jp-ii_exh_25031992_pastores-dabo-vobis .html, §47.

into it."[23] The text, Gregory the Great says, grows with the reader. And readers grow with study. Academic study, Simone Weil has argued, develops our ability to pay attention. And it is precisely attention which we need, both for prayer, understood as paying attention to God, and for learning to really see the suffering of others.[24] In *Evangelii gaudium* 146, Pope Francis begins his discussion of homily preparation with the themes of attention and of study as reverence of the truth. This is an important text and worth quoting at length:

> The first step, after calling upon the Holy Spirit in prayer, is to give our entire attention to the biblical text, which needs to be the basis of our preaching. Whenever we stop and attempt to understand the message of a particular text, we are practicing "reverence for the truth" [*Evangelii nuntiandi*, §78]. This is the humility of heart which recognizes that the word is always beyond us, that "we are neither its masters or owners, but its guardians, heralds and servants" [*Evangelii nuntiandi*, §78]. This attitude of humble and awe-filled veneration of the word is expressed by taking the time to study it with the greatest care and a holy fear lest we distort it.[25]

There are several biblical texts in the Wisdom corpus that could be used to show the roots of this approach to the Word of God. Ecclesiastes 12:9 connects study, wisdom, and teaching in a way suggestive of aspects of the priestly vocation: "Besides being wise, the Teacher also taught the people knowledge, weighing and studying and arranging many proverbs." Ezra the scribe is described in Ezra 7:10 as having "set his heart to study the law of the LORD, and to do it, and to teach the statutes and ordinances in Israel." Here, study of the Word is linked with both doing and teaching. Ben Sira's description of the scribe's vocation in Sirach 39 speaks of study of both the law and of tradition (38:34–39:1) as well as meditation (39:7), prayer, (39:5), praise (39:6), and preaching (39:8).

Similarly, Psalm 101:1–2 begins by speaking of divine praise (liturgy) and then turns to study "I study the way of integrity; when will you come to me?" Here, the word translated "study" is a wisdom term (Hebrew root שׂכל/*śkl*) that could equally be translated "understand" or "contemplate." In the Grail psalter used in the breviary for Morning Prayer of Tuesday Week IV, this word "study" or "contemplate" is replaced by another image: "I will walk in the way of perfection." The Revised Grail translation corrects this toward the Hebrew: "I will

---

23. John Cassian, *Collationes*, conference 14, chapter 11, as cited in Magrassi, *Praying the Bible*, 41.

24. See Weil's essay, "Reflections on the Right Use of School Studies with a View to the Love of God," in Simone Weil, *Waiting for God* (New York: Harper Collins, 2009), 57–65.

25. Pope Francis, *Evangelii gaudium* (November 24, 2013) (Washington, DC: USCCB, 2013), §146.

ponder the way of the blameless." Showing the connection the Psalmist makes between prayer (verse 1) and study and contemplation (verse 2) and the use of this wisdom term elsewhere in the Psalms could help the students to see a closer connection between their life of study and their celebration of the Liturgy of the Hours.[26] On the connection between study and preaching, Aquinas writes: "That the study of scripture is particularly appropriate for people who are appointed to the task of preaching is clear from what the Apostle says in 1 Timothy 4:13, 'Until I come, apply yourself to reading, to exhortation, and to teaching,' which makes it clear that studious reading is a prerequisite for people who propose to exhort and teach."[27]

Lectio divina, *Prayer, and Wisdom Literature*

Many contemporary Christians look outside the biblical tradition for teaching on ascetical and meditative practices, often unaware of the rich and developed biblical teaching on prayer, fasting, and almsgiving and the deep roots of meditation in the Old Testament.[28] Sirach 6:37 offers a good example of the traditional teaching on meditation found throughout the Old Testament: "Reflect on the statutes of the Lord, and meditate (Hebrew: הגה/*hgh*; Greek: μελετάω/ *meletaō*) at all times on his commandments. It is he who will give insight to your mind, and your desire for wisdom will be granted." This verse from Sirach employs one of several Hebrew words used to refer to the meditative pronouncing of the words of the Torah.[29] In the New Testament the common Septuagint verb for meditation (μελετάω/*meletaō*) is used in Paul's exhortation to Timothy in 1 Timothy 4:13–16. Timothy is counseled not to neglect (ἀμέλει/ *amelei*) the gift of ordination, but rather meditate (μελέτα/*meleta*; Vulgate: *meditare*) on it and on the things Paul has been commending (reading, exhortation, and teaching), devoting himself to them so that all may see his progress. Consideration of this text in class could help show the continuity between the mediation counseled in the wisdom tradition of the Old Testament, the pastoral paraenesis of the New Testament, and the daily life of the contemporary priest.

26. Another text on the connection between study and prayer, though not in the Wisdom books, is Neh 8:13, where study leads to liturgical prayer, the celebration of the feast of Booths (Neh 8:14–18) and a penitential liturgy (Neh 9).

27. Thomas Aquinas, *Contra impugnantes Dei cultum et religionem*, chapter 11, in *Albert and Thomas, Selected Writings*, ed. Simon Tugwell, CWS (New York: Paulist, 1988), 609.

28. Luke Dysinger, OSB, has made this point in several publications and has a website with valuable biblical and patristic texts on *lectio divina*.

29. The same word is used elsewhere as well, e.g., in Josh 1:8 and Ps 1:2; see also the nominal form in Psalm 49:3. Other terms include "thoughts"/"meditations" (הִגָּיוֹן / *higāyôn*; Ps 19:15) and "pondering"/"thoughtful contemplation" (שִׂיח/*śiḥ* and שִׂיחָה/*śiḥâ*; Pss 77:13, 119:97).

Of the many excellent books on *lectio divina*, the one cited above by Archbishop Mario Magrassi, OSB, stands out, not least for its numerous patristic and medieval quotations. It will be liberating to many students familiar only with the four-step model of *lectio divina* to discover the wide range of approaches to the faithful reading of Scripture practiced in the great tradition. Many of the quotations can be used to lead students back to the biblical text which the Fathers and medieval writers were commenting on. That exercise, especially with the Psalms, can become an opportunity to compare the Latin or Greek texts of earlier centuries with the Grail translation in our own breviary and with the Revised Grail now proposed for its replacement. This models one way of reading the Bible within what Cardinal Sarah has called "the great river that carries all the riches accumulated over the course of Church history by the fervent readers of God's Word."

A valuable resource for introducing the topic of praying with the Psalms is the article "Psaumes en prière," by Jean-Luc Vesco, OP, published in 1999 and translated into English in 2001.[30] Vesco introduces the breadth and depth of the tradition in a masterful way. He explores in detail both the important teaching found in the Rule of St. Benedict 19:7 that in praying the psalms our minds should be conformed to the words our voices are singing (*ut mens nostra concordet voci nostrae*), as well as the injunctions found in Psalm 47:8 on singing with understanding (*psallite sapienter*) and in 1 Corinthians 14:15 on praying with the spirit but also with the mind.[31] Vesco includes a rich selection of patristic and medieval citations on psalmody and prayer and concludes by presenting three approaches to praying the psalms: praying with a single verse; a kind of psalmody in which the interior movement from psalmody to prayer occurs already as the text is read; and the familiar four-step model of *lectio divina*, described in a succinct and helpful manner.

Preachers and Confessors for the New Evangelization

Preaching and the Form of Wisdom Literature

Over a third of the Old Testament is poetry, characterized in varying degrees by such features as concision, parallelism, attention to lexical choice, word-pairing,

---

30. Jean-Luc Vesco, "Psaumes en prière," *Revue Thomiste* 99 (1999): 331–368. This essay was translated into English by Sr. Maria of the Cross, OP, and is available in *Dominican Monastic Search* 20 (2001): 32–63, available online at archive.org/details/dominicanmonasti2ounse.

31. The *General Instruction of the Liturgy of the Hours*, §§105–106 treats elements of this, though only briefly. Its section on praying the psalms (100–139) is well done and deserves periodic rereading.

alliteration, and assonance. "The ability and practice of perceiving the poetic word," Karl Rahner has said, "is a presupposition for hearing the word of God."[32] Teaching students to pay closer attention to poetry, and to the theological significance of this form of language, can help them both to hear the word of God with greater acuity and to develop a poet's attentiveness and sensitivity to the power of language and to word choice in preaching.[33]

"The Teacher sought to find pleasing words," we read in Ecclesiastes 12:10, "and he wrote words of truth plainly." The pleasing or felicitous word can refer to a word which is "apt and timely."[34] Striving to find a word in due season, a memorable expression, or an arresting image is part and parcel of the preaching office, the one our students are preparing for. In Ecclesiastes 12:9, a series of three verbs describe Qohelet's own manner of fulfilling this office: he listened (אִזֵּן/'izzēn), investigated (חִקֵּר/ḥiqqēr), and composed (תִּקֵּן/tiqqēn).[35] Preaching and teaching well, it would seem, have to include these same elements: listening in silence, careful study, and attention to form. Ambrose, whose eloquence aided Augustine's conversion, cites this text in offering advice to a preacher: "Therefore let your sermons be flowing, let them be clear and lucid so that . . . by the grace of your words [you] may persuade the crowd to follow willingly where you lead."[36]

Ecclesiastes is said to have spoken words of truth. There is something important here for preachers. Paul VI identified "reverence for the truth" as essential to evangelization, and Pope Francis refers to this phrase in *Evangelii gaudium* as well.[37] Reverence for the truth implies as well an "obedience to the

---

32. Karl Rahner, "Poetry and the Christian," *Theological Investigations Vol. 4: More Recent Writings* (Baltimore: Helicon, 1966), 363.

33. In class, I introduce and summarize an article by Patrick Miller on this theme: "The Theological Significance of Biblical Poetry," in *Language, Theology, and the Bible, Essays in Honour of James Barr*, ed. Samuel E. Balentine and John Barton (Oxford: Clarendon, 1994), 213–230.

34. Choon-Leong Seow, *Ecclesiastes*, AncB 18C (New York: Doubleday, 1997), 385. The apt, timely word is described in Prov 15:23: "To make an apt answer is a joy to a man, and a word in season, how good it is!"

35. Here I rely on the interpretation of Eccl 12:9 in Peter Enns, *Ecclesiastes* THOT (Grand Rapids MI: Eerdmans, 2011), 111.

36. St. Ambrose, *Letter 15, To Constantius*, as cited in J. Robert Wright, *Proverbs, Ecclesiastes, Song of Solomon*, ACCSOT 9 (Downers Grove, IL: InterVarsity, 2005), 282. Ambrose is writing to a bishop, therefore a preacher, and though he explicitly cites Eccl 12:11, not v. 10, his words seem to offer an interpretation of that verse as well.

37. The *Directory for the Ministry and the Life of Priests*, §62, entitled "Fidelity to the Word" has a valuable section on fidelity and truth in the preaching office. The document was published by the Congregation for the Clergy in a new edition in 2013.

truth [*oboedentia veritatis*]," an obedience which is said in 1 Peter 1:22 to purify the soul. Benedict XVI has offered an important discussion on this theme. He writes:

> Obedience to the truth must "purify" our souls and thus guide us to upright speech and upright action. In other words, speaking in the hope of being applauded, governed by what people want to hear out of obedience to the dictatorship of current opinion, is considered to be a sort of prostitution: of words and of the soul. The "purity" to which the Apostle Peter is referring means not submitting to these standards, not seeking applause, but rather, seeking obedience to the truth. And I think that this is the fundamental virtue for the theologian, this discipline of obedience to the truth, which makes us, although it may be hard, collaborators of the truth, mouthpieces of truth, for it is not we who speak in today's river of words, but it is the truth which speaks in us, who are really purified and made chaste by obedience to the truth. So it is that we can truly be harbingers of the truth.[38]

Obedience to the truth in preaching could be introduced in connection with several biblical texts: Job 42:7 (Job has spoken rightly), the "pleasing words" (דִּבְרֵי־חֵפֶץ/*dibrê-ḥēpeṣ*) and "words of truth" (דִּבְרֵי אֱמֶת/*dibrê 'ĕmet*) of Ecclesiastes 12:10, or the "goads" (דָּרְבֹנוֹת/*dārəbōnôt*) of Ecclesiastes 12:11. On this latter verse, Jerome comments: "Thus, anyone's discourse that has not sting in it, but instead gives pleasure to the audience, is not the discourse of a wise man, because *the words of the wise are as goads*. These words challenge the offender to conversion."[39]

Preparing Confessors for the New Evangelization

Wisdom literature can help prepare confessors for the New Evangelization in each of the four areas of formation. Before briefly outlining these, I want to recall the words of Benedict XVI in an address given at the Vatican in 2012: "The New Evangelization begins in the confessional." He explains: "The celebration of the Sacrament of Reconciliation is itself a proclamation, and therefore a path to take for the work of the New Evangelization."[40] In the first

---

38. Pope Benedict XVI, Homily at the Eucharistic concelebration with the members of the International Theological Commission (October 6, 2006), www.vatican.va/content/benedict-xvi/en/homilies/2006/documents/hf_ben-xvi_hom_20061006_commissione-teologica.html.

39. Jerome, *St. Jerome: Commentary on Ecclesiastes*, trans. Richard J. Goodrich and David J. D. Miller, ACW 66 (New York: The Newman Press, 2012), 132.

40. Pope Benedict XVI, "Address to the Annual Course on the Internal Forum organized by the Apostolic Penitentiary" (March 9, 2011), www.vatican.va/content/benedict-xvi/en/speeches/2012/march/documents/hf_ben-xvi_spe_20120309_penitenzieria-apostolica.html.

instance the sacrament brings about new life for the members of the Church, allowing penitents to receive "God's transforming and renewing action" and to walk in newness of life. It brings people into contact with Jesus Christ, "in whom God made himself so close that he may be seen and heard." Priests are instruments of the grace of contact with God, of the offer of a newness of life, of a new beginning. Having experienced these realities, penitents "themselves will become credible witnesses of that holiness which is the aim of the New Evangelization." Each confession, Pope Benedict concluded, "from which each Christian will emerge renewed, will be a step ahead in the New Evangelization."

Although it is true that all of Scripture can play a role in the human formation of seminarians, it is in the Wisdom literature that we encounter sustained teaching about when to speak and when to refrain from speaking. Speaking well and knowing when to speak may not be prerequisites for becoming a good confessor, but they are the kind of raw material which the grace of ordination can elevate and perfect. Reflection on these texts and memorization of sayings on this topic can aid in the human formation of our students.

In terms of intellectual formation, a thematic approach intended to help prepare confessors for the New Evangelization could include a presentation of Wisdom texts on compunction of heart, repentance, mercy, and the call to conversion. There are a number of texts one could include, but one suggestion would be to briefly identify several (e.g., Sir 21:6 "Those who hate reproof walk in the sinner's steps, but those who fear the Lord repent in their heart"; or Sir 17:29 "How great is the mercy of the Lord, and his forgiveness for those who return to him!") while concentrating on just one. Psalm 130, the *De profundis*, and the commentary on that Psalm by St. John Fisher would serve well. Another way to approach the topic would be to identify and introduce the Wisdom texts recommended in the most recent Rite of Penance (e.g., Wis 5:1–16; Sir 28:1–7; Pss 13, 22, 25, 31, 32, 36, 50, 51, 130, 143, 146). The refrains for these psalms as presented in the ritual often capture a brief phrase that could be used as part of the rite, even if the longer passage was not read (e.g., "With the Lord there is mercy and fullness of redemption").

There is grace present in the celebration of the Sacrament of Penance and an openness to the Word in contrite hearts, so the power of even a short word of Scripture spoken in faith in such a context should not be underestimated. Identifying and committing to memory a few passages from the psalms to be used in this way could be recommended to students. Even to introduce the topic of the pastoral use of the Bible in the sacraments of the Church and in the daily and Sunday lectionaries can be helpful to those students who wonder whether anything they are learning will ever be of practical use.[41] Their intellectual labors during the semester ("it is no light matter but calls for sweat and loss of sleep," 2 Macc 2:26) are, we can assure them, intended to bear fruit in a variety of ways, and especially in the pulpit and the confessional.

New Hearing: Theological Dimensions of the Wisdom Books

The call from many quarters for a renewed attention to the theological dimensions of Scripture, a reading made under the influence of the *lumen fidei*, that is, in the light of the same Spirit by whom it was written, is starting to be answered. Still, we appear to be in the early stages of assimilating and implementing the conciliar teaching of *Dei verbum* and more recent magisterial teaching. The way forward has nonetheless been shown: sustained and careful attention to 1) the unity of Scripture, 2) the living Tradition of the whole Church, and 3) the analogy of faith. The succinct summary of the great tradition given in *Dei verbum* 12, unpacked a bit more in the *Catechism of the Catholic Church*, and again in *Verbum Domini*, is a great gift and relatively easy to describe to students. But it is no easy thing to apply this teaching in any programmatic way in the classroom. In what follows I outline several ways of using these "three fundamental criteria" (*Verbum Domini*, §34) in teaching an introduction to the Wisdom books of the Old Testament.

The First Criterion: Old Testament Wisdom, the Incarnate Lord, and the Unity of Scripture

If the providential plan of God gives Scripture its unity, and Christ himself is the center and heart of that plan (*CCC*, §112), what might it mean in practice to be especially attentive (*diligenter respiciendum*) to the *contentum et unitatem totius Scripturae* in reading the Wisdom books? Erasmo Leiva-Merikakis points us toward an answer and offers a concrete example.

In his commentary on Matthew 12:14 ("they took counsel against him, how they might utterly destroy him"), Erasmo Leiva-Merikakis notes how different

---

41. Indicating where passages from the Wisdom books are used in the Liturgy of the Hours and the lectionary is an important way to teach the Bible in its ecclesial context and helps students to learn how the Church uses the Bible during the liturgical year. The recent document from the Congregation for the Clergy entitled *The Gift of the Priestly Vocation* speaks of seminarians interiorizing the scriptural texts of the liturgy in this way: "In the journey of formation, the liturgical year offers the pedagogical mystagogy of the Church, allowing its spirituality to be absorbed by interiorizing the scriptural texts and liturgical prayers." *The Gift of the Priestly Vocation: Ratio Fundamentalis Institutionis Sacerdotalis* (December 8, 2016) (London: Catholic Truth Society, 2017), §102.

this is from the way of God, who has no need to take counsel with anyone: "Who has directed the Spirit of the Lord, or as his counselor has instructed him?"[42] (Isa 40:13–14). The way of Jesus, who heals a man in this passage, is then contrasted with the way of those who plotted against him. His radiant simplicity is revealed in his simple and direct healing of the man in Matthew 12:13. His "whole attitude and presence appears to be the very embodiment of Wisdom," Leiva-Merikakis writes, citing here the description of personified Wisdom in Wisdom 7:22–23, a description replete with divine attributes: "In her there is a spirit that is intelligent, holy, unique, . . . clear, unpolluted, certain, . . . loving the good, keen, unhampered, beneficent, kindly, firm, secure, tranquil, all-powerful, all-seeing." He comments, "If Jesus ever 'took counsel', it was only with his Father on the subject of how best to accomplish his coming among us in order to save us, for instance when he speaks as eternal Wisdom before the Incarnation."

Leiva-Merikakis then cites several texts in which personified Wisdom speaks (Sir 24:6–8, 12; Wis 8:9, 16), hearing in these texts the voice of Christ, "eternal Wisdom before the Incarnation." None of this, of course, is found simply in Matthew 12. Nor is it rank eisegesis. The New Testament itself identified Christ with Wisdom (1 Cor 1:24; Heb 1:3), borrowing language from the Wisdom of Solomon to do so. The Old Testament, Leiva-Merikakis argues, is necessary for any correct understanding of Christ. "Such Old Testament texts are not decorative; they are essential for our understanding of who this Jesus is who walks into our midst." By these interpretative moves he helps us to see a new depth, a *sensus plenior*, in both the Wisdom texts in the Old Testament and in Matthew 12. He brings us close to the Christological center, to the heart of the plan of God and of the Bible, to Christ, the power of God and the Wisdom of God. "We do not have, on the one hand," he continues, "the lavish sapiential richness of Old Testament mysticism and, on the other, an antithetical historical presence of Jesus of Nazareth. In the latter we encounter God's Wisdom incarnate, bringing close to us in unsurpassable brightness the full depth of those sublime Hebrew glimmerings concerning God's inner life that proved to be the dawn of redemption." In this way, Leiva-Merikakis moves from the known, from the incarnate Lord revealed in the "unsurpassable brightness" of the whole New Testament, to the less well known, to "those sublime Hebrew glimmerings concerning God's inner life."

42. Erasmo Leiva-Merikakis, *Fire of Mercy, Heart of the Word*, vol. 2 (San Francisco: Ignatius, 2003). The passages excerpted here are found on pages 79 and 80, within his commentary on Matt 12:14.

Robert Wilken has shown how the importance of wisdom in the Old Testament "opened up a rich vein of associations for thinking about the person of Christ and his relation to God the Father."[43] He notes that Origen in his treatise *First Principles* "mentions wisdom first in his list of titles for Christ."[44] Christ, the Wisdom of God, lies hidden in the Old. And the Old Testament is opened, unveiled, revealed, given a new hearing in the New. "The title Wisdom," Wilken writes, "provided a secure foothold in the Old Testament, that is, in Israel's history, that spoke of the activity of Christ prior to the Incarnation."[45] It is helpful on this point to recall the teaching of the *Catechism of the Catholic Church* 129: "Christians therefore read the Old Testament in the light of Christ crucified and risen. Such typological reading discloses the inexhaustible content of the Old Testament. . . . As an old saying put it, the New Testament lies hidden in the Old and the Old Testament is unveiled in the New."

Leiva-Merikakis, toward the end of his reflection on Matthew 12:14 points to the fulfillment of the Old Testament in the New, a fulfillment in which the Old is taken up and included but also transcended: "The apostles and all those who come into intimate contact with Jesus could not respond to that event and person with any less interior delectation than Solomon found in his experience of Wisdom. On the contrary, for now Wisdom can be encountered more than just interiorly, since in Jesus she has become the Word of Life."

The Second Criterion: Old Testament Wisdom, Philosophy, and Reading Scripture from Within the Tradition

To read the Wisdom books "within the living Tradition of the whole Church" means that we do not read Scripture alone or on its own, divorced from the body of Christ. The biblical text comes to us from the Church and tends toward communion. Any idiosyncratic approach, any focus exclusively on what catches my own fancy, is to be avoided in any ecclesial interpretation, such as in the act of preaching. It is the great river of tradition, the living stream flowing from the side of the Temple and from Christ's side which is normative. Reading the text with earlier commentators and with attention to the liturgical contexts of Scripture are clearly essential. The Liturgy of the Hours trains seminarians in precisely these approaches.

Here I will briefly describe a complementary approach, a way of reading

---

43. Robert Wilken, *The Spirit of Early Christian Thought* (New Haven, CT: Yale University Press, 2003), 94.

44. Wilken, *The Spirit of Early Christian Thought*, 94.

45. Wilken, *The Spirit of Early Christian Thought*, 95.

the Wisdom books within the philosophical tradition of the Church. In the second chapter of *Fides et ratio*, which begins with a quotation of Wisdom 9:11 ("Wisdom knows and understands all") and is entitled *Credo ut intellegam*, John Paul II discusses the contribution of the Old Testament Wisdom literature to the question of the relationship of faith and reason. In sections 16–21 he cites a number of important primary texts from the Wisdom books, notes similarities with ancient Near Eastern wisdom (mentioning wisdom texts from Mesopotamia, Egypt, and Greece), and goes on to discuss Paul's understanding of wisdom in Romans and 1 Corinthians. Joseph Koterski, SJ, a philosopher with a longstanding interest in the Wisdom of Solomon, has provided a helpful resource which uses this important encyclical as a lens to consider the significance of Old Testament Wisdom literature. In his article *"Fides et ratio* and Biblical Wisdom Literature," Koterski offers a model for reading both the Wisdom books and magisterial texts within the living tradition, in this case the philosophical tradition of the Church.[46] "The purpose of this essay," Koterski writes in his introduction, "will be to reflect on biblical Wisdom Literature in light of *Fides et ratio.* After examining what the encyclical itself says about this portion of the Bible, we will explore some additional themes of a generally philosophical nature important to these writings, and then we will comment on the general question of the relations of faith and reason in light of biblical Wisdom Literature."[47] The Wisdom books speak to a theme of great relevance to the New Evangelization, namely the relationship of faith and reason (see *Fides et ratio*, §§102–107), and Koterski's article can help students see that their own intellectual formation in both philosophy and theology inscribes them in an ancient and powerful intellectual tradition with a great deal to offer the world. It can give them courage and confidence.

The Third Criterion: Old Testament Wisdom and the Analogia fidei

The third fundamental criterion is perhaps the most difficult to understand and to illustrate. A gloss in the *Catechism of the Catholic Church* 114 is helpful: "By 'analogy of faith' we mean the coherence of the truths of faith among themselves and within the whole plan of Revelation."[48] To simplify, we might say

46. Joseph Koterski, *"Fides et ratio* and Biblical Wisdom Literature," in *The Two Wings of Catholic Thought: Essays on* Fides et ratio, ed. David Ruel Foster and Joseph W. Koterski, SJ (Washington, DC: Catholic University of America Press, 2003), 129–162. Koterski's 2009 course on Biblical Wisdom literature is available in written and audio formats from The Teaching Company.

47. Koterski, *"Fides et ratio,"* 130.

48. Francis Martin describes it as "a traditional phrase that emphasizes two facts: [1] that

that it means to read the Bible with the Creed. Here I will offer two very brief illustrations.

The first illustration of the analogy of faith, drawn from Cardinal Avery Dulles, uses a dogma of the Church, the Immaculate Conception, to point to a deeper meaning of the rare word 'favored one' (κεχαριτωμένη/*gratia plena*) in Luke 1:28. Cardinal Dulles writes: "The dogmas serve as negative norms for excluding misinterpretations. More than this, they throw positive light on what the Holy Spirit was intimating in various biblical texts. The dogma of the Immaculate Conception, for example, permits a deeper understanding of the expression "full of grace" (translating the rare Greek word, *kécharitôménê*) applied to Mary by the angel at the Annunciation."[49]

Dulles goes on to cite a comment of Cardinal Aloysius Grillmeier: "[T]he living tradition of the Church helps us through its growing understanding of faith to a deeper understanding of Scripture."[50] There is a reciprocal relationship between Scripture and the living faith of the Church. The Bible requires faith to be properly understood, and it in turn tests, purifies, and strengthens the faith of its readers. All three fundamental criteria locate particular biblical passages in larger interpretive contexts.

A second illustration of the analogy of faith suggests a way of reading the Wisdom of Solomon through the lens of the three theological virtues: faith, hope, and love.[51] The purpose of the Wisdom of Solomon, the message the author wished to communicate, is found in the book's last line: "For in everything, O Lord, you have exalted and glorified your people, and you have not neglected to help them at all times and in all places" (19:22). The book encourages and strengthens the faith of the Jewish community in Alexandria by arguing that as the Lord sustained his people in the past, in their Egyptian slavery, and in the Exodus, so he will not neglect to help them now. The NABRE introduction

---

the Bible is a whole with a multifaceted but consistent message, and [2] that each part of the sacred text must be understood as compatible with others in the canon, indeed as deriving from and contributing to an understanding of the whole." Francis Martin, "Revelation and Its Transmission," in *Vatican II: Renewal Within Tradition*, ed. Matthew Lamb and Matthew Levering (New York: Oxford University Press, 2008), 68.

49. Dulles, "Vatican II on the Interpretation of Scripture," *Letter & Spirit* 2 (2006): 22.

50. Aloysius Grillmeier, "The Divine Inspiration and the Interpretation of Sacred Scripture," 199–246 in *Commentary on the Documents of Vatican II*, vol. 3, ed. Herbert Vorgrimler (New York: Herder and Herder, 1969), 245; Dulles, "Vatican II," 23.

51. In his commentary on Deuteronomy, Telford Work adopts a similar approach, identifying four senses: a plain sense; faith, corresponding to allegory or the Christological sense; hope, corresponding to the anagogical; and love, corresponding to the moral sense. See Telford Work, *Deuteronomy*, BTCB (Grand Rapids, MI: Brazos, 2009).

to this book summarizes it thus: "The primary purpose of the author was the edification of his co-religionists in a time when they had experienced suffering and oppression, in part at least at the hands of apostate fellow Jews." His purpose, we could say, was to strengthen his people's faith in God, their hope in God, and their love for God. Let us take each in turn, beginning with faith.

Faith: The Wisdom of Solomon is a book in the first instance about the faithfulness, the fidelity of God. This is the primary mystery being revealed. God is faithful to his word, and faithful to his people, "at all times and in all places" (19:22). The response Israel is to make is to turn away from idols (chapters 13–15), to be faithful in response to God's fidelity. Faith is not only loyalty but also an illumination of the mind, a way of knowing. "Those who trust [πεποιθότες/pepoithotes] in him will understand truth [συνήσουσιν ἀλήθειαν/synēsousin alētheian]" (3:9).[52] When God's people do sin, the Lord corrects them little by little to purify and renew their faith: "Therefore you correct little by little those who trespass, and you remind and warn them of the things through which they sin, so that they may be freed from wickedness and put their trust [πιστεύσωσιν/pisteusōsin] in you, O Lord" (12:2). Even the manna had a pedagogical goal ordered toward faith—"so that your children, whom you loved, O Lord, might learn that it is not the production of crops that feeds humankind but that your word sustains those who trust [πιστεύοντας/pisteuontas] in you" (16:26).

Hope: The Wisdom of Solomon is also a book about hope because it is a book about divine presence, about divine providence in history, and about immortality. "For though in the sight of others they were punished, their hope is full of immortality" (3:4). It is significant that the Greek noun "immortality" is introduced here for the first time in the Old Testament. The adjective 'immortal' is found once, in 1:15 ("For righteousness is immortal") and the noun "immortality" five times (3:4; 4:1; 8:13, 17; 15:3). Immortality in this book is considered to be a gift of God given in response to fidelity, not a natural property of the soul. Immortality is closely associated both with knowing God and with living justly: "For to know you is complete righteousness, and to know

---

52. The comments on the Greek translation of Isa 7:9 ("unless you believe, you will not understand") in *Lumen fidei* 23 are relevant here: "Because God is trustworthy, it is reasonable to have faith in him, to stand fast on his word. He is the same God that Isaiah will later call, twice in one verse, the God who is Amen, 'the God of truth' (cf. Isa 65:16), the enduring foundation of covenant fidelity.... Augustine was concerned to show that this trustworthy truth of God is, as the Bible makes clear, his own faithful presence throughout history, his ability to hold together times and ages, and to gather into one the scattered strands of our lives." Pope Francis, *Lumen fidei* (June 29, 2013) (San Francisco: Ignatius, 2013), §23.

your power is the root of immortality" (15:3). Michael Kolarcik comments: "Wisdom brings a knowledge of God that makes one an intimate friend of God and enables one to acknowledge God's dominion. Acknowledging the sovereignty of God is the root of immortality."[53]

Hope, the book teaches, is a gift that comes from God and is based on his mercy: "You have filled your children with good hope, because you give repentance for sins" (12:19). The wicked are those who seek too little in life, who do not dare to hope in God: "They did not know the secret purposes of God, nor hoped for the wages of holiness, nor discerned the prize for blameless souls" (2:22). The hopes they do harbor are either "in vain" (3:11), "set on dead things" (13:10), "cheaper than dirt" (15:10) or ephemeral, "like thistledown carried by the wind" (5:14). Hope and gratitude are related, "for the hope of an ungrateful person will melt like wintry frost and flow away like waste water" (16:29).

Love: Finally, the Wisdom of Solomon is also a book about love.[54] In the first place it reveals the love of God for his creatures: "For you love all things that exist" (Wis 11:24), "you spare all things, for they are yours, O Lord, you who love the living" (Wis 11:26). The book begins with three imperatives: love (ἀγαπήσατε/*agapēsate*), think (φρονήσατε/*phronēsate*), seek (ζητήσατε/*zētēsate*). "Love righteousness, you rulers of the earth, think of the Lord in goodness and seek him with sincerity of heart" (Wis 1:1). It commends the love of justice and righteousness as well as the love of wisdom, philosophy in its root sense. "Wisdom . . . is easily discerned by those who love her, and is found by those who seek her" (Wis 6:12). Although the book does not speak as directly of our love for God as does the famous command in the Shema (Deut 6:5), since Wisdom is a divine attribute and a divine gift the frequent injunctions to love Wisdom point to the same reality. Finally, in Wisdom 3:9 we can find all three theological virtues of faith, hope, and love: "Those who trust [πεποιθότες/pepoithotes] in him will understand truth, and the faithful [πιστοί/pistoi] will abide with him in love [ἀγάπη/agapē], because grace and mercy are upon his holy ones, and he watches over his elect." This certainly comprises grounds for hope, even if it does not name that virtue.

---

53. Michael Kolarcik, SJ, "The Book of Wisdom," in *The New Interpreter's Bible*, vol. 5 (Nashville: Abingdon, 1997), 563.

54. The noun "love" (ἀγάπη/*agapē*) occurs three times in the book, and the verbal form nine times. Other words from this same semantic domain (such as "friendship," φιλία/*philia*) occur in the Wisdom of Solomon and could be included for a complete survey of the theme.

A New Proclamation: Friendship, Wisdom, and the New Evangelization in Evangelii Gaudium

When divine Wisdom enters a soul, "she produces friends of God and prophets" (Wis 7:27). It is worth dwelling on this image, this joining of friendship with God and the conferral of a prophetic office. At the heart of the Gospel is the invitation to become friends of God in the person of his beloved Son (John 15:15—ὑμᾶς δὲ εἴρηκα φίλους/*humas de eirēka philous*). Pope Francis reflects on the transformative power of an encounter with Christ, with his love, and his offer of friendship, at the beginning of his 2013 exhortation on the proclamation of the Gospel in today's world: "Thanks solely to this encounter— or renewed encounter—with God's love, which blossoms into an enriching friendship, we are liberated from our narrowness and self-absorption. We become fully human when we become more than human, when we let God bring us beyond ourselves in order to attain the fullest truth of our being. Here we find the source and inspiration of all our efforts at evangelization" (*Evangelii gaudium*, §8). What is remarkable here for our purposes is the central role of friendship, which he places at the heart of human, spiritual, and pastoral formation. In fact, much of the Holy Father's writing about accompaniment can be understood as emphasizing the importance of spiritual friendship in the process of evangelization. The two, friendship and evangelization, are linked in *Evangelii gaudium* 8 as they are in Wisdom 7:27.

The theme of friendship with Christ recurs throughout *Evangelii gaudium*. "If something should rightly disturb us and trouble our consciences," Pope Francis writes, "it is the fact that so many of our brothers and sisters are living without the strength, light and consolation born of friendship with Jesus Christ, without a community of faith to support them, without meaning and a goal in life" (*Evangelii gaudium*, §8). Friendship with God leads the prophet, the evangelizer, the friend of God to deep concern for his brothers and sisters who are like sheep without a shepherd, who are without divine strength, divine light, or the consolation born of divine friendship. The love of God and his offer of friendship is at the center of the Gospel, Francis reminds us. This is "the fundamental message: the personal love of God who became man, who gave himself up for us, who is living and who offers us his salvation and his friendship" (*Evangelii gaudium*, §8). Our forgetting this, the pope adds, is why we lose our enthusiasm for mission—"we forget that the Gospel responds to our deepest needs, since we were created for what the Gospel offers us: friendship with Jesus and love of our brothers and sisters" (*Evangelii gaudium*, §265).

It is particularly in the Wisdom books that God himself teaches us how to have true and lasting friendships. Sirach deals with friendship more extensively than any book of the Bible.[55] Proverbs probably comes a close second, containing, for example, teaching on friendship with wisdom ("Say to wisdom, 'You are my sister,' and call insight your intimate friend," Prov 7:4) and on the nature and importance of fidelity in friendship (Prov 17:17; 18:24; 27:10). The Song of Songs, Ellen Davis notes, is about healthy desire, about the desire for friendship with God, affirming that "longing for intimacy with God is a necessary desire for a healthy soul."[56] Job is about innocent suffering, but also, importantly, about friendship in suffering. Job calls his friends "miserable comforters" or "torture comforters" with windy words (Job 16:2–3). Job himself had been a friend repeatedly to the needy and the oppressed (Job 29:12–17), had wept for the hardships of others (Job 30:24–25), and after suffering became capable of interceding for his friends for the remission of their punishment (Job 42:9–10).

This biblical teaching on friendship, though it remains largely unknown, offers a vision of the good life, the blessed life, that is both accessible and directly relevant to men and women at every stage of life. Old Testament Wisdom literature can help to build a solid foundation for responding to the divine invitation to friendship that is at the heart of Gospel. Sharing that gift, that divine offer, is the prime motive for evangelization. Teaching this material offers us the great gift of dwelling on these texts year in and year out, and so also the opportunity to assimilate their teaching. Over a hundred years ago Leo XIII urged us to teach Scripture in a way that leads to love of the Word of God, "in such a way that the students may learn . . . to love and use the remainder of the sacred Book during the whole of their lives."[57] May this volume, and the Monsignor Quinn Institute of Biblical Studies, help us all to find a way to do this.

---

55. Patrick W. Skehan and Alexander A. Di Lella, *The Wisdom of Ben Sira*, AncB 39 (New York: Doubleday, 1987), 187. Excellent treatments are found in Jeremy Corley, *Ben Sira's Teaching on Friendship*, BJSt 316 (Providence, RI: Brown Judaic Studies, 2002); Daniel Harrington, SJ, *Jesus Ben Sira of Jerusalem: A Biblical Guide to Living Wisely* (Collegeville, MN: Liturgical Press, 2005), 115–7; and Jan Liesen and Laurie Watson Manhardt, *Come and See Catholic Bible Study: Wisdom* (Steubenville, OH: Emmaus, 2009), 181–184. In the accompanying DVD Liesen, now a bishop and member of the International Theological Commission, offers a lecture on the theme of friendship based largely on Proverbs and Sirach.

56. Ellen F. Davis, *Proverbs, Ecclesiastes, and the Song of Songs* (Louisville: Westminster John Knox, 2000), 235.

57. Pope Leo XIII, *Providentissimus Deus* (November 18, 1893), www.vatican.va/content/leo-xiii/en/encyclicals/documents/hf_l-xiii_enc_18111893_providentissimus-deus.html, §13. The pope also offers this helpful reminder, one which I wish I had read and taken to heart during my first years of teaching: ". . . and not to overload the minds of the students with a mass of information that will be rather a hindrance than a help."

CHAPTER 5

Free Will and the Hardening of Pharaoh's Heart: Integrating Modern and Ancient Interpretations into the Seminary Classroom

Juana L. Manzo

> The Spirit said to Philip, "Go and join up with that chariot." Philip ran up and heard him reading the prophet Isaiah and said, "Do you understand what you are reading?" He replied, "How can I, unless someone instructs me?"
>
> ACTS 8:29–30 NAB

Introduction

Scripture, being the Word of God, provides a powerful and credible narrative that illuminates the nature of human existence. It narrates the story of Israel, Jesus, and the Church. On every occasion the divine Word is heard and celebrated in the Liturgy of the Church, the Word spiritually nourishes the faithful, strengthening them to give witness to their faith.

Yet, although Scripture indeed is a compelling narrative that is transformative, often the Word of God is riddled in mystery. Scripture contains many passages that for the faithful may call into question God's love for his people. Often Catholic students enter seminary with little knowledge of the historical and theological background of Scripture. As I reflect on the New Evangelization and Scripture, I consider the necessity of not only the instructors and students' familiarity with the Word of God but also helping students navigate faith challenges posed by difficult scriptural passages. As *Verbum Domini* states,

> It would be a mistake to neglect those passages of Scripture that strike us as problematic. Rather, we should be aware that the correct interpretation of these passages requires a degree of expertise, acquired through a training

that interprets the texts in their historical-literary context and within the Christian perspective.[1]

A theological theme that is often problematic for students of the Hebrew Bible is the hardening of Pharaoh's heart in Exodus 4–14. Inevitably, students will raise questions. Is God responsible for Pharaoh's hardening? Has God predestined Pharaoh to damnation? Has Pharaoh's free will been compromised? How are we to reconcile God's hardening to Pharaoh's own hardening?

In the *Instrumentum laboris* for the 2012 Synod of Bishops, "The New Evangelization for the Transmission of the Christian Faith," the synod states that the aim of the New Evangelization is the diffusion of the faith.[2] The synod emphasizes as well the correlation between faith and education: "If evangelization is to be true to itself, it cannot take place apart from education; it is directly related to it. In this regard, the Church possesses a tradition of educational resources, studies, research, institutions and people."[3] Indeed, the Church throughout its history has benefited from the scholarly contribution of many gifted thinkers who have treated the subject of the hardening of Pharaoh's heart from a literary, historical, and theological perspective. In this paper, I provide three different scholarly views that will break open the meaning of the hardening motif in Exodus and a pedagogical strategy that helps students with this difficult theme. These three scholars are: Brevard Childs, St. Gregory of Nyssa, and St. Augustine.

Childs, a modern scholar, provides a literary study of the theme. In his form critical analysis, he challenges the notion that the hardening motif functioned as an editorial tool by the redactor to connect independent plague narratives. Gregory of Nyssa, a father from the Eastern Christian tradition, deals with the issue by addressing free will. St. Augustine, a theologian from the Western Church, discusses the theological problem of the hardening of the heart as just retribution. In the following section we begin with Childs first, for his contribution on the subject based on the Documentary Hypothesis. Subsequently, the contributions of Gregory of Nyssa and St. Augustine are presented to introduce theological aspects of the text.

---

1. Pope Benedict XVI, *Verbum Domini* (September 30, 2010) (Boston: Pauline Books and Media, 2010), §42.

2. Synod of Bishops, XIII Ordinary General Assembly, *Instrumentum laboris* "The New Evangelization for the Transmission of the Christian Faith" (December 19, 2012), www.vatican .va/roman_curia/synod/documents/rc_synod_doc_20120619_instrumentum-xiii_en.html, §90.

3. Synod of Bishops, "The New Evangelization," §147.

Helping Students Navigate Faith Challenges: Three Different Voices on the Hardening Motif

Brevard Childs

The hardening of Pharaoh's heart occurs twenty times between Exod 4:21 and Exod 14:17 as an important theological motif of the liberation of the Israelites from Egyptian slavery by the hand of YHWH. Form critics have identified the literary and theological function of the motif as it appears within the J, P and E narratives.[4] The following chart illustrates the occurrences of the Pharaoh's actions regarding his heart and the literary tradition to which it has been attributed.[5]

	TEXT	TRANSLATION	SOURCE
4:21	וֽאני אחזק את־לבו	I will make his heart strong	E
7:3	וֽאני אקשה את־לב פרעה	I will harden the heart of Pharaoh	P
7:13	ויחזק לב פרעה	The heart of Pharaoh was strong	P
7:14	כבד לב פרעה	The heart of Pharaoh was heavy	J
7:22	ויחזק לב־פרעה	The heart of Pharaoh was strong	P
7:23	ולא־שת לבו	He did not set his heart to it	J
8:15[11]	והכבד את־לבו	He weighted down his heart	J
8:19[15]	ויחזק לב־פרעה	The heart of Pharaoh was strong	P
8:32[28]	ויכבד פרעה את־לבו	Pharaoh weighted down his heart	J

---

4. Franz Hesse, *Das Verstockungsproblem im Alten Testament: Eine frömmigkeitsgeschichtliche Untersuchung*, BZAW 74 (Berlin: Topelmann, 1955), 31–98; James Plastaras, *The God of Exodus* (Milwaukee: Bruce, 1966), 133–137; Karl L. Schmidt, "Die Verstockung des Menschen durch Gott," *Theologische Zeistchrift* 1 (1945): 1–17.

5. Matthew McAffee, "The Heart of Pharaoh in Exodus 4–15," *Bulletin for Biblical Research* 20, no. 3 (2010): 347. McAffee gives an insightful treatment of the subject based on a lexical, grammatical, and contextual study of the motif. In his summary chart, he incorporates the Hebrew root and stem for חזק, קשה, and כבד, as well as the subject of the "hardening." I have adapted his work by incorporating the source to which the hardening motif has traditionally been attributed.

	TEXT	TRANSLATION	SOURCE
9:7	ויכבד לב פרעה	The heart of Pharaoh was heavy	J
9:12	ויחזק יהוה את־לב פרעה	YHWH made the heart of Pharaoh strong	P
9:34	ויכבד לבו הוא ועבדיו	He weighed down his heart, he and his servant	J
9:35	ויחזק לב פרעה	The heart of Pharaoh was strong	E
10:1	כי־אני הכבדתי את־לבו ואת־לב עבדיו	For I weighted down his heart and the heart of his servants	J
10:20	ויחזק יהוה את־לב פרעה	YHWH made the heart of Pharaoh strong	E
10:27	ויחזק יהוה את־לב פרעה	YHWH made the heart of Pharaoh strong	E
11:10	ויחזק יהוה את־לב פרעה	YHWH made the heart of Pharaoh strong	E
14:4	וחזקתי את־לב־פרעה	I will strengthen the heart of Pharaoh	P
14:8	ויחזק יהוה את־לב פרעה מלך מצרים	YHWH made the heart of Pharaoh, the king of Egypt, strong	P
14:17	ואני הנני מחזק את־לב מצרים	I am strengthening the heart of Egypt	P

Brevard Childs studied the hardening motif within its literary context to provide an answer to the theological problem.[6] Childs identifies the three Hebrew terms used for hardening: כבד, חזק, and קשה. He attributes to the Yahwist the passages using the verb כבד, meaning "to be heavy."[7] When the root is applied to bodily organs, it indicates that the organ is not working properly.[8] For example, the heavy eye is incapable of seeing (Gen 48:10), and the heavy ear of hearing (Isa 6:9–10; 59:1). When the Yahwist refers to a heavy heart, he

6. Brevard S. Childs, *The Book of Exodus: A Critical, Theological Commentary*, OTL (Philadelphia: Westminster Press, 1974), 170–175.

7. Childs, *Exodus*, 171.

8. Wilhelm Caspari, *Die Bedeutung der Wortsippe כבד, in Hebräischen* (Leipzig: Deichert, 1908), 8–10.

is speaking of an organ that has failed to be receptive to any external stimuli.[9] The verb is used either in the hiphil (Exod 8:11 [15], 28, [32]; 9:34) or in the qal (Exod 7:14; 9:7) and YHWH is never the agent of the hardening. Pharaoh himself is the subject or the subject is unmentioned, as in Exod 9:7: "The heart of Pharaoh was heavy."

In contrast to the Yahwist, Childs points out that the Priestly writer prefers the term חזק (Exod 7:13, 22; 8:19 [15]; 9:12; 14:4, 8, 17), but once uses the root קשה (Exod 13:15).[10] חזק means "to be firm or secure."[11] The term, however, may also have the sense of being "courageous" (Isa 41:6). According to G. K. Beale, חזק in reference to Pharaoh, functions similar to that in Josh 11:20, where YHWH gives the Canaanites a strong desire to fight against Israel:[12] כי מאת יהוה היתה לחזק את־לבם לקראת המלחמה את־ישׂראל ("For it was from [YHWH] to strengthen their hearts to meet Israel in battle"). Here the חזק is used in conjunction with לב in a military action that is similar to the meaning found in Exod 14:8, where Pharaoh exhibited a strong refusal to let the Israelites depart from Egypt.[13] In his assessment of the passages, Childs states that the Elohist source is parallel to P.[14] This means that the Elohist uses חזק as well to express the hardening of Pharaoh's heart. The word appears only in four passages (Exod 4:21; 9:35; 10:20, 27). In Exod 4:21; 10:20, and 10:27, the Elohist uses the piel of the verb חזק to present YHWH as the agent of the hardening. In Exod 9:35, the Elohist uses the qal of חזק to describe the condition of Pharaoh's heart.[15]

Having identified the Yahwist and the Priestly strand, Childs explains the hardening motif in each. In the Yahwist, the hardening phrase appears always after the plague has been removed and Pharaoh himself is the agent. Pharaoh's hardening is therefore a reaction of a plague being removed by Moses' intercession. This is found in Exod 7:11 and 8:15, where Pharaoh, seeing a reprieve,

---

9. Aubrey R. Johnson, *The Vitality of the Individual in the Thought of Ancient Israel* (Cardiff: University of Wales, 1964), 75–87.

10. Childs, *Exodus*, 171.

11. Francis Brown, et al., *The Brown-Driver-Briggs Hebrew and English Lexicon* (London: Hendrickson, 1996), 304.

12. Gregory K. Beale, "An Exegetical and Theological Consideration of the Hardening of Pharaoh's Heart in Exodus 4–14 and Romans 9," *Trinity Journal* 5 (1984): 131.

13. McAffee, "The Heart of Pharaoh," 334–335.

14. Childs, *Exodus*, 171.

15. Of all the passages mentioning the hardening of Pharaoh's heart, Childs says that Exod 7:14 and 10:1 may not be attributed either to the Yahwist, Elohist or Priestly writer. He argues that 7:14 is a redaction passage resulting by a fusion of the Priestly and Yahwist source and influenced by P in 7:13. Exod 10:1 is a foible, using Yahwist vocabulary (כבד) but being Priestly in form and theology. He attributes it to a Deuteronomic redactor. See Childs, *Exodus*, 171.

hardens his own heart. Because of the hardening, the plagues did not produce the intended reaction—that is, the plagues' function as signs to reveal God.[16] The phrase, "so that you may know that I, the LORD, am your God," accompanies the announcement of a plague (Exod 6:6–7; 7:17; 8:10, 22; 9:14, 29; 11:7). The phrase recalls the beginning of the Exodus narrative where Pharaoh provides the reason for not listening to Moses and Aaron as not knowing YHWH: "Who is the LORD, that I should heed him and let Israel go? I do not know the LORD, and I will not let Israel go" (Exod 5:2). The plagues are signs given to Pharaoh for the acknowledgement of YHWH, and the hardening is the refusal of this knowledge.[17] Childs sees the hardening of Pharaoh's heart as a motif that developed after the plague tradition as a "specific negative reaction to the plagues as divine signs."[18]

In his further assessment of the Priestly sources, Childs ascertains that hardening is analogous to Pharaoh's failure in listening. He finds a strong proof in the ab-abc structure found in Exod 7:3–4:[19]

a   But I will harden Pharaoh's heart
   b   That I may increase my signs and wonders in the land of Egypt
a'   When pharaoh will not listen to you
   b'   I will lay my hand upon Egypt
      c   and lead out my hosts, my people, the Israelites, from the land of Egypt by great acts of judgment.

The two cola of verse 3 parallel the first two cola of verse 4. Thus, the expression, "I will harden Pharaoh's heart" (v. 3a) is analogous to "Pharaoh will not listen" (v. 4a). God hardens Pharaoh's heart to increase his signs (v. 3b) and lay his hand upon Egypt (v. 4b). The Priestly writer proclaims the power of God being applied to a people in judgment (v. 4c).[20] This same meaning is found in 11:9–10 in the announcement of the death of the first-born. Pharaoh's refusal to listen to Moses allows YHWH to harden Pharaoh's heart so that his deeds may be multiplied in the land of Egypt. Here the writer turns abruptly from the interior feelings of Pharaoh to God's actively making his heart unrelenting.[21]

Childs summarizes as follows: "This means that for the P writer the plagues

---

16. Childs, *Exodus*, 171.

17. Childs, *Exodus*, 171. See also Dorian G. Coover Cox, "The Hardening of Pharaoh's Heart in its Literary and Cultural Contexts," *Bibliotheca Sacra* 163 (2006): 296–299.

18. Childs, *Exodus,* 172.

19. Childs, *Exodus*, 172.

20. Childs, *Exodus*, 171.

21. Childs, *Exodus*, 173.

are not the result of Pharaoh being hardened, but rather the reverse. Pharaoh is hardened in order to effect plagues."[22] From the Yahwist and the Priestly strands, the hardening is to be understood in light of the function of signs. In the Yahwist, the hardening of Pharaoh's heart thwarts the sign from revealing the knowledge of YHWH. For the Priestly writer, the hardening effects the multiplication of the signs as judgments. For Childs, the hardening motif should not be interpreted as a theological issue of divine causality that deals with the problem of free will and predestination.[23] He concludes:

> All attempts to relate hardness to a psychological state or derive it from a theology of divine causality miss the mark. The motif of the hardening in Exodus stems from a specific interpretation of the function of signs. . . . The motif has been consistently over-interpreted by supposing that it arose from a profoundly theological reflection and seeing it as a problem of free will and predestination.[24]

The interpretation of the hardening motif should be studied from the perspective of the writer who sought to provide the reason as to why the plagues, as divine signs, failed in their purpose and especially on how the motif functions in the rescuing of Israel from Egypt. Childs concludes from his analysis of the two strands that the hardening motif presents the degree of Pharaoh's failure to acknowledge and to know YHWH. In the Yahwist, the hardening of the heart is a deliberate refusal to hear the revelation of "he who is." In the Priestly account, the hardening of the heart is a refusal to acknowledge the judgment that YHWH passes upon Egypt. The hardening of the heart pertains to what ought to be a proper response to YHWH in light of his revelation and might. Both the Yahwist and the Priestly writers make a strong connection between the hardening, not listening to the word of the prophet, and not being able to interpret the divine signs as YHWH's judgment for their refusal to acknowledge him.

Childs's approach presents students with a clear example of how form-critical and traditional-historical approaches have served to postulate the theory that the hardening motif was developed by the author after the plague tradition, but Childs does not offer a concrete response to the more pressing theological themes of free will, predestination, and grace.

---

22. Childs, *Exodus*, 173.
23. Childs, *Exodus*, 174.
24. Childs, *Exodus*, 174.

St. Gregory of Nyssa

Whereas in our time Childs studied the correlation of the hardening of the heart to signs, avoiding the themes of divine causality and predestination, St. Gregory of Nyssa addresses the issue of free will in his work the *Life of Moses*.[25] Written around 390 CE, the work is a commentary on the life of Moses based on a pre-modern Christian exegesis that provides guidance concerning the perfect life. Gregory begins his argument of Pharaoh's hardened heart by questioning divine justice:

> Let us not be astonished if the history says that the rod of virtue did these things to the Egyptians, for it also says that the tyrant was hardened by God. Now, how could he be condemned if he were disposed by divine constraint to be stubborn and obstinate? Somewhere the divine Apostle also expresses the same thought: "Since they refuse to see it was rational to acknowledge God, he abandoned them to shameful passions," speaking about those who commit sodomy and those who disgrace themselves by dishonorable and unmentionable profligacy.[26]

Paul asserts that God is manifesting his wrath against the Gentiles by permitting them to pursue the desires of their heart which has been rendered incapable of living virtuously by their refusal to acknowledge the existence of God in their lives.[27] Gregory makes a comparison between Pharaoh's condition and Paul's assessment of the Gentiles' behavior in Romans 1:26 and 28 by making a distinction between virtue and vice. Gregory, following Paul's argument, says that some people follow a virtuous life while others slide into vice. It will be useful at this point to define Gregory's definition of free will and its correlation with virtue and vice. Gregory understands free will as the inner capacity to choose between virtue and vice, life and death, God and Satan.[28] Two paths exist in life:

---

25. Gregory of Nyssa, *The Life of Moses*, trans. Abraham J. Malherbe and Everett Ferguson (New York: Harper One, 2006).

26. Gregory, *Life of Moses*, book 2, paragraph 51.

27. Frank J. Matera, *Romans*, PCNT (Grand Rapids, MI: Baker Academic, 2010), 47–56.

28. Andrew P. Klager, "Free Will and Vicinal Culpability in St. Gregory of Nyssa's *De Vita Moysis*," *Greek Orthodox Theological Review* 55 (2010): 153. See also, Paul M. Blowers, "Maximus the Confessor, Gregory of Nyssa, and the Concept of Perpetual Progress," *Vigiliae Christianae* 46, no. 2 (1992): 156; Anthony Meredith, *Gregory of Nyssa*, ECF (New York: Routledge, 1999), 24. Joseph T. Muckle defines Gregory's understanding of virtue and vice as follows: "For Gregory the virtues are an integral part of man's original possession in virtue of his being made in the image of God. St. Gregory does not make the classification found in scholastic times of the moral and theological, the acquired and infused virtues. For him all virtues were originally implanted in man by God when He created Him," in "The Doctrine of St. Gregory of Nyssa on Man as the Image of God," *Medieval Studies* 7 (1945): 79. Gregory does not understand the

vice results in a life of perdition, while virtue leads toward the Good. The capacity to choose either path is based on rational free choice. The virtuous life begins when the person chooses the good based on evidence. A virtuous life leads the soul back to its original state of purity and participation in true Goodness.[29] The life of vice is the result of succumbing to sensual and irrational emotions.[30] The ability to live a life of virtue or vice cannot be attributed to divine constraint, but to human freedom. In fact, freedom is a constitutive attribute of the human person. In a text from the *Great Catechism* Gregory says:

> For He who made man . . . would never have deprived him of the most beautiful and precious of all goods; I mean the gift of being without a master and having self-determination. For if necessity in any way was the Master of Human life, the "image" would have been falsified in that particular part by being altered through this unlikeness to its archetype. How can that nature which is under a yoke and bondage to any kind of necessity be called an image of a Master Being? Was it not, then, most right that that which is in every detail like the Divine should possess in its nature a self-ruling and independent principle . . . ?[31]

Gregory's statement must be understood in light of his teaching of human beings created in the image and likeness of God (Gen 1:27). For him, image and likeness are synonyms. One is part of the other and the original is replicated in both, with image being the impress, that which can be transferred, whereas the likeness is the result. As in a statue, if the image impressed on the matter is good enough, the resulting statue bears the likeness fully. Humanity, made in the image and likeness of God, shares both in the real, active God-like impression and in the resultant resemblance to God, sharing his attributes.[32]

---

divine image as something external that is attached to the soul; it is intrinsic to the fundamental make-up of human nature. By pursuing a virtuous life, humans return to their original pure state prior to the disobedience of Adam and Eve.

29. Sara J. Denning-Bolle, "Gregory of Nyssa: The Soul in Mystical Flight," *Greek Orthodox Theological Review* 34, no. 2 (1989): 107.

30. Robert W. Jensen, "Gregory of Nyssa: The Life of Moses," *Theology Today* 62 (2006): 534. Gregory, *Life of Moses*, 2.78 says that "he who would approach the knowledge of things sublime must first purify his manner of life from all sensual and irrational emotion . . . when he is purified, then he assaults the mountain." The knowledge of God is like a mountain that is difficult to climb.

31. Gregory of Nyssa, *The Great Catechism*, book 2, chapter 5, as cited in Verna E. F. Harrison, *Grace and Human Freedom According to St. Gregory of Nyssa*, SBEC 30 (Lewiston, NY: Edwin Mellen, 1992), 140.

32. Harrison, "Grace," 142–143; Muckle, "The Doctrine of St. Gregory," 61–70; 77–84, states that according to St. Gregory among the many attributes that a person possesses are free

Because God possesses freedom, the human person must also be characterized by freedom. The passage emphasizes the person's freedom to choose a path of life without being coerced.[33] For Gregory, the person has the interior power to be self-governed.

Because humans are inclined to pursue that which is evil, Gregory says that God's grace is necessary to aid us in choosing goodness. However, in every case, human freedom initiates the process through which divine grace is received, either by living a virtuous life or by requesting it though prayer.[34] Divine grace is accessible to every human being and becomes known to every individual when their life is oriented toward a pursuit of divine goodness and avoidance of sin.[35] Conversely, a person's failure to choose divine grace is not the effect of divine intervention, but the result of rejecting grace. V. Harrison summarizes as follows:

> This means that even when, in our freedom, we turn away from God and so lose our participation in other divine attributes such as the virtues, we are still free. We remain free through all the vicissitudes of fall and restoration, and that same freedom that enabled us to turn away from our Creator also enables us to turn toward him again and enter through grace into a renewed and ever-increasing participation in all his attributes. In other words, it is through our freedom that we have access to all the other resources of the divine image.[36]

Gregory's understanding of the human openness to God's grace provides the theological interpretation to Pharaoh's hardening and Paul's assertion of God's abandonment of the Gentiles to shameful passions (Rom 1:26). He states:

> Who it is who is delivered up to shameful affections can be clearly learned from the Apostle: It is he who does not like to have God in his knowledge.

---

will, reason, virtue, intellect, love, word, etc. Although man possesses God's attributes in virtue of being created in God's image and likeness, they are not the same as those in God. In man they are finite; they are created and subject to change. In God they are infinite: "For that which is made according to the image has in every respect an utter likeness to the archetype, intellectual of intellectual, and incorporeal of incorporeal, free from any bodily bulk as the archetype, and like it evading measurement, yet in its own proper nature it is something else than the latter. For it would no longer be an image if it were identically the same in all respects as the other. But in those respects, in which the archetype is disclosed in the uncreated nature, in the same respects does the created manifest the image." Muckle, "The Doctrine of St. Gregory," 61–62.

33. Harrison, *Grace,* 141; Klager, *Free Will,* 153.

34. Harrison, *Grace,* 241.

35. Gregory, *Life of Moses,* 2.44.

36. Harrison, *Grace,* 143.

> God delivers up to passion him whom he does not protect because he is not acknowledged by him. But his failure to acknowledge God becomes the reason why he is being pulled down into the passionate and dishonorable life. . . . In the same way, the thought of the apostle should be clear, that it is those who do not acknowledge God who are delivered up to shameful affections, and that the Egyptian tyrant is hardened by God not because the divine will places the resistance in the soul of Pharaoh but because the free will through its inclination to evil does not receive the word which softens resistance.[37]

Gregory affirms that "God delivers up to passion him whom he does not protect."[38] What brings God's lack of protection is the person's failure to acknowledge God. A reference to this is made by Pharaoh who says: "Who is the LORD that I should heed his plea to let Israel go? I do not know the LORD" (Exod 5:2).[39] The divine grace that would have protected the person from being allured into a dishonorable life is not present. Klager summarizes as follows: "God permitted, at most perpetuated, the sedition that was already an unaffected expression of Pharaoh's heart, hence he does not coerce. If God were to coerce with the desire of his own will, then human choice would fall into line in every case, so that no distinction between virtue and vice will be observed."[40] Recognizing God, the true good, leads to virtue, the opposite leads to vice and judgment.

In conclusion, human freedom is an essential element in Gregory's anthropology; free will is essential to be considered a person. Gregory's theological position refuses to even entertain the possibility of denying free will to Pharaoh. Thus, Pharaoh's stubborn refusal to follow a life of virtue in accordance to his own free will resulted in God's just judgment.

St. Augustine
Whereas Gregory's treatment of the motif of the hardening focuses on free will, Augustine, in his work *Eighty-Three Different Questions*, addresses the theological problem of the hardening in response to the broader theological issue raised

37. Gregory, *Life of Moses*, 2.52.

38. Gregory, *Life of Moses*, 2.52.

39. Martin Laird in *Gregory of Nyssa and The Grasp of Faith: Union, Knowledge and Divine Presence* (Oxford: Oxford University Press, 2005), 63–78, says that according to Gregory humans can assert certain truths about God's essence using apophatic discourse, but this leads only to the unknowability of God. God may only be known through faith. To illustrate this point, he refers to the life of Abraham. Abraham responded to the unknown God in faith (trust, loyalty, and obedience).

40. Klager, *Free Will*, 154; Gregory, *Life of Moses*, 2.51.

by Paul in Romans 9.[41] The theological issue focuses on God's apparent injustice. Although all persons deserve eternal damnation, God nevertheless shows mercy to some apart from any prior merit. The basis for God's mercy is granted through faith, so that the sinner may be saved through grace.[42] Thus, their sins are forgiven and rendered capable of seeing God.[43] Conversely, others are hardened. Augustine says:

> By all means he has mercy on whom he wants, and he hardens whom he wants, but this will of God cannot be unjust. For it springs from deeply hidden merits, because, even though sinners themselves have constituted a single mass on account of the sin of all, still it is not the case that there is no difference among them. Therefore, although they have not yet been made righteous, there is some preceding thing in sinners whereby they are rendered worthy of righteousness, and again there is some preceding thing in other sinners whereby they are deserving of obtuseness.[44]

The statement "he has mercy on whom he wants, and he hardens whom he wants, but this will of God cannot be unjust" must be studied within the context of Romans 9:14–18 where Paul responds to the objection of God's injustice by recounting Israel's dwelling in Egypt to demonstrate how God's elective purpose resulted in divine mercy and protection for the Israelites. Paul, according to F. Matera, recounts the story from the theological theme of divine election.[45] Quoting the LXX of Exodus 33:19, Paul says, "For he says to Moses, 'I will have mercy on whomever I have mercy, and I will have compassion on whomever I have compassion'" (9:15).[46] The statement follows the episode of the golden

41. Augustine, *Eighty-Three Different Questions*, trans. David L. Mosher, FaCh 70 (Washington, DC: Catholic University of America Press, 1982), q. 68.

42. According to Augustine in *Saint Augustine Letters 204–270*, trans. Wilfrid Parsons, FaCh 5 (New York: Fathers of the Church Inc., 1956), 78, God prepares the will to receive faith: ". . . the true grace of God is presented to us, that is, that when it is given, it gives merit because it goes before the good will of men and does not find it in any heart but produces it . . ."

43. Augustine, *Questions*, q. 68.2.

44. Augustine, *Questions*, q. 68.4. According to Augustine, *Saint Augustine Letters 165–203*, trans. Wilfrid Parsons, FaCh 4 (New York: Fathers of the Church, 1955), 308, the mystery of unbelief is hidden in the depth of the riches of God's wisdom: "The reason why one believes and another does not believe, although both hear the same thing, and, if a miracle is worked in their sight, both see the same thing, is hid in the depth of the riches of the wisdom and of the knowledge of God whose judgments are unsearchable, and with whom there is no injustice, when He 'has mercy on whom He will and whom He will He hardens' (Rom 9:14, 18) for His judgments are not unjust because their meaning is hidden."

45. Matera, *Romans*, 224–225.

46. Matera, *Romans*, 224–225.

calf (Exod 32), after which YHWH instructs Moses to travel toward the land he promised the patriarchs, but because the people has broken the covenant YHWH informs Moses that "he would not be among them" (Exod 33:3). Upon hearing YHWH's decision, Moses pleads on Israel's behalf and YHWH yields to Moses' request. From this event, Paul draws the following conclusion: "So it depends not upon a person's will or exertion, but upon God, who shows mercy" (Rom 9:16). For Paul, God manifesting his mercy upon Israel was an indication of their divine call and election, and not as a result of any previous deeds.[47]

After Paul describes the merciful way in which God has dealt with his people, he proceeds to explain God's treatment of Pharaoh at the time of the exodus. Paul states: "For the Scripture says to Pharaoh, this is why I have raised you up, to show my power through you that my name may be proclaimed throughout the earth" (Rom 9:17). Matera points out that by "raising up" Pharaoh, YHWH had chosen him for his redemptive purpose on behalf of Israel. He states: "God 'elected' him to play a role in Israel's redemptive history, of which he was not even aware. For by refusing to obey Moses, the servant of God, Pharaoh enabled the Lord to show his power to redeem Israel. Thus, the Lord's name was proclaimed throughout the earth."[48] Paul concludes by saying: "Consequently, he has mercy upon whom he wills, and he hardens whom he wills" (9:18). Verse 18a refers to Moses and Israel, 18b to Pharaoh. For Paul, God's redemptive plan resulted in mercy toward Moses for the salvation of Israel, but it hardened Pharaoh's heart revealing God's glory.[49]

Paul clearly attributed the hardening to Pharaoh, echoing the many references found in Exodus, but he does not allude to any specific passage. Paul is not interested in presenting a solution to the problem of God's sovereignty and human freedom, but in accenting God's purpose in Israel's history.[50] If this is the case, how are we to understand Augustine's position on the subject? We must consider his teaching on God's mercy.

Augustine affirms that God's mercy or hardening stems from "deeply hidden merits." Although all individuals are sinners and deserving of God's punishment, those who receive mercy obtain it by virtue of their repentance and outcry to God.[51] If a person is deemed worthy of receiving God's mercy through repentance, it is achieved through God, but the person must will it. Within the

47. Matera, *Romans*, 224–225.
48. Matera, *Romans*, 224–225.
49. Matera, *Romans*, 226.
50. Matera, *Romans*, 226.
51. Augustine, *Questions,* q. 68.5. A clear example of God showing mercy is found in Exod 2:23 where the Israelites' delivery resulted from God's response to their prayer and lament.

Exodus account, God provides the spoken word and visible signs, which were understood as God's sovereign power and mercy. In Pharaoh's case, the word and the signs were also revealed to him. But because he "could not believe the most obvious signs decreed by God," he warranted God's judgment for his failure to acknowledge God.[52] Augustine affirms that such persons are destined for destruction.[53] He says,

> To mercy belongs the calling; to judgment belongs the blessedness of those who have come when called and the punishment of those who did want to come. Therefore, was Pharaoh ignorant of how much good came upon the land through Joseph? The acknowledgement of that fact, therefore, was Pharaoh's invitation to a gratitude expressed through merciful treatment of the people of Israel. However, because he did not want to obey this invitation, but exercised cruelty on those to whom he owed humanity and mercy, he deserved punishment. As a consequence, his heart was hardened, and he suffered such a blindness of the mind that he did not believe God's signs, though so many and so great and so manifest.[54]

Augustine views the hardening of Pharaoh as just retribution for his own actions. God allows the consequences of sin to take their natural course. Thus, Pharaoh did not suffer any injustice, but through his actions God chooses to reveal his justice. In essence, the fate of Pharaoh is deserved by all humanity because of sin. None are worthy of God's mercy. But God bestows grace, through no merit of our own. When a person responds to God's invitation mercy is imparted and salvation granted. If grace is refused, God's justice is revealed in judgment.

Augustine in *On Grace and Free Will* again states that the hardening of Pharaoh's heart is just retribution. In this work, Augustine illustrates how the will is not destroyed by grace and how the will of the unredeemed is subject to God's power without their free will being compromised. To make his point, Augustine references 2 Samuel 16. According to the text, Shimei curses David as he flees from Absalom. "Was it not of his own will that the wicked son of Gera cursed King David?" asks Augustine. "And yet what says David . . . ? Let him alone and let him curse, because the Lord hath said unto him, Curse David."[55]

Augustine explains that God did not command Shimei to curse David: if

---

52. Augustine, *Questions,* q. 68.4.
53. Augustine, *Questions,* q. 68.4.
54. Augustine, *Questions,* q. 68.4.
55. Augustine, "On Grace and Free Will," in *Nicene and Post Nicene Fathers: Volume 5*, ed. Philip Schaff (Buffalo, NY: Hendrickson, 1994), chapter 20, paragraph 41.

this had been the case, he would have been lauded.[56] Instead, God disposed Shimei's will, which was already perverted to commit this sin according to His own just and hidden judgment.[57] Thus, Augustine affirms a person's responsibility for his action without compromising free will and once again avows that there is no injustice in God.

> When you read that truth of the Scriptures and find that men are led astray by God, or that their hearts are dulled and hardened by Him, have no doubt that it was their previous evil merits that made them suffer their just penalties.[58]

Furthermore, he says that one must not deny Pharaoh's free will simply because God says, "I have hardened Pharaoh."

> For it does not by any means follow that Pharaoh did not, on this account, harden his own heart. For this too, is said of him, after the removal of the fly-plague of the Egyptians. . . . Thus it was that both God hardened him by his just judgment, and Pharaoh by his own free will.[59]

In summary, Augustine taught that a hardened heart results from God withholding his grace from a sinful individual, resulting in condemnation, but God's action did not violate Pharaoh's free will. As we look at these passages, we must be satisfied with the affirmation that there is no injustice in God. To seek to determine why God saves some and leaves others for perdition is seeking the impossible.

Helping Students Gain Theological Understanding of the Motif of the Hardening of the Heart

When teaching the theme of the hardening of Pharaoh's heart, I use a pedagogical strategy that helps students acquire the theological insights of the subject. The purpose of the assignment is to expose the students to contemporary scholarship as well as previous (pre-modern) authors' opinions, in conjunction with the professor and their peers.

Knowledge gained thus, caught as much as taught, will remain better in their memory. At the same time as the discussion, students complete a three-part worksheet concerning interpretation: occurrences of the motif plus at

---

56. Augustine, "On Grace and Free Will," 20.41.
57. Augustine, "On Grace and Free Will," 20.41.
58. Augustine, "On Grace and Free Will," 21.43.
59. Augustine, "On Grace and Free Will," 23.45.

least ten observations. This should demonstrate attentive reading: content, repetition, comparison, purpose, verse tense, subject, etc. In class I offer my observations to facilitate discussion. The goal is to have students carefully attend to the passage. Students are then assigned to read Childs's contribution on the subject. At this point, they are able to understand his position and present the limitations and advantages of form analysis. For worksheets two and three, they are given selected passages dealing with St. Gregory of Nyssa's and St. Augustine's treatment of the motif. Students are again required to write down their observations and identify the theological approach of the authors. In class, I help students make connections between their initial questions and those gained by each scholar. By the end of our study, students will have approached the text in its literary form and then moved to a discussion of virtue, vice, free will, humanity created in the image of God, and God's justice—all within the context of the hardening motif. Through being exposed to diverse interpretative voices, they learn to analyze texts critically, to gain theological insights, to be receptive to different voices, and to be patient (attending to the same theme from three different perspectives).

Conclusion

I have presented, in accordance with the suggestion made in "The New Evangelization for the Transmission of the Christian Faith" concerning the importance of the transmission of the faith in education and the *Verbum Domini* recommendation that difficult passages in scripture should not be avoided, three different scholarly methodologies to the understanding of the hardening of Pharaoh's heart. Modern scholars, such as Brevard Childs, analyze the variance of sources and the development of the narrative structure to interpret the motif within the function of divine signs, whose purpose was to reveal God's knowledge and judgment. In St. Gregory of Nyssa's treatment, free will is an essential anthropological element. St. Augustine, on the other hand, attributes the hardening of the heart to a refusal to accept God's grace and asserts God's justice. Each of these authors provides a different insight into the hardening motif based on their own hermeneutics. Ultimately, however, the question of the hardening of the heart is a deep mystery that is rooted in God's sovereignty and its interaction with human freedom. It would be imprudent to think that an easy resolution is to be found; nevertheless, a systematic approach to the study of the theme broadens the theological understanding for students.

PART TWO

CHAPTER 6

The Father of Proverbs 1–9:
A Spiritual Father for Seminary Professors

Kelly Anderson

Proverbs 1–9 is largely composed of ten lectures delivered by a father to his son, a young man on the cusp of independence and adulthood.[1] Through these speeches the father educates his son in the religious traditions to form him to be a mature, pious man.[2] But the father of Proverbs 1–9 is more than an educator.

1. R. Norman Whybray, through form criticism, was the first to identify ten instructions in Proverbs (1:8–19; 2:1–22; 3:1–12, 21–35; 4:1–9, 10–19, 20–27; 5:1–23; 6:20–35; 7:1–27) (*Wisdom in Proverbs: The Concept of Wisdom in Proverbs 1–9* [Chatham, UK: SCM, 1965], 33–37). He delineated several distinguishing characteristics. Each begins with "my son(s)," each commands the pupil/son to "hear," "receive," or "not forget" the instruction which follows, and each asserts the personal authority of the teacher. Further, each implies or asserts the great value and utility of the teacher's words. Finally, there is no reference to any authority beyond the teacher himself (the only reference to God is found in 3:4) (R. Norman Whybray, *The Composition of the Book of Proverbs* [Sheffield, UK: Sheffield Academic, 1994], 13). Michael V. Fox says that each instruction develops a central topic in a tripartite structure: the *exordium* comprising an address, an exhortation, and motivations; the *lesson*; and the *conclusion* ("Ideas of Wisdom in Proverbs 1–9," *Journal of Biblical Literature* 116, no. 4 [1997]: 613–633). There is a general scholarly consensus regarding the presence of ten instructions, though Roland Murphy questions the existence of ten instructions because it is difficult to find an ending to the speeches, and therefore "poems" or "interludes" (1:20–33; 3:13–20; 6:1–19; 8:1–36; 9:1–18) have been identified in order to explain the presence of other material (*Proverbs*, WBC 22 [Nashville: Thomas Nelson, 1998], 8–9).

2. While there is general agreement that the ten instructions are textually composite, some scholars maintain that the ten instructions were delivered or composed by various authors and then shaped into their final form by a redactor (R. Norman Whybray, *Proverbs* [Grand Rapids, MI: Eerdmans, 1994], 24–25; William McKane, *Proverbs*, OTL [Philadelphia: Westminster, 1970], 7–10). But Fox points out that this would require a widespread knowledge of the genre

He is truly a *father* who can serve as a meaningful example of a spiritual father for seminary professors who, like the father, are instructing and forming young men on the cusp of independence. This essay will first examine how the father of Proverbs acts as a spiritual father, and then will present the father's method for persuading his son to follow the right path.[3] Finally, the father's method will be applied to seminary professors today.

The Father of Proverbs as a Spiritual Father

God is the Eternal Father and from him we receive our understanding of fatherhood.[4] The father of Proverbs, in his act of instructing his son, shows some striking affinities with the Eternal Father whom Jesus Christ definitively reveals centuries later. Speech is the only "activity" in which the father engages; that is, he gives his *word*. He delivers ten instructions to his son, and, in doing so, he patterns the activity of God the Father in two ways. First, he gives himself, his very being, through his words, and second, he gives life through his words.[5] Each of these will be examined.

"instruction" as it is found in Proverbs 1–9. Though the genre "instruction" is a well-recognized genre in the Ancient Near Eastern Wisdom literature, it is more flexible and widespread than the highly uniformed instructions found in Proverbs (with the tripartite structure of *exordium, lesson*, and *conclusion*). Michael Fox instead posits that the ten instructions are all the work of a single author composed as a unit, and I agree with this conclusion (Fox, "Ideas of Wisdom," 615–616; *Proverbs 1–9*, AncB 18A [New York: Doubleday, 2000], 322–330).

3. Since this essay focuses on the father of Proverbs as a model for seminary professors, I will use exclusively the term "father." Motherhood with all its traits could also be applied in this study.

4. "It is not any earthly father but God, from whom all fatherhood is derived (Eph 3:15), who defines what true fatherhood is . . . God's fatherhood, being the source, is also the norm of paternal authority and the critical standard by which it is judged" (Walter Kasper, *The God of Jesus Christ*, trans. Matthew J. O'Connell [New York: Crossroad, 1984], 139–140). Hilary of Poitiers says, "Remember that the revelation is not of the Father manifested as God, but of God manifested as the Father" (*On the Trinity*, book 3, paragraph 22 in *Nicene and Post-Nicene Fathers of the Christian Church: Second Series, Vol. 9*, eds. Philip Schaff and Henry Wace [New York: Scribner, 1899], 68). The Catechism says, "By calling God 'Father,' the language of faith indicates two main things: that God is the first origin of everything and transcendent authority; and that he is at the same time goodness and loving care for all his children" (*CCC*, §239).

5. I am indebted to Father Chris Christensen, whose reflections on this theme spurred this paper. It was during the course, "Wisdom Literature and the Psalms," in Spring 2014, when I was presenting the Book of Proverbs that then Deacon Christensen remarked that the father in Proverbs seemed to be much like God the Father who pours himself out in his Word to give life to the Son. Much of this paper is an outgrowth of Father Christensen's profound reflection, and he should rightfully be considered the "author" of it.

The Father Gives His Being

The father of Proverbs imitates the Eternal Father in the way he gives himself. The Fourth Lateran Council says that the Father gives his *substance* to his Son, generating him from all eternity (DS, §805). The father of Proverbs similarly pours out his very *being* to his son through his teachings. He has deeply assimilated the traditions of the past in such a way that they come to constitute his very being. Thus, in his teaching, something new and yet organic flows forth from him through his words. What follows are three ways that show how the father's instructions are informed by the religious and familial traditions, but also how he teaches them creatively.

THE TEN COMMANDMENTS

Given that there are ten lectures, it can be reasonably concluded that the father encourages his son to regard his instructions as an authoritative body of texts patterned upon and informed by the Ten Commandments. And the father's teachings closely resemble the teachings of the Decalogue. He teaches his son not to steal (1:13–14; 4:17), not to kill (1:11–12; 6:17), nor to commit adultery (2:16–17; 6:32; 7:10–27), not to bear false witness (4:24; 6:17, 19) nor to covet another's wife (5:18–19). Of course, he expects his son to obey him and his mother's teaching (1:8; 6:20), and thus the Ten Commandments can be viewed as the scaffolding or foundation of the father's teachings.

But the father does not simply repeat the Ten Commandments. He has amalgamated the Mosaic tradition within himself and teaches it creatively and colorfully, and in doing so he creates from within him something new and different: a primitive form of Wisdom.[6]

Interspersed among the father's instructions are five interludes: three are wisdom speeches (1:20–33; 3:13–20; 8:1–36); one is a series of admonitions and warnings (6:1–19); and, the last is an invitation by both Wisdom and Folly to the young man to dine with them (9:1–18). Thus, four of the five interludes deal with Wisdom and they show a more developed theology regarding Wisdom than the ten speeches of the father.[7] Given the differences in the theology of

---

6. The identity of Wisdom remains debated among scholars. Richard Clifford has summarized the four theories: wisdom as a hypostasis of YHWH; wisdom as a model of a Syro-Palestine goddess, such as Astarte, or an Egyptian goddess Maat; wisdom as a derivation from Mesopotamian mythology; and wisdom as a pure literary personification (*Proverbs*, OTL [Louisville: Westminster John Knox, 1999], 23–24). See also Alice M. Sinnott (*The Personification of Wisdom* [Burlington, VT: Ashgate, 2005], 10–52) for an overview of the proposed origins of wisdom.

7. Wisdom gives life to the young man (3:16, 18; 9:6, 11) and is preexistent to creation (8:22–26). She is the means by which God created the world (3:19–20; 8:30), the one through

the ten speeches and the interludes, it seems likely that the father is not the author of the interludes. On the other hand, given their context and similarity to the ten speeches, it may be that they are contiguous to his teachings or outgrowths of them, particularly since the ideas of the interludes are found in a primitive and inchoate form in the father's teaching (Prov 2:3–4; 4:8–9; 6:22; 7:4).[8] Therefore, taking into account the juxtaposition of the interludes, as well as their similarity to the father's speeches, it is probable that the father has deeply reflected on and imbibed the Ten Commandments and its relations to the creation tradition, and this leads him to develop a new insight, Wisdom, which he communicates in his instructions.[9] The community then seizes upon

---

whom kings rule (8:15–16) and the means by which the man can achieve life, honor, and wealth (8:18–21). Wisdom calls out to the young man, and thus she is similar to the prophets (1:20–21; 8:1–5; 9:6); she desires to be in a relationship with him, and thus she is similar to a wife.

8. "Given the diverse authorship of at least some of the interludes, along with the continuity of the interludes with the lectures, we can picture the process of growth as a series of insertions by scribes learning from and building on the lectures rather than as compilation and reorganization of unrelated texts by a redactor. The connection among the wisdom interludes can be explained not from their having a single author but from a process of organic growth with each successive author reading the earlier text and elaborating on it" (Fox, "Ideas of Wisdom," 618; see also Alan Lenzi, "Proverbs 8:22–31: Three Perspectives on Its Composition," *Journal of Biblical Literature* 125, no. 4 [2006]: 690).

9. The presence of ten instructions or ten words also can recall the act of creation. In the Genesis creation account, the words "God said" appear ten times, and the creation narrative anticipates the Ten Commandments. "This makes us realize that these Ten Commandments are, as it were, an echo of the creation; they are not arbitrary inventions for the purpose of erecting barriers to human freedom but signs pointing to the spirit, the language and the meaning of creation; they are a translation of the language of the universe, a translation of God's logic which constructed the universe" (Cardinal Joseph Ratzinger, *"In the Beginning...": A Catholic Understanding of the Story of the Creation and the Fall*, trans. Boniface Ramsey [Grand Rapids, MI: Eerdmans, 1995], 26). It is plausible that the father of Proverbs is aware of the creation tradition. The whole of Proverbs, and the Wisdom literature in general, views creation as ordered and rational. The sages study the created order, learn its patterns and natural rhythms, apply those lessons to life, and teach that a person can become wise by studying the world and the cosmos and by learning from them. The connection between the created order and the law is explicitly stated in Psalms 19 and 93 through the juxtaposition of hymns of creation with texts that extol the Torah. Further, the father sees no disjunction between the ordered cosmos and the Law (6:6–9; 27–28). God commands the created order, it obeys him, and chaos and darkness are defeated. Likewise, humans who follow the commands of God and participate in that harmony and order will enjoy lives of prosperity and peace. It may be that the creation tradition influenced the father's understanding of Wisdom. If that is the case, then the father merged within himself the creation tradition and the law tradition (at least the Ten Commandments) and produced the idea of Wisdom.

his contemplative insights and develops his general ideas which are expressed in the interludes.[10]

To summarize, the father assumes the normative teachings of the Decalogue and presumes them in his teaching. But the father does not simply echo these ideas. He has first deeply contemplated them and dwelled upon them, and thus in his teachings he expounds a primitive form of personified Wisdom. This primitive tradition will be expanded by subsequent sages and their reflections placed side by side with the instructions of the father.[11]

THE BOOK OF DEUTERONOMY

The influence of the Book of Deuteronomy on the father's speeches is well attested.[12] The father deploys Deuteronomy most notably in Proverbs 3:1–5, 6:20–24 and 7:1–5, three instructions which share several similarities. First is the word *tôrāh* in 3:1, 6:20, and 7:2, followed by the idea of guarding (*šmr* and *nṣr*; 3:1; 6:22; 7:2). Further, the words of the father are to adhere to the person: they should be bound to the heart and the neck (6:21; 3:3); they should also be bound to the finger (7:3); and, they should be written on the tablet of one's heart (3:3; 7:3). Finally, all three instructions promise the son a successful life,

10. Michael Fishbane describes the process of "traditioning": "The inner–biblical dynamic of Torah and tradition, as thus far analyzed, reveals the reuse (controlled or creative) transformation, readaptation or blending of transmitted teachings having an authoritative aspect. Tradition emerges as a relationship to a past authority – be that an historical memory, a theological proclamation, or a commanded behavior. Tradition, in its relationship to the Torah, has thus far been seen to be both conservative and innovative. As an innovative process, tradition is a mode of hermeneutics, a process of interpretation, which *actualizes* a received, authoritative text in a new context. Through tradition, a sacred teaching remains effective in new life situations. As a conservative force, tradition provides for cultural continuity and cohesion by *preserving* the authoritative memories of the past" ("Torah and Tradition," in *Tradition and Theology in the Old Testament*, ed. Douglas A. Knight [Philadelphia: Fortress, 1977], 286).

11. Juxtaposing the father's teachings with the wisdom interludes creates a powerful effect: the father's speeches are mirrored, and even undergirded, by Wisdom herself. The father figure speaks of Wisdom, but with his instructions juxtaposed with wisdom texts, his message is grounded not only in the law and in authoritative figures, but also in Wisdom.

12. To illustrate the connections, I will draw largely from the observations of Bernd U. Schipper who has used several previous studies and developed them further ("Das Proverbienbuch und die Toratradition," *Zeitschrift für Theologie und Kirche* 108, no. 4 [2011]: 383–390; cf. A. Robert, "Les attaches littéraires bibliques de Pr. I–IX (Suite)," *Revue Biblique* 44, no. 3 [1935]: 344–365). I also make use of Paul Overland's study, where he outlines six correlations between Prov 3:1–12 and Deut 6:4–9 ("Did the Sage Draw from the Shema? A study of Proverbs 3:1–12," *Catholic Biblical Quarterly* 62 [2000]: 427–433). Finally, I also draw from Fishbane who demonstrates an intertextual relationship between Prov 6:20–34 and Deut 5, 6 ("Torah and Tradition," 284; cf. Fox, *Proverbs 1–9*, 230).

and all three expressions have a word which derives from *ḥyh* ("years of *life*" 3:2; "way of *life*" 6:23; "keep my commandments and you will *live*" 7:2).

These three texts share some notable similarities with Deuteronomy 6:5–9 and 11:18–20. First is the command of Deuteronomy 6:7 and 11:19 that repeats the words *yšb, hlk, škb*, and *qûm*.[13] Two of these terms are found in Proverbs 6:22 where the father, after bidding his son to follow his commands (v. 21), equates them with the Torah, which guides the son where he walks (*hlk*) and guards him when he sleeps (*škb*). Also, both Deuteronomy 6:5 and Proverbs 3:5 modify heart (*lēb* or *lēbāb*) with "all" (*kōl*), a phrase that we see only two other times in the Wisdom literature[14] and that only in Greek (Sir 7:27; Wis 8:21), and ten times in the Psalms.[15] Finally, in all the Wisdom literature, the command to do something with "all your heart" occurs only in Proverbs 3:5 and Sirach 7:27.

Further, Moses teaches that his words should be bound on one's wrist (Deut 6:8; 11:18). The father also teaches that his words should be bound to one's body, whether it be the neck (Prov 3:3 and 6:21) or the finger (Prov 7:3). The writer also makes a connection with the command to write (*ktb*). In Deuteronomy 6:9 and in 11:20, Moses commands the Israelites to write his words on the doorposts of the houses, while in Proverbs 3:3 and 7:3, the father commands that his words are to be written on the tablets of their hearts. Finally, the combination of "to bind" (*qšr*) and "to write" (*ktb*) occurs in the whole Hebrew Bible only in Deuteronomy 6:8, 11:18 and Proverbs 3:3 and 7:3.[16]

I could add Proverbs 3:21–24 to illustrate further links to Deuteronomy. This instruction does not begin with the word *tôrāh*; but the young man is promised life (*ḥyh*), and that prudence will adorn his neck (3:22). Also, the combination of *hlk* and *škb* is found in Proverbs 3:23–34 where the teachings promise the son security and freedom from anxiety.

The father uses the powerful language of Deuteronomy to show that his words should be taken as seriously as the *Šᵉmaʿ* and the Torah because his teachings have the same effect as they do! The father's teachings are bold and

---

13. "Drill them into your children. Speak of when you are at home (*yšb*), walking along the road (*hlk*), lying down (*škb*), or getting up (*qûm*)" (Deut 6:7); "Teach them to your children, reciting them when you are at home (*yšb*), walking along the road (*hlk*), lying down (*škb*), or getting up (*qûm*)" (Deut 11:19). The biblical translations in this chapter are the author's.

14. Overland illustrates this, as well as pointing out that *lēb* and *lēbāb* are interchangeable, as is demonstrated by the account of Josiah's piety: 2 Kgs 23:3 has *kōl lēb* while 23:5 has *kōl lēbāb* with no difference in meaning ("Draw from the Shema?," 429).

15. The phrase "all your heart" in the Wisdom literature is found in Prov 3:5, Pss 9:2, 85:12; 111:1; 119:10, 34, 58, 69, 145; 138:1; Sir 7:27.

16. Schipper, "Proverbienbuch," 386.

even daring. He so considers himself a font of authentic teaching that obedience to his words is paralleled with obedience to God himself, and his words will be a source of well-being and life to his son. Conversely, disobedience to the father's words is tantamount to disobedience to God, and that will result in a lack of life.

FAMILIAL AUTHORITIES

The father appeals to authority figures in the family. In Proverbs 4:4–9, he cites a speech of his father, the son's grandfather. The grandfather's aim is much like that of the father's: to encourage the son to accept and to obey his words. He attempts to persuade the son by personifying his teaching as Wisdom and by equating his words and commandments (4:4) with wisdom and insight (4:5).[17] He further promises that Wisdom will bring the young man protection (4:6), honor (4:8), and a crown of splendor (4:9).

Twice the father calls his own words the *tôrāh* of "your mother" (1:8; 6:20), thereby showing how another authoritative figure in the son's life accepts and upholds his teachings. The father never calls this woman "my wife," but only "your mother," stressing her authoritative role. By showing that his words are synonymous with those of respected, authoritative figures, he gives his own teachings further credence. Given that his teachings are informed by his own father's life and words and parallel those of his wife, the words he hands onto the son ought to inform the young man's life.

CONCLUDING REFLECTIONS ON THE FATHER'S GIVING HIS BEING

The father does not robotically recite ancient precepts or memorized laws to his son. Instead, he has allowed the religious and familial traditions to penetrate his essence and to become mingled with his own being, particularly those of creation and the Ten Commandments. Through his penetrating contemplation of these past traditions, he grasps something of a primitive form of Wisdom, which while being a genuinely new concept, is still deeply faithful to the past and is an outgrowth of it. He then presents his creative ideas and teachings to his son in the form of ten speeches, and using the wording of Deuteronomy, encourages his son to intensely and profoundly adhere to them. Finally, he

---

17. See Glenn D. Pemberton (PhD diss., *The Rhetoric of the Father: A Rhetorical Analysis of the Father/Son Lectures in Proverbs 1–9* [University of Denver, Iliff School of Theology, 1999], 138) who also points out that he is unaware of any other instruction in the Old Testament or in the Wisdom literature of the Ancient Near East in which the father/rhetor cites the speech of his father/teacher.

undergirds his teachings by ensconcing them in the familial life. In actuality, the father proclaims *himself* as the tradition to be upheld and trusted. He is both the medium of a dynamic, living tradition (*traditio*) but also that tradition itself (*traditum*). The father graciously gives himself through his teaching to his son, and in doing so, he can be likened to the Eternal Father who gives his substance to his Word.

The Father Creates Through His Word

This section will examine the similarities between the Eternal Father's act of creating the world through his word (Gen 1:1–2:1; John 1:3), and those of the father.

The first creation account in Genesis (Gen 1:1–2:4a) teaches that human-kind, through its participation in the liturgy and in work, imitates the Father as creator.[18] The father in Proverbs broadens this message and shows that a person can also imitate the creative activity of the Father through speech and instruction.

The father maintains numerous times that his *words* will bring life to the young man (3:2, 22; 4:10, 13, 22; 5:6), and he is concerned that the son will not accept his words. He is aware of two temptations that may lead his son into disobeying the father and even bring the young man to his death: wicked men; and, the strange or foreign woman. Both persuade the young man with their *words*, and both promise him pleasures without negative consequences.[19] Both represent a value system that is antithetical to that of the father: the impious

18. Humankind is to extend and complete God's work in creation through the building of the tabernacle and proper worship of God, particularly by participating in Sabbath rest. There are significant parallels between God's work in creation and the Israelites' work on the Taberna-cle. See respectively Gen 1:31; 2:1; 2:2; 2:3 and Exod 39:32; 39:43; 40:33. Further, both accounts are structured around a series of seven acts: "And God said," (Gen 1:3, 6, 9, 14, 20, 24, 26) and "the LORD said," (Exod 25:1; 30:11, 17, 22, 34; 31:1, 12) (Gregory K. Beale, *The Temple and the Church's Mission: A Biblical Theology of the Dwelling Place of God* [Downers Grove, IL: Inter-Varsity, 2004], 60–61). Further, Pope John Paul II wrote, "When man, who had been created 'in the image of God . . . male and female,' hears the words: 'Be fruitful and multiply, and fill the earth and subdue it' (Gen. 1:27–28), even though these words do not refer directly and explicitly to work, beyond any doubt they indirectly indicate it as an activity for man to carry out in the world. Indeed, they show its very deepest essence. Man is the image of God partly through the mandate received from his Creator to subdue, to dominate, the earth. In carrying out this mandate, man, every human being, reflects the very action of the Creator of the uni-verse" (Pope John Paul II, *On Human Work: Encyclical* Laborem exercens [September 14, 1981] [Washington, DC: United States Catholic Conference, 1981], §4).

19. Jean-Noël Aletti, "Seduction et Parole en Proverbes I–IX," *Vetus Testamentum* 27, no. 2 (1977): 129–144.

men tempt the son to resort to violent means to satisfy his longing for money and honor, and the foreign woman tempts the man to have an affair with her, assuring the young man that her husband is far away and will never find out. The father must counter their messages to show that his words, and not theirs, are what the son should trust and obey.[20]

The question for the son comes down to: whom does he trust more? Whose words will he accept? In the end, the father is concerned about his son's heart, for to believe the word of another means to yield one's heart to him and to give him a certain authority. The father understands this, and therefore warns his son, "Above all, guard your heart, for from it flows the sources of life" (4:23), and he continuously exhorts his son concerning his heart.[21]

The father knows that his words, if accepted and believed, will bring his son life, protection, wealth, and honor, and so he willingly pours himself out in his instructions to his son. At stake is nothing less than the life of his son.

Concluding Reflections on the Father of Proverbs as a Spiritual Father

God the Father is the Eternal Father who teaches humankind the essence of fatherhood. The father imitates the activity of God the Father. Just as the Eternal Father gives his substance to his Son, the Word and Wisdom, so too, does the father of Proverbs give his very self to his son through his word. The father's word, however, is informed by the religious and familial traditions. Thus, in

---

20. The father knows that his son's search for knowledge and truth cannot be limited to the intellectual sphere alone. Ultimately, knowledge and truth cannot be divorced from relationships. John Paul II explains this well in *Fides et ratio* wherein he delineates three types of knowledge: empirical, philosophical, and religious (*Faith and Reason: Encyclical Letter* Fides et ratio [September 14, 1998] [Washington, DC: United States Catholic Conference, 1998], §30). Empirical knowledge can be gained by experimentation and everyday observations. Since it is impossible, however, for any one person to validate for himself all scientific findings and critical information, a person must necessarily trust what other people have told him (*Fides et ratio*, §31). Gaining knowledge and coming to know the truth necessarily entails relationships and the willingness to entrust oneself to what others say. The father of Proverbs knows that he must protect his son against trusting in a thought and value system that is antithetical to his own and that will lead the son to harm. "It is the nature of the human being to seek the truth. This search looks not only to the attainment of truths which are partial, empirical or scientific; nor is it only in individual acts of decision-making that people seek the true good. Their search looks towards an ulterior truth which would explain the meaning of life. And it is therefore a search which can reach its end only in reaching the absolute. Thanks to the inherent capacities of thought, man is able to encounter and recognize a truth of this kind. Such a truth—vital and necessary as it is for life—is attained not only by way of reason but also through trusting acquiescence to other persons who can guarantee the authenticity and certainty of the truth itself" (*Fides et ratio*, §33).

21. Prov 2:2, 10; 3:1, 3, 5; 4:4, 23; 5:12; 7:3, 7, 10, 25.

order to be a true father who imitates the activity of the Eternal Father through instruction, the father must first receive and be taught; in other words, to be a good father, the father must first be a son.

Second, the father imitates God the Father in his act of creation. Just as the Eternal Father *out of love* creates the world through his Word, the father of Proverbs *out of love* attempts to give his son life through his word. He does not call the young man to follow him or his way of life, but to follow his *words*, grasping them because they are life-giving. And he presents himself as an example to be followed, as one who first obeyed, and as one who has grasped wisdom, all in hopes of showing his son that his words are trustworthy so that the son will listen and obey. In this, the father shows himself to be an example of good fatherhood.

The Method of the Father

As noted, the father in Proverbs presents no new substantive ethical teachings. His speeches are grounded in the religious traditions, but the father re-presents them in a creative way, mainly by focusing on desires. The father's speeches reveal his strong desires for his son, and his instructions address his son's desires for power and pleasure.

The Desire of the Father

The father continuously implores his son to trust his words and to follow them. In fact, most of the speeches contain exhortations to trust the words of the father. The father's continual appeal discloses a heart brimming with love, concern, and his longing for the life and well-being of his son.

Ultimately, the father desires his son's life and knows that by following the religious tradition the son will come to life. Therefore, he asks his son to trust him and his words, and to choose paths that are difficult and do not appear to be fruitful or satisfying at first glance. This request involves a certain vulnerability, and even condescension on the part of the father who reveals a heart full of love for his son in the hopes that the son will choose life.

The Desire of the Son

The father understands that his son is filled with strong desires, which unsavory characters can use to tempt him. He is particularly concerned with his son's desires for honor, wealth, and women. These desires are not sinful, but they do need to be properly directed, and the father attempts to show his son how to do that. He accomplishes this by vividly portraying the temptations that the young man will encounter, and how the young man can be protected from their powerful influence. In these portrayals, the father envisions people approaching his son in order to lure him to engage in sinful activities to fulfill his desires.

As noted above, the first temptation the young man might face comes from a group of wicked men who invite the young man to join their group (1:10–19; 2:12–15; 4:14–17). These men come together to obtain wealth through aggressive and violent means. The father knows that these impious men appeal to the son's desire for companionship, honor, and wealth. Following the greedy, violent men is an easy and painless way to belong to a group and to enjoy accessible riches, but the father points to the long-term consequences of joining the wicked men. He warns the son that they delight in evil and their ways are devious and perverse (2:14–15). If the young man walks their dark paths, he actually sets a trap for his own life (1:17–18). So, although they appear to be the means of satisfying desire, they are in fact the means to death.

The father also warns of the strange or foreign woman (2:16–19; 5:3–8; 6:23–29; 7:6–27; 9:13–18). In several speeches the father focuses on her and on her smooth words, and she may also represent an idolatrous way of life. She presents a quick and easy way for the son to fulfill his sexual desires without the messiness and responsibilities of a relationship. The woman tries to seduce the man by assuring him that her husband is not home, meaning that he can experience satisfaction without any negative consequences (7:19–20). But the father insists that her words are untrue. He compares the foolish man who goes to her to an ensnared animal whose fate is only death (5:22; 7:22–23). Instead of suffering no consequences, the woman's husband will come to know of the illicit relationship and punish the young man (6:34–35). A man caught in the throes of the foolish woman will find himself travelling inescapably to his death (2:18–19; 5:5; 7:26–27).

The warnings are complemented with advice on the correct way the son should fulfill his desires: he should trust God with his wealth (3:9–10); work hard to obtain good things (6:4–11); and develop his relationship with his wife (5:15–19). The father's ways will bring the man honor, money and sexual satisfaction. These paths are more difficult, but they will produce lasting fruits and true fulfillment.

Finally, the father knows that simply having knowledge of the good is not enough. The father also promises the young man succor from Wisdom (2:6–11). If the young man seeks her, he will find her and she will protect him from the duplicitous words of the tempters (2:12, 16).

The father thus concentrates on the young man's desires, and explicitly shows his son the various temptations he will encounter and the consequences of following those paths. However, he does not leave the son mired in his strong desires; rather, he shows him how to channel these desires properly and advises him to pray for the help that he needs.

But why should the young man listen? He has no way of knowing whether the father's difficult way will bring him happiness or not. The easier path can seem the better one to choose. And this is precisely why the father presents himself as the bearer of tradition, almost as one taking the place of God. The father's essential appeal is to ask the young man to love him and trust him enough to pattern his life upon the father's teachings. To obey the father means to love him and to trust him, and at the heart of the father's teachings is an appeal for a relationship. The son may not love God and his teaching in the Torah enough to love and trust him but he may love his father enough to listen to him and to obey him. And the father, who stands in the place of God and who strains himself to present the traditional teachings creatively and color-fully, can say that his own teachings are as binding as those of Deuteronomy, for they are a mirror and reflection of them.

Application: The Seminary Professor

I suggested in the introduction that the father of Proverbs can serve as a model for seminary professors. Considering the above analysis, it appears to me that three things can be drawn from the father's own life which could be imitated. First, he has meditated on the traditions profoundly and in some sense, they form part of his being. Second, he responds personally and creatively to his son, considering his son's personal dilemma and offering frank—and possibly even uncomfortable—teachings about them. The father is not a mere conveyer of information but a life-giver whose goal is to bring his son to life and well-be-ing. Third, he appeals to their own relationship to bring his son to trust him. Each of these will be examined.

The seminary professor's first task is to deeply assimilate the religious tra-dition and allow it to be mingled with one's own being and etched in the heart. It seems an important part of classroom preparation is to spend time in prayer with the Lord, listening to his word and letting it take form in us. Through prayer, the professor imbibes the stream of our life-giving tradition, allow-ing it to flow through him, and he pours it into the garden of his seminarians to water and give life (Sir 24:28–31). Seminary professors are not conduits of information but those who, through their teaching, water and give life to their students. A professor ought to strive to be a synthesis of both the *traditio* and the *traditum* because, as a teacher of the tradition, his own personal witness cannot be divorced from the message that he teaches.

The second and third points can be examined from the perspective of desire. At times, the desire of the professor is often for his *own well-being*, but the father demonstrates a complete reversal of this familiar setting by being wholly unconcerned with himself. Although it is necessary for a professor to be respected, the father teaches that the *telos* of respect and success is for the well-being of the *son*, not for *himself*. A professor can learn from such an example and seek to be a life-giver in the classroom, desiring the good of the students more than he desires his own good. This comes about by loving the students with a love that is not a veneer but springs authentically from the heart and is exhibited in sacrifice, justice, and even tenderness. Professors who love their students allow themselves to be moved by that love in their preparation and teaching, creating lessons which are focused on the good of the student. The father's pure heart yearns for his son's life, sanctification, and salvation; so too can seminary professors endeavor for the life and sanctification and salvation of their students. Such a person can appeal to the students to love and trust him, not for his own sake, but because something of the divine shines through in him.

As noted, the father presents his teaching by concentrating on the son's desires. The father knows well the temptations his son will face, but by describing them as extraneous to the young man or as possibilities that might occur, he speaks of the young man's temptations without a direct confrontation. The father acknowledges what is genuinely tempting in these situations of sin and how they seem to bring a person fulfillment. But he does not hesitate to combat these false promises of happiness by showing how sinful actions have dire consequences.

It seems to me that two points can be emphasized. First is the compassion of the father in presenting the difficult teachings to his son. The father confronts the most painful and difficult temptations a young man could face, but he manages this situation with such delicacy and subtlety that the son surely is neither embarrassed nor feels himself condemned. By depicting his son's fierce temptations and desires as extraneous to him, in the form of people who might try to corrupt him, the father communicates that he is aware of his son's painful struggles against sin, but never defines his son by his sin or by his temptations.

Seminary professors can learn from the father, and they can be more effective if they are aware that the students are young men who are perhaps caught in the throes of sinful desires and that certain discussions and teachings actually might be painful for them. Confronting the burning purity of the Scriptures can be a trying experience for them. Teaching can have force and impact if professors communicate delicately and subtly that they are aware of their students' painful temptations and conflicting desires, present such temptations as extraneous to the students (to save them from unnecessary humiliation), and show compassion and understanding.

And the second point is that the father does not mistake compassion for indulgence, and he presents the consequences of sin in full force. He is convinced of the ferocious nature of sin, and his compassion for his son's real struggle does not blind him to the reality of sin and to its dire consequences. The father makes clear that to ignore his words is foolish and deadly, and so he continually implores his son to follow them.

Seminary professors, too, can warn their students of the consequences of sin. Like the father, they must be convinced of the deadly slavery of sin and its consequences, and present God as the savior and protector from such evil forces. The goal is not that they fear God and live out their spiritual lives perfunctorily but rather that they see God as the one who can rescue them from evil and the slavery of sin. With gentleness inflamed by passion and motivated by burning charity, seminary professors can speak poignantly of the deadly consequences of sin and implore their students continually to follow the roads which may not seem immediately good. Professors will be credible to the extent that they are trustworthy and genuinely seek the good of their students. If the students know they are loved, even the difficult lessons of life become more palatable.

In conclusion, the father understands his son's desires and the real struggle he might be having. The father does not avoid the difficult discussions but rather speaks honestly of the trials his son might experience—acknowledging the young man's temptations (which the father presents as extraneous to his son) and warning him of the false promises of fulfillment.

Such paternal love is not to be confused with indulgence. The father spells out the real consequences should the young man refuse to listen to his father and to the venerable tradition. All his teachings are motivated by a desire for his son to have life. By following the example of the father, seminary professors can become more than conduits of information: they can become spiritual fathers who give life to their students.

I have been blessed to have worked with a faculty member who mirrors the father of Proverbs. He is a charming, intelligent man who could have been successful in life but instead was obedient to the call of God to become a priest and has employed his gifts in the service of the Church, particularly at the seminary. I enjoy watching his interactions with the seminarians and I would describe them as such: this priest genuinely delights in his students but without being emotionally dependent upon them. He towers above them intellectually but uses his intellect to form his students, particularly by spending long hours with them at lunch and engaging in robust, stimulating discussions. I have served on a comprehensive exam board with him and have seen his paternal care for the students. He asks difficult questions, and if they stumble, he works with them to try to elicit the best answer from them. Though sometimes he must give a bad grade, he never humiliates them during their trials. At times the students have told me that when they are struggling with some theological dilemma, this priest is the one they will seek out. They know that he will take them seriously, reflect on their question, and even engage in research to help them. Though he is close to them, he also takes no nonsense from them, and the students know better than to cross him. Such a priestly activity patterns the father of Proverbs who acts to bring life to his son.

Conclusion

Scholars debate whether the father of Proverbs is a biological father or a sage in a school.[22] There is no definitive consensus, but it seems to me therein lies the point. Should not a seminary professor also be indistinguishable from a true expression of fatherhood? It is true that an educator does not give his students biological life, but in a very real way, the seminary professor engages in the creative activity of God the Father who gives life through his word. Through pouring themselves out in their teaching, seminary professors constitute in truth those who listen to them, give them courage and strength to make radical decisions, console broken and wounded hearts, and clarify confusion and chaos.

I would like to conclude with a quote from John Paul II who saw his ministry as a life-giving one in the manner of Saint Joseph:

> He became a father in an extraordinary way, without begetting his son in the flesh. Isn't this, perhaps, an example of the type of fatherhood that is proposed to us, priests and bishops, as a model? Everything I did in the course of my ministry I saw as an expression of this kind of fatherhood . . . a way of living out that fatherhood.[23]

22. Clifford, *Proverbs*, 6–7.
23. Pope John Paul II, *Rise, Let Us Be on Our Way*, trans. Walter Ziemba (New York: Warner, 2004), 141.

CHAPTER 7

Honey in the Comb:
Toward a Spiritual Reading of Sacred Scripture in the Twenty-First Century

Scott Carl

Not only the homily has to be nourished by the word of God. All evangelization is based on that word, listened to, meditated upon, lived, celebrated and
witnessed to. The sacred Scriptures are the very source of evangelization.
Consequently, we need to be constantly trained in hearing the word. The
Church does not evangelize unless she constantly lets herself be evangelized.
It is indispensable that the word of God "be ever more fully at the heart of
every ecclesial activity" [*Verbum Domini*, §1]. God's word, listened to and celebrated, above all in the Eucharist, nourishes and inwardly strengthens Christians, enabling them to offer an authentic witness to the Gospel in daily life.

POPE FRANCIS[1]

Introduction

In the wake of Pope Emeritus Benedict XVI's *Jesus of Nazareth*, there has been
increased recognition of the importance of developing a hermeneutic that operates on two methodological levels, the historical-critical and the theological as
given in *Dei verbum* 12—a hermeneutic that engages the faith-reason dynamic.[2]
Given that such a hermeneutic is the stated direction for biblical interpretation
in *Dei verbum*, perhaps the frustration of many seminarians with their seminary courses in sacred Scripture is in part understandable. They yearn for a

1. *Evangelii gaudium* (November 24, 2013) (Washington, DC: USCCB, 2013), §174. See
also Pope Benedict XVI, *Verbum Domini* (September 30, 2010) (Boston: Pauline Books and
Media, 2010).

2. Cf. Ignacio Carbajosa, "Una exégesis a la vez científica y creyente. Comentario a *Verbum
Domini* 29–38," *Estudios Bíblicos* 69, no. 4 (2011): 462.

meaningfully spiritual encounter with God through the biblical word. Yet it also must be acknowledged that many seminarians would tend to throw aside reason in favor of faith, especially when it comes to sacred Scripture. Applying such an inclination to Scripture can lead perhaps to a sort of pietism at best and a sort of Docetism[3] at worst.

However, the New Evangelization calls us to engage the world in which we find ourselves, so such a deemphasizing of reason applied to the sacred Scripture would undermine the Church's mission of making known Jesus Christ to the modern world. The need for a reliable hermeneutic in which both faith and reason are taken seriously and complement each other becomes all the more necessary not only in seminary formation but in the Church more broadly as the movement of the New Evangelization gains momentum. If such evangelical outreach is to be lasting it needs solid intellectual underpinnings.

The present paper is a humble attempt to reach toward such a hermeneutic. My hope is that, although it needs much refinement, it will move us from conversation about a hermeneutic to the actual development and exercise of one. To set the stage for such a hermeneutic I will state in further detail the need for it. Secondly, I will propose principles for such a hermeneutic. Finally, I will indicate a direction for its application. This final step will draw upon a fine example of one author's historical and literary exegesis that is ripe to produce solid spiritual fruit.

The Need for Honey—Spiritual/Theological Interpretation

Dei verbum 12 stresses two aspects of interpreting Scripture. Section 12.1 begins by saying the goal of the interpreter of sacred Scripture is "to see clearly what God wanted to communicate to us."[4] Then it mentions two parts for the interpreter to accomplish this goal. The interpreter should carefully investigate "what meaning the sacred writers really intended, and what God wanted to manifest by means of their words."

In section 12.2, *Dei verbum* describes the first of these two parts as an effort

---

3. The implication of such a Docetism is the denial not of the full humanity of Christ but of the role that the humanity of the human authors played in the writing of sacred Scripture (DV, §11).

4. The ".1" of DV 12.1 refers to the first paragraph in the English translation on the vatican.va website; DV 12.2 refers to the second and so on. The Latin on the same website has more than three paragraphs. See Second Vatican Council, *Dei verbum* (November 18, 1965), www.vatican.va/archive/hist_councils/ii_vatican_council/documents/vat-ii_const_19651118_dei-verbum_en.html, §12.

to arrive at what the human author intended to say. To accomplish this inter-pretation, the interpreter pays attention to different forms of discourse (e.g., historical or prophetic or poetic), to contemporary literary forms, and to the characteristic styles of feeling and speaking. Thus, *Dei verbum* 12.2 stresses the modern historical and literary interpretation of Scripture.

Dei verbum 12.3 describes the second of these parts as an effort to see clearly what God wanted to communicate to us. "Holy Scripture must be read and interpreted in the same spirit [*eodem Spiritu*] in which it was written."[5] Thus, "no less serious attention must be given" to three aspects. The interpreter should take into account, first, the content and unity of all of Scripture; second, the living tradition of the whole Church; and, third, the harmony which exists between elements of faith (i.e., the analogy of faith).

In Augustin Cardinal Bea's commentary on *Dei verbum* 12.3, he mentions that there is a *sensus plenior*, a "fuller" sense of Scripture. Bea says, "This means a sense which, although latent in the text and intended by the primary author, is nevertheless one which the human author did not fully understand, or did not even perceive."[6] He moreover stresses that we need to determine both the literal sense and this "fuller sense," saying, "Only by so doing shall we be able to give a wise and profound interpretation of God's word."[7]

The post-synodal Apostolic Exhortation of Pope Benedict XVI *Verbum Domini* reminds us of these points by first recalling the prudent and balanced interventions of the Magisterium "regarding the correct response to the intro-duction of new methods of historical analysis" (VD, §33), namely:

1) "Pope Leo XIII's intervention [i.e., *Providentissimus Deus* (November 18, 1893)] had the merit of protecting the Catholic interpretation of the Bible from the inroads of rationalism, without, however, seeking refuge in a spir-itual meaning detached from history" (VD, §33).

2) "The Encyclical *Divino afflante Spiritu* [of Pope Pius XII (September 30, 1943)] . . . affirmed both the 'theological significance of the literal sense, methodically defined' and the fact that 'determining the spiritual sense . . . belongs itself to the realm of exegetical science'[8]" (VD, §33).

---

5. Translation amended to include the word "same," which is present in the Latin.

6. Augustin Bea, *The Word of God and Mankind*, trans. Dorothy White (Chicago: Francis-can Herald Press, 1967), 210.

7. Bea, *Word of God*, 211.

8. Cf. Pope John Paul II, Address for the Celebration of the Centenary of the Encycli-cal *Providentissimus Deus* and the Fiftieth Anniversary of the Encyclical *Divino afflante Spiritu* (April 23, 1993), pp. 232–243 in *Acta Apostolicae Sedis* 86 (1994), §5.

3) "In this way, both documents rejected 'a split between the human and the divine, between scientific research and respect for the faith, between the literal sense and the spiritual sense'.[9] This balance was subsequently maintained by the 1993 document of the Pontifical Biblical Commission" (VD, §33).

Even though *Dei verbum* 12.3 says "no less serious attention must be given" to investigating "what God wanted to manifest by means of their words" (DV, §12.1), Pope Emeritus Benedict, writing as a private theologian, pointed out in the foreword of volume two of *Jesus of Nazareth* that the type of interpretation directed in *Dei verbum* 12 is "a task that unfortunately has scarcely been attempted thus far."[10] Toward such an interpretation, Benedict mentions the need for biblical studies to have a twofold methodology which would involve an appropriate faith-hermeneutic to be combined "with a historical hermeneutic, aware of its limits."[11] Our Pope Emeritus goes on to say, "Naturally, this combination of two quite different types of hermeneutic is an art that needs to be constantly remastered. But it can be achieved, and as a result the great insights of patristic exegesis will be able to yield their fruit once more in a new context."[12]

Theologians have recognized the same need. Brian Daley, SJ, who teaches at Notre Dame, says,

> Some sense of the historical trajectory of meaning borne by a Biblical passage—from its reconstructed "original" form and content, through its various stages of redaction and interpretation, to the life of the present Church—seems to be an indispensable prerequisite for any honest, intellectually plausible treatment of the text in contemporary exegesis.[13]

At the same time he says,

> A more positive perception of early Christian exegesis, however, as not merely "pre-critical" but as thoroughly and—in many cases, at least—successfully *theological*, can open our eyes to what seems to be the other, less fulfilled need in Biblical interpretation today: its need to recapture an understanding of its own role within the Church, and of its centrally

---

9. Cf. Pope John Paul II, Address for the Celebration, §5.

10. Joseph Ratzinger, *Jesus of Nazareth, Part Two: From the Entrance into Jerusalem to the Resurrection*, trans. Philip J. Whitmore (San Francisco: Ignatius, 2011), xv.

11. Ratzinger, *Jesus of Nazareth, Part Two*, xv.

12. Ratzinger, *Jesus of Nazareth, Part Two*, xv.

13. Brian Daley, "Is Patristic Exegesis Still Usable?," *Communio* 29, no. 1 (2002): 213.

theological task as reading not just texts, but sacred and normative texts, texts that relate to the overarching story of Jewish and Christian faith.[14]

In a similar line of thinking, Robert Louis Wilken says, "To understand the Christian Old Testament, the ancient near east is the place to begin but hardly the goal toward which interpretation moves."[15]

Developing such a hermeneutic involves a search for "honey in the comb," so to speak. I draw this expression from a Dominican priest, Fr. Hugues Vincent, OP, living in Jerusalem, who wrote to another priest (Msgr. Bruno de Solages, April 26, 1950) about his great teacher and mentor, Fr. Marie-Joseph Lagrange, OP:

> [Lagrange] told me over and over again . . . how mutually fruitful it would be for historico-critical exegetes, spiritual-allegorist exegetes (or any other label!) to arrive at a sympathetic understanding of each other, rather than remain compartmentalized and hostile towards one another.[16]

The same Fr. Vincent, a historical-critical exegete, later wrote Fr. de Lubac (June 21, 1950) about de Lubac's book on Origen:

> Today's generation can fruitfully learn from it that there are much better things to do than waste one's time in swordplay *for* or *against* literalism or spiritual meaning; tomorrow's can derive from it the guiding principles of an integral catholic exegesis, worthy of Holy Scripture and fully capable of answering all the needs of the intellect and soul. And, since the labor is infinitely too great for the same men to be able to undertake it with the desired precision, historians will learn that their arduous task simply puts them in the presence or in the possession of the honey-in-the-comb, and spiritualists will reckon with the fact that, before one can extract the honey from the wax with any profit for the soul, it is necessary to check on the quality of the comb and see whether it was produced by the divine Bee or by common hornets.[17]

In other words, a solid historical method establishes a solid honeycomb from which spiritual/theological exegesis can extract the sweet honey of "what God wanted to manifest" beyond the human author's intention (DV, §12).

14. Daley, "Is Patristic Exegesis Still Usable?," 214. Emphasis in the original.

15. Robert Louis Wilken, "The Inevitability of Allegory," *Gregorianum* 86, no. 4 (2005): 752.

16. Henri de Lubac, *The Sources of Revelation*, trans. Luke O'Neill (New York: Herder, 1968), 232.

17. De Lubac, *The Sources of Revelation*, 234. Emphasis in the original.

Extracting the Honey: Principles for a Spiritual Reading of Scripture in the Twenty-First Century

To lay the groundwork for such a spiritual/theological interpretation, two verses from the New Testament are particularly significant. The Risen Jesus appears to His disciples, shows them His wounds, eats in their presence . . .

> Then he said to them, "These are my words which I spoke to you, while I was still with you, that everything written about me in the law of Moses and the prophets and the psalms must be fulfilled." Then he opened their minds to understand the scriptures.[18]

> [The] sacred scriptures . . . are capable of giving you wisdom for salvation through faith in Christ Jesus.[19]

That there is more to the literal meaning of Scripture as intended by the human author is stressed in the above verses. The first demonstrates Jesus interpreting the Old Testament with Himself being the hermeneutical key. Secondly, 2 Timothy speaks about a wisdom from the Old Testament that leads to Jesus Christ.

Such an interpretive key offered by these verses of the New Testament speaks to the essential role that the inspiration of the Bible has in extracting honey.[20] In Marius Reiser's terms,

> The dogma of inspiration touches on a decisive point. Accepting the inspiration of holy scripture (however that is understood) leads to—and in fact presupposes—allegory [i.e., spiritual interpretation]. Without inspiration, allegory is merely playing games. According to the church fathers, it is the Holy Spirit who unifies scripture and who has created the references and connections that can be discovered through allegory. If the exegete lacks the Holy Spirit, then those references and connections cannot be discovered through allegory. It is the Holy Spirit, finally, who is concerned with the connection of everything else.[21]

In developing such a hermeneutic, one has to be clear that spiritual interpretation cannot just be a random free-for-all. In fact, a principle from the early Church, the *regula fidei*, helps to protect from such abuses. The *regula fidei* is the norm of revealed truth. Clement of Alexandria (died ca. 215) summarized

---

18. Luke 24:44–45 RSV.

19. 2 Tim 3:15 NABRE.

20. Allegorical interpretation/allegory as Reiser (cf. de Lubac) uses it here is in its most general sense, which encompasses the three spiritual senses.

21. Marius Reiser, "Biblical and Postbiblical Allegory," *Theology Digest* 51, no. 1 (2004): 26.

the "Rule of Faith" as "the concord and harmony between the Law and the Prophets and the covenant brought into being by Jesus Christ."[22] Reiser mentions the importance of the *regula fidei*, the rule of faith, to protect the interpreter from inappropriate interpretations as he or she seeks to demonstrate how everything is connected to everything else,

> The rule of faith sets clear limits to any random or arbitrary use of allegory. The seemingly "open field" practice of patristic allegory follows rules. It takes these rules to make sense of what the fathers are doing—substantially linking [diverse] scriptural passages. Without the rules, it is . . . "pure yarn-spinning."[23]

The Fathers acknowledged the literal sense but did not develop it to the extent that we do today. De Lubac says, "Doubtless again, in principle, all were in agreement with the following declaration of Origen: 'It was first necessary to discuss historically the things that are being read, and in this way . . . to seek the spiritual understanding in them.'"[24] Yet what frustrates modern exegetes is how quick the Fathers are to move from the literal sense, as seen in St. Jerome's comment on the Gospel of Mark, "We do not deny the history, but we prefer the spiritual understanding."[25] De Lubac continues,

> For these believers, which they all were, the history or the letter was again merely the threshold giving access to the interior of the Temple of God: "The temple of God is the whole Church . . . but the threshold of the temple is the historical sense in the Scriptures, since we enter into the temple of God . . . through faith in the history. But the depth of the allegories lies hidden beneath this threshold."[26]

Cardinal Bea offers a principle for the interpreter seeking the intention of the primary author: the passages interpreted "must be checked by the text itself, and explained with all the means offered by linguistic, literary and historical research."[27] By applying this principle, other similar passages will arise.

---

22. Clement of Alexandria, *Stromata*, book 6, chapter 15, quoted in William R. Farmer, "The Church's Gospel Canon: Why Four and No More?," in *The International Bible Commentary: A Catholic and Ecumenical Commentary for the Twenty-first Century*, ed. William R. Farmer (Collegeville, MN: Liturgical Press, 1998), 1247.

23. Reiser, "Biblical and Postbiblical Allegory," 27.

24. Henri de Lubac, *Medieval Exegesis: Vol. 2, The Four Senses of Scripture*, trans. E. M. Macierowski (Grand Rapids, MI: Eerdmans, 2000), 75.

25. St. Jerome, *Tractatus in Marci Evangelium*, chapter 9, verses 1–7, in AMar 3, vol. 2 (Maredsous, Belgium: Morin, 1895), 348; quoted in de Lubac, *The Four Senses of Scripture*, 78.

26. De Lubac, *The Four Senses of Scripture*, 79.

27. Bea, *Word of God*, 209.

Such interpretive work may deepen the text's meaning for us; it may render a richer meaning than that rendered by its obvious meaning. "But," Bea adds, the interpretation "may never be completely extraneous to [the text]."[28] There can be a "fuller sense" (*sensus plenior*) "which, although latent in the text and intended by the primary author, is nevertheless one which the human author did not fully understand, or did not even perceive."[29]

Verbum Domini offers insight on such a hermeneutic by stressing that Scripture be read in light of the Paschal Mystery. There is a unity and interrelation between the literal sense and spiritual sense (VD, §37). Following the 1993 Pontifical Biblical Commission document, *Verbum Domini* speaks about a definition of the spiritual sense as the meaning of the biblical texts when read under the influence of the Holy Spirit and in the context of the Paschal Mystery and the new life that flows from it. The apostolic exhortation quotes directly from the 1993 PBC document (thereby making this portion of the document part of the ordinary Magisterium): as a general rule, the spiritual sense can be defined as

> the meaning expressed by the biblical texts when read under the influence of the Holy Spirit, in the context of the paschal mystery of Christ and of the new life which flows from it. This context truly exists. In it the New Testament recognizes the fulfillment of the Scriptures. It is therefore quite acceptable to reread the Scriptures in the light of this new context, which is that of life in the Spirit.[30]

Moreover, such a hermeneutic also should involve the interpreter's integrity of life. The way the interpreter lives out his or her life in charity, i.e., Christian love, affects the interpretation of Scripture. In the words of St. Augustine, "Anyone who thinks that he has understood the divine scriptures or any part of them, but cannot by his understanding build up this double love of God and neighbor, has not yet succeeded in understanding them."[31]

Prior to indicating the direction for applying such a hermeneutic, it is worth summarizing in a concise manner the principles which make it up. The starting point is to ascertain what the human author intended to say as sought

---

28. Bea, *Word of God*, 209.

29. Bea, *Word of God*, 210.

30. Pontifical Biblical Commission, *The Interpretation of the Bible in the Church* (April 15, 1993), II.B.2, in *Enchiridion Vaticanum. Vol. 13, Documenti ufficiali della Santa Sede, 1991–1993*, ed. Erminio Lora and Bruno Testacci, 3rd ed. (Bologna: EBD, 2004), §3003; quoted in Pope Benedict XVI, *Verbum Domini*, §37.

31. Augustine, *De doctrina Christiana*, book 1, paragraphs 35–36; quoted in Michael Cameron, "Augustine and Scripture," in *A Companion to Augustine*, ed. Mark Vessey and Shelley Reid (Chichester, UK: Wiley-Blackwell, 2012), 206.

through modern methods of biblical exegesis, i.e., examine the honeycomb. Then, through a Christian spiritual interpretation, one needs to draw out the meaning that leads to love of God and neighbor, i.e., extract the honey. I propose that such a method would include:

1) The presumption that what we study is the inspired Word of God, different in kind from any other literature;

2) Being expressly open to the influence of the Holy Spirit (VD, §37) who inspired the text and to living in accord with the charity of Christ;

3) The patristic principle of the *regula fidei* subsuming what *Dei verbum* 12.3 describes as the role of tradition and the analogy of faith (which will protect the contemporary interpreter from an inappropriate application of the spiritual sense);

4) Interpreting a passage in light of the content and unity of all of Scripture (DV, §12), which in the terms of *Verbum Domini* means, "the person of Christ [giving] unity to all the 'Scriptures' in relation to the one 'Word'" (VD, §39);[32]

5) Following *Verbum Domini* 37 (referring to the 1993 PBC document, II.B.2), which stresses that to interpret a text spiritually, one must read it in the context of the Paschal Mystery *and* in the context of the new life that flows from the Paschal Mystery (cf. moral and anagogical interpretation); and

6) Studying other passages that arise from applying to the passage at hand the content and unity of all Scripture, tradition, and the analogy of faith *and* checking these passages "with all the means offered by linguistic, literary and historical research."[33] Such a study of complementary passages will protect the interpreter from a fanciful use of imagination rather than a solid method of interpretation.

By applying such a method, one will be able to extract the honey in the comb, which is latent in the text and intended by the primary author, although not being fully understood or even perceived by the human author. To draw such honey we need a solid honeycomb, which we find in good exegetical work. One such example is Gianni Barbiero's exegesis of Psalm 87. It will give a base from which to indicate how one can apply the principles of the hermeneutic I have proposed here.

---

32. We can think of St. Augustine's principle referenced in *Dei verbum* 16 (and *Verbum Domini* 41): The New Testament is hidden in the Old and the Old Testament is made manifest in the New.

33. Bea, *Word of God*, 209.

The Honeycomb of Psalm 87—A Contemporary Historical/Literary Reading of Psalm 87[34]

Psalm 87:1b–2: "His foundation on the holy mountains . . . . [2] The Lord loves the gates of Zion more than all the dwelling places of Jacob."[35]

In v. 1b, "His foundation on the holy mountains . . .," "foundation" is central to the Psalm. It is taken up again in v. 5c "He, the Most High, *will keep her solid.*" Verse 1b says "His" foundation . . . but whose foundation is that? That is, to whom does the "His" in "His foundation" refer? The parallel in v. 5c clarifies that the 3rd m s suffix on "foundation" (יסודתו) refers to God (v. 5c "He, the Most High, will keep her solid."); i.e., God will keep her solid.[36] In v. 1b, "the holy mountains" refers to the mountain of God, i.e., the primordial mountain which emerged from the chaos of water; God conquered the primitive chaos.[37] "The land belongs to God because he founded it (Ps 24:1–2). . . ." So too the city of Jerusalem belongs to God; He founded it.[38] The "mountains" (pl.) here refer to Zion (the temple mount) and Mishneh (which became part of the city at Hezekiah's time), the two mountains that make up Jerusalem.[39] The psalmist transposes the ideology of the Temple to the city Jerusalem.[40] Jerusalem is preferred because only there is the Temple where God dwells; God is present in the city. It is, as v. 3 says, the "city of God"; the stress is put on the whole city.[41]

In v. 2a, Jerusalem has a universal sense not in itself but because God loves (אהב) her (v. 2). This is similar to Zechariah 2:14–16,[42] where God comes to live in Jerusalem and on the "day of the Lord" many nations will join the people of God and dwell there.[43] The form (אהב) in v. 2a as a participle is atemporal and with such "love" language "the Psalmist transfigures the city into a woman" and, indeed, a spouse.[44] The image of woman is taken up again in vv. 4–6 with

---

34. The historical/literary commentary on Psalm 87 (the "honeycomb") that follows is from Gianguerrino Barbiero, "'Di Sion si dirà: Ognuno è stato generato in essa'. Studio esemplare del Sal 87," in *Biblical Exegesis in Progress: Old and New Testament Essays*, ed. Jean-Noël Aletti and Jean Louis Ska, AnBib 176 (Rome: Editrice Pontificio Istituto Biblico, 2009), 209–264. English translations are mine.

35. Barbiero, "Di Sion si dirà," 216.

36. Barbiero, "Di Sion si dirà," 217, 224–225.

37. Barbiero, "Di Sion si dirà," 225.

38. Barbiero, "Di Sion si dirà," 225.

39. Barbiero, "Di Sion si dirà," 225.

40. Barbiero, "Di Sion si dirà," 225.

41. Barbiero, "Di Sion si dirà," 226.

42. Following the Hebrew and NAB verse numbering.

43. Barbiero, "Di Sion si dirà," 226.

44. Barbiero, "Di Sion si dirà," 226.

the reference to motherhood in the theme about being born.[45] The object of the love in v. 2a is the "gates of Zion." This phrase "gates of Zion" is a synecdoche to refer to the whole city.[46]

87:3 Glorious things are said regarding you, O City of God![47]

This verse separates from vv. 1–2 by having the discourse turn directly to Jerusalem.[48] "O City of God" (עיר האלהים) restates vv. 1b–2 where there is a reference to the holiness of Jerusalem in v. 1b (בהררי-קדש), literally "mountains of holiness."[49] Because Jerusalem is "his foundation" (v. 1b), it is "the city of God" (v. 3). Like Isaiah and Ezekiel, Psalm 87 has a non-political character; it has, rather, a religious one. There is no role for the king but only God's temple. Thus, there is a universal dimension which is important because on the political level Israel can have a conflict with other kingdoms but on the religious level it can be open to them.[50] Thus, "city of God" takes on a universal function because God dwells in Jerusalem and God is God of all humanity. Verses 1–3 affirm "the divine character of Jerusalem."[51] The verses that follow delineate its universal mission.[52]

87:4 "I will mention Rahab and Babylon among those who know me. Look, Philistia, Tyre, with Cush; this one was born there."[53]

In v. 4a "the ones who know me" (ידעי), the use of (ידע) is strong, equivalent to an act of faith: "the ones who know me" are "the ones who believe in God."[54] In v. 4a Rahab and Babylon, enemies of Israel, are included "among those who know me [God]" (ידעי) (N.B. the 1st common singular suffix). Rahab, a name that refers to Egypt, i.e., an enemy in the southwest (cf. Isa 30:7), and Babylon, i.e., an enemy in the East, are used together as a merism to indicate all of Israel's enemies.[55] These historic enemies are now "among those who know me [God]," i.e., among those who believe in God, the ones who trust in Him. Thus, the

---

45. Barbiero, "Di Sion si dirà," 227.
46. Barbiero, "Di Sion si dirà," 227.
47. Barbiero, "Di Sion si dirà," 216.
48. Barbiero, "Di Sion si dirà," 217.
49. Barbiero, "Di Sion si dirà," 228.
50. Barbiero, "Di Sion si dirà," 228.
51. Barbiero, "Di Sion si dirà," 228.
52. Barbiero, "Di Sion si dirà," 228.
53. Barbiero, "Di Sion si dirà," 216.
54. Barbiero, "Di Sion si dirà," 230.
55. Barbiero, "Di Sion si dirà," 230.

stress is put on the relation of people with God without mentioning Jerusalem. But since she is "city of God" (v. 3b), "all those who know God belong to Jerusalem."[56] The nations are not converting as much as recognizing a common faith in this one God.[57]

In v. 4b "Philistia and Tyre, with Cush," these three nations together likewise function as a merism, thereby indicating all the surrounding nations through the mention of the two closest enemies, Philistia (on the coastal plain of Palestine) and Tyre (in Lebanon), and the one farthest away, Cush (which is south of Egypt in modern day Sudan).[58] Thus, the sense here of Philistia, Tyre, and Cush is "all the peoples of the earth"[59] and pairs well with the two preceding names, Rahab and Babylon, who know God. Verse 4b continues, "this one was born there." "This one" refers to "the peoples," i.e., Rahab, Babylon, Philistia, Tyre, and Cush. "There" refers to Jerusalem. Thus, "all the peoples who know God (v. 4a) were generated in Jerusalem (v. 4c)"; this is Zion's privileged role.[60] Jerusalem is the mediator between God and the peoples.[61] "Was born" shows the image of the woman or the spouse giving way to that of the mother.[62] The children of whom she is mother are made from their enemies. Such an image evokes the lion and lamb image of Isaiah 11 or the image of Isaiah 2, where they will turn their swords into plowshares.[63] Enemies become children of the same mother, an eschatological image.

87:5 And of Zion it shall be said, "Everyone was born in her; and, He, the Most High, will keep her solid."[64]

In v. 5b "and, He, the Most High, will keep her solid" shows complementarily the relation between God and Zion (cf. the 3rd feminine singular pronoun, ה-):[65] God founded Zion (v. 1b) and now God "will keep her solid (v. 5b). In v. 5b the title "Most High" recalls "holy mountains" of v. 1b and thus "Zion" and "city of God" (v. 3). The "and" of v. 5c shows "the connection between the universal maternity of Zion and her belonging to God."[66] "Everyone was born in her"

---

56. Barbiero, "Di Sion si dirà," 231.
57. Barbiero, "Di Sion si dirà," 231.
58. Barbiero, "Di Sion si dirà," 233–234.
59. Barbiero, "Di Sion si dirà," 234.
60. Barbiero, "Di Sion si dirà," 234.
61. Barbiero, "Di Sion si dirà," 234.
62. Barbiero, "Di Sion si dirà," 234–235.
63. Barbiero, "Di Sion si dirà," 235.
64. Barbiero, "Di Sion si dirà," 216–217.
65. Barbiero, "Di Sion si dirà," 237.
66. Barbiero, "Di Sion si dirà," 237.

(v. 5b) expresses universal maternity. "The Most High will keep her solid" (v. 5c) expresses she belongs to God.

87:6 The Lord will count in writing the peoples, "This one was born there."[67]

In v. 6a, "in writing the peoples" (בכתוב עמים) conveys a common metaphor in the Ancient Near East and in the Old Testament, that of the "writing of God."[68] In the Old Testament, some think of the census in 2 Samuel or of the returned exiles under Ezra/Nehemiah or even Exodus 32:32, where Moses says, "Cancel me from your book!" But more helpful to understand v. 6a is Psalm 69:29, where by implication the just are recorded in the book of life: "May they be blotted from the book of life; not registered among the just" (NABRE). "The 'peoples' are written in the 'book of the living', where God makes note of the 'just' (Ps 69:29), that is, those 'who know him' (Ps 87:4)."[69]

In v. 6b, "there" (שם) refers to Jerusalem. God counts the single peoples (יהוה יספר בכתוב עמים) by saying "This one was born there."[70] Thus, an indissoluble link is made between being saved and being generated in Jerusalem.[71] The nations are spiritually generated in Zion. They, then, are counted in writing which is an eschatological image for being saved. The Assyrian (Akkadian) use of *manû*, "to count," as meaning "to consider as belonging to" sheds light on "to count" (ספר) in v. 6a. The Assyrians had a way to transform conquered peoples into citizens of their empire; it involved in part being "counted" among the citizens. Thus, we can see in the Hebrew word "to count" (ספר) a divine declaration that juridically makes enemies to be citizens just as the Assyrian ruler would transform conquered peoples to be citizens of his empire.[72] The age-old enemies of Israel are becoming, in a certain way, citizens, but not in a political sense rather in a religious one. In Psalm 87, it is a second or a spiritual birth, a spiritual citizenship since these peoples retain their national identities.[73]

87:7 And they will sing while they dance, "All my springs are in you."[74]

Verse 7 is the reaction of the people to the declaration the Lord (יהוה) made in v. 6.[75] The "counting" (ספר) of the Lord in v. 6a is different than that of the

---

67. Barbiero, "Di Sion si dirà," 217.
68. Barbiero, "Di Sion si dirà," 238.
69. Barbiero, "Di Sion si dirà," 239.
70. Barbiero, "Di Sion si dirà," 239.
71. Barbiero, "Di Sion si dirà," 240.
72. Barbiero, "Di Sion si dirà," 240.
73. Barbiero, "Di Sion si dirà," 241.
74. Barbiero, "Di Sion si dirà," 217.
75. Barbiero, "Di Sion si dirà," 241.

Assyrian rulers who required taxes and labor. The evidence for the difference is the explosion of joy coming from the people in v. 7.[76] Verse 4 and v. 6 pass from a particular affirmation of the Lord to a universal affirmation of the people in v. 5 and v. 7.[77] Verse 4 and v. 6 show an indissoluble link between being saved and being generated in Jerusalem. Verse 5 and v. 7 show that all the peoples born in Jerusalem express their joy in singing and dancing. Verse 7b "All my springs are in you" refers to the "mountain of God" evoked in v. 1b, "the holy mountains," and again in v. 5c, "the Most High."[78] Such springs are characteristic of post-exilic eschatological prophecy, e.g., Ezekiel 47:1–12 where the water of the Temple flows out even to the Dead Sea.[79] Jerusalem is the "spring" from which flows the joy of these peoples.[80] God is usually seen as the "spring of living water," e.g., Jeremiah 2:13. God is in Zion and any access to Him "comes through the holy city"; in Zion "are found the springs of every life and every joy."[81]

In summary, there are certain key themes and concepts produced by a historical/literary reading of Psalm 87. God founds Jerusalem, the holy city, the city of God. All Israel's enemies and all the nations are spiritually generated in Jerusalem, indicating her future glory, an eschatological image like that of Zechariah 2:14–16. Zion is thus spouse of the Lord and mother of all nations; she has a privileged role mediating between God and the peoples, an eschatological image like that of Isaiah 11 and Isaiah 2. The nations, as the ones who know the Lord, are counted, and being counted announces their salvation, an eschatological image like that of Psalm 69:29. Finally, the joys of the peoples flow like springs from Jerusalem, the city of God, an eschatological image like that of the post-exilic prophecy like Ezekiel 47.

A Drop of Honey Extracted from Psalm 87: Applying the Method

To point toward what such a spiritual interpretation would look like, I will suggest avenues of how to apply the method I have proposed. With the key themes and concepts produced by the historical/literary study of Psalm 87 in mind, we need to investigate the spiritual meaning of this psalm according to the principles proposed in this paper. A first step is to gather passages that came to mind

---

76. Barbiero, "Di Sion si dirà," 241.
77. Barbiero, "Di Sion si dirà," 242.
78. Barbiero, "Di Sion si dirà," 242.
79. Barbiero, "Di Sion si dirà," 243.
80. Barbiero, "Di Sion si dirà," 243.
81. Barbiero, "Di Sion si dirà," 243.

as we did the historical and literary interpretation. These include: Zechariah 2, Psalm 69, Isaiah 2, and Isaiah 11. Moreover, further reflection on the significance of the historical and literary interpretation brings to mind other passages. Among the possibilities are Isaiah 61, where Jerusalem as mother abundantly nourishes her children, and other parts of Isaiah and Ezekiel that describe the new Jerusalem. It might also be worth investigating a negative image of Jerusalem, as in Lamentations 1–2.

The next step would be to research passages that come to mind through *the context of the Paschal Mystery and of the new life that comes from it*. The role of Jerusalem in the Gospel of Luke would be fruitful for this Psalm. It is the beginning and ending point of that Gospel. It is the place where Jesus' words and deeds culminate. It is also the place from which the evangelization of the world begins (cf. Acts 1:8).

Also worthwhile would be a study of the role of Jerusalem elsewhere in the New Testament.[82] Studying Galatians 4, where St. Paul presents a spiritual Jerusalem as mother and heiress of the divine promises,[83] leads to meaningful implications of Psalm 87's depiction of Jerusalem. Likewise, in the Letter to the Hebrews, Jerusalem is the heavenly city of the living God to which Christians have already drawn close through baptism; it is the divine home of the temple not made by human hands.[84] Moreover, the Book of Revelation "takes up the description of [the heavenly Jerusalem] to contemplate the Church in its final perfection: the spouse of the Lamb" (Rev 21:1–22:5).[85]

Another aspect of Psalm 87 to be studied in the context of the Paschal Mystery is the consequences of "knowing" (ידע) in relation to the Lord. "Before knowing God, man is known to God. This is the mystery of divine election and concern as appears when God is said to know Abraham (Gen 18:19) . . ." or Jeremiah even before his birth (Jer 1:5).[86] Likewise, Psalm 87's sense of knowing has meaningful contact with the Johannine sense, "The Son of God has come and given us understanding to know the true one" (1 John

---

82. A tool such as Xavier Léon-Dufour, ed., *Dictionary of Biblical Theology* (Gaithersburg, MD: Word Among Us, 1988; repr., 1995), would be particularly helpful for this task.

83. Michel Join-Lambert and Pierre Grelot, "Jerusalem," trans. Joseph R. Sweeney, in *Dictionary of Biblical Theology*, 263.

84. Join-Lambert and Grelot, "Jerusalem," 263.

85. Join-Lambert and Grelot, "Jerusalem," 263.

86. Jean Corbon and Albert Vanhoye, "Know," trans. W. Jared Wicks, in *Dictionary of Biblical Theology*, 296–297.

5:20; 2:14).[87] In the Gospel of John eternal life is to know the one true God and Jesus Christ whom He has sent (John 17:3). At its fullest, to know God is to share "communion" with Him since to know Him is to share in His life (1 John 1:3; John 14:19ff.).[88]

Similarly, images of baptism resound powerfully through such a method. Baptism is the means by which Christians become citizens of the kingdom, i.e., counted in writing by the Lord, hence Psalm 87 is connected to baptism by the analogy of faith. Furthermore, there is John 3 speaking about being born from above and Romans 6 where St. Paul describes the consequences of baptism. To ensure the solidity of the spiritual interpretation, these passages "must be checked by the text itself, and explained with all the means offered by linguistic, literary and historical research."[89] Such study verifies that the connections made are not tenuous or eisegetical but rather render insight into the intentions of the primary author. This insight is not in conflict with that of the human author but rather exists in a manner beyond his capacities. We are now in a position to reread Psalm 87 in light of these further insights to draw out the honey.

Conclusion

Based on *Dei verbum* 12.3, it is clear that a method of interpretation is needed that seeks the intention of the primary author, which may not have been fully understood or even perceived by the human author. A method to determine the spiritual meaning of a passage does not need to be an arbitrary and subjective process, e.g., an eisegetical meditation on the text or a fanciful use of imagination. The task is rather daunting if we consider that it should involve more than the Scriptural focus expressed in this paper. In fact, it should include three areas of study: sacred Scripture, Patristics, and Liturgy. One immediate line of thinking from the standpoint of liturgy is that Psalm 87 is used in the Office of Readings for the Common of the Dedication of a Church. The fruit of that fact would add to the work begun here. While daunting, we can be consoled by Cardinal Bea's words,

> [The] difficulty of the interpreter's task must not alarm him unduly or cause him to doubt the validity of the principles of interpretation laid down by the Council. They are a logical consequence of the doctrine of inspiration and

---

87. Corbon and Vanhoye, "Know," 298.
88. Corbon and Vanhoye, "Know," 298.
89. Bea, *Word of God*, 209.

are deduced from sacred tradition itself. And, after all, as every scientific study is faced with similar difficulties it is not surprising that they occur in the interpretation of a book of which God himself is the primary author! Certainly the exact application of these principles is not easy for it requires great and laborious care.[90]

In establishing a solid honeycomb, there is much honey to be had!

---

90. Bea, *Word of God*, 211.

CHAPTER 8

"We Have Found Him!":
The Joy of Discovery in the Fourth Gospel

Michael Magee

As a French writer affirmed so eloquently, "Joy is the infallible sign of the presence of God."[1] Pope Francis in *Evangelii gaudium* begins his Apostolic Exhortation by describing joy as an essential quality of effective evangelization. Indeed,
the joy of the Christian proclamation and the joyful witness of Christian life
confound the critics of Christian evangelization by captivating human hearts
with an experience that is elusive to secular humanistic analysis.

According to a materialistic understanding of the human person, joy seems
at first glance to fall simply into the category of the human emotions that may
be elicited by behavior that stimulates or deadens them—as with those emotions generated or managed by medication, sometimes indulged, at other times
repressed, and at other times sublimated. In such a view, the task of life might
seem to be a self-centered pursuit of maximum enjoyment by means of avoiding the stimuli of painful emotions and pursuing those of pleasant ones.

Quite different, however, is the actual lived experience of Christian joy
that by its nature cannot be sought for its own sake but "fills the hearts of those
who encounter Jesus."[2] Even as this joy means that Jesus' disciples "are set free

---

1. A web search for this quotation will yield a multitude of attributions of the statement
to the Jesuit Pierre Teilhard de Chardin, who seems to have repeated it in his writings, but
the original source, according to George Weigel, is the author Leon Bloy, who is said to have
written it in a letter to Jacques Maritain. See George Weigel, "Joy is the Infallible Sign of God's
Presence," at Ethics and Public Policy Center, July 19, 2001, at eppc.org/publications/joy-is-the
-infallible-sign-of-gods-presence/.

2. Pope Francis, *Evangelii gaudium* (November 24, 2013) (Washington, DC: USCCB,
2013), §1.

from sin, sorrow, inner emptiness and loneliness," it is anything but a self-centered pursuit of any subjective experience for its own sake, as Jesus' disciples in fact "are liberated from our narrowness and self-absorption" and "become fully human . . . when we let God bring us beyond ourselves in order to attain the fullest truth of our being."[3]

The Gospel of John, in particular, vividly depicts the response of joy on the part of those who come to know the truth who *is* Jesus. Likewise, it displays the joy that lends credibility to the apostles' message as they seek out others with whom to share the truth that has been revealed to them. It is joy, in fact, that cements into the minds of the disciples the memory of that which they have to share with others.

Pope Francis sees this joy exemplified by the loving attention to a detail of the sort that lovers remember: "The joy of evangelizing always arises from grateful remembrance: it is a grace which we constantly need to implore. The apostles never forgot the moment when Jesus touched their hearts: 'It was about four o'clock in the afternoon' (John 1:39)."[4] The significance of John's giving that precise hour may be multifold: it may be a detail given to underscore the eyewitness nature of the account; it may be suggestive of the length and importance of the encounter, since the visit began at the "tenth hour" calculated from sunrise—that is about 4 p.m. (and thus not long before nightfall, which in the Hebrew reckoning is the beginning of the day). Verse 1:39 therefore seems to indicate that the visit lasted overnight and perhaps even through the following daylight hours.[5] In any case such detail also bespeaks the vivid memory of a cherished event, as in the exchange between Henry II and Eleanor in the movie *The Lion in Winter*, based on James Goldman's 1966 play:

HENRY: Do you remember when we met?
ELEANOR: Down to the hour and the color of your stockings.

This essay, then, will consider the role that the Gospel of John ascribes to joy in that configuration of Christian existence that can be termed *missionary discipleship*. Joy constitutes an essential part of the bridge that joins those two elements of Christian identity—becoming a disciple and becoming a missionary—into one inseparable configuration of Christian life. Pope Francis

3. Pope Francis, *Evangelii gaudium*, §8.
4. Pope Francis, *Evangelii gaudium*, §13.
5. J. H. Bernard, *A Critical and Exegetical Commentary on the Gospel According to John,* vol. 1, ICC (Edinburgh: T&T Clark, 1999), 56; Raymond Brown, *The Gospel according to John (I–IX),* AncB (Garden City, NY: Doubleday, 1966), 75; Samuel Marie-Joseph Lagrange, *Évangile selon Saint Jean* (Paris: Librairie Victor Lecoffre, 1925), 46.

describes this quality of joy in his exhortation to all who read his words, with reference to certain key Johannine texts:

> Every Christian is a missionary to the extent that he or she has encountered the love of God in Christ Jesus: we no longer say that we are "disciples" and "missionaries", but rather that we are always "missionary disciples". If we are not convinced, let us look at those first disciples, who, immediately after encountering the gaze of Jesus, went forth to proclaim him joyfully: "We have found the Messiah!" (Jn 1:41). The Samaritan woman became a missionary immediately after speaking with Jesus and many Samaritans come to believe in him "because of the woman's testimony" (Jn 4:39). So too, Saint Paul, after his encounter with Jesus Christ, "immediately proclaimed Jesus" (Acts 9:20; cf. 22:6–21). So what are we waiting for?[6]

Joy and the Fulfillment of Nature's Desire

Certainly relevant to the role that the Fourth Gospel ascribes to joy is the insight that the Anglican exegete John Painter considers foundational for his life's work in regard to that Gospel, namely, his "recognition of the way that John holds together a theology of creation and redemption."[7] A further insight listed by Painter as distinct but clearly related to this one is that "God's love is not coercive but seeks to woo all people, indeed the whole of creation, that all may be made whole."[8] Here Painter seems to be viewing the Fourth Gospel as a corrective to any undue (Lutheran/Calvinist) suppression of the dignity of human nature or its incorporation into the work of salvation.

The role ascribed to joy in the Gospel of John thus brings into relief the importance of an integral Christology as well as an integral theology of grace (whether provided by Christian tradition or by the fuller context of biblical revelation) as a hermeneutical key to understanding the Gospel message. Without Jesus' true and full participation in human existence, he could bestow gifts on humanity but would not be seen as the fulfillment of its own inherent yearnings. By the same token, without the possibility of the full engagement of the human will and heart in the enterprise of discipleship, the life of grace would appear as something extrinsic to human nature rather than as its own highest expression.

---

6. Pope Francis, *Evangelii gaudium*, §120.

7. John Painter, "The Signs of the Messiah and the Quest for Eternal Life," in *What We Have Heard from the Beginning: The Past, Present, and Future of Johannine Studies*, ed. Tom Thatcher (Waco, TX: Baylor University Press, 2007), 235.

8. Painter, "The Signs of the Messiah," 235.

A Johannine phenomenon closely linked to these insights is the importance ascribed to human initiative in the Johannine narratives of discovery. Rather than denigrating all human longings as impure, John often depicts them as stepping stones to higher aspirations: "In the signs (the Johannine miracle stories), what is significant for everyday life becomes a sign (narrative symbol) of the source of eternal life (John 20:30–31)."[9] A woman's natural thirst becomes emblematic of her deeper thirst for the water that "will become in her a spring of water welling up to eternal life" (4:14 NAB; cf. 7:38), and the crowds' hunger for "food that perishes" prepares for the invitation to approach "the food that endures for eternal life" (6:27). A blind man's passage from his native darkness into the light of physical sight prepares for, and then pales into insignificance in comparison to, his passage into the light of the faith by which he now sees and worships the Son of Man.

The joy of the Gospel is thus rooted in the fact that the gift of salvation that Jesus brings to the believer—even while it does outstrip every merely human expectation—is not extraneous to his own hopes and needs as a creature; rather, it satisfies these in superabundance and in a manner that he could never have expected. For this reason it should not be surprising, and neither does it detract in any way from the greatness of God's gift, that so many of the disciples' most electrifying moments of joyful discovery in the Gospel occur in the course of inquiries initiated by the disciples themselves rather than by Jesus.[10]

The Disciples' Seeking and the Path of Discovery

Such a path of discovery, initiated by the disciple himself but carrying him even so beyond his own expectations, is the paradigm established in the first chapter of the Gospel of John. When Jesus first speaks in this Gospel, it is to those who are already "following" him (1:37–38), though they are not yet doing so in the manner that he will call them to follow him. Indeed, they are already "seeking" as he recognizes by his question to them, "What are you looking for?" (1:38), but at this point they can only express their quest in simple, earthly terms: "Rabbi . . . where are you staying?"

It seems an important clue for all evangelization to recognize here that the transition to a deeper quest and the discovery of a deeper truth, unveiled so exquisitely by the Evangelist, is not merely a correction to the conscious quest that they have already initiated. Neither is it even a detour from that quest.

9. Painter, "The Signs of the Messiah," 237.
10. Painter, "The Signs of the Messiah," 236.

Instead, this path of discovery is already hidden within their quest, needing only to be drawn out skillfully by the evangelizer. As Alan Culpepper comments on the above-mentioned initial dialogue between Jesus and his disciples starting with his question "What are you looking for?": "This is a natural question to ask if two people are following you. At a deeper level, of course, it is one of the great existential questions of life: What are you searching for?"[11] Their question, "Rabbi . . . where are you staying?" (*Rabbi . . . poû meneis?*), admits of many possible levels of meaning, and each level opens up the way to an answer of corresponding depth.

If the question is allowed to rest at its most basic level, it is answered purely and simply by showing the followers a place where the Rabbi lays down his head at night for his physical rest. But as the Gospel unfolds, still deeper answers to the same question will be given, not contradicting the former answers but filling them with still more content: Jesus dwells also in those who eat his flesh and drink his blood (6:56), and the one privileged to dwell with him and believe in him will find that he remains (i.e., the same verb *menei*) forever (8:35; 12:34). The ultimate and unsurpassable answer to the question is finally reached in the Last Discourses as Jesus opens his heart fully to the disciples to reveal to them not only that his true dwelling place is in the Trinitarian communion of the Father's love (15:10) but also that he wishes them to dwell with him precisely there. Indeed, in 15:4–9 that exhortation and invitation occurs in almost every verse. The groundwork is being laid for this dwelling in everything that Jesus is presently accomplishing, as he has already assured them: "If I go and prepare a place for you, I will come back again and take you to myself, so that where I am you also may be" (14:3).

Indeed, the disciples may even be in the intimacy of Jesus' own transcendent communion with the Father, in that chapter that Pope St. Paul VI describes as lifting a sacred veil to reveal the secret of the unfathomable joy that dwells within Jesus. Here Jesus will speak of this intention: "I wish that where I am they also may be with me, that they may see my glory that you gave me" (17:24).[12] As one looks down from that mountaintop on the whole path of the disciples' unity with Jesus that has been traversed from that first day, it is astoundingly wonderful to see again the potential that lay hidden already in the

---

11. R. Alan Culpepper, *The Gospel and Letters of John*, IBT (Nashville: Abingdon, 1998), 122.

12. Pope St. Paul VI, Apostolic Exhortation *Gaudete in Domino* (May 9, 1975), w2.vatican.va /content/paul-vi/en/apost_exhortations/documents/hf_p-vi_exh_19750509_gaudete-in -domino.html, §3.

disciples' innocent question—"Where are you staying?"—and the surpassing joy afforded by the revelation of an answer that was far more profound than they could have imagined!

The nature of this quest and the infinitude in which its true fulfillment consists gives rise to a series of partial discoveries in which the reader is given various clues to enable him to sense the joy being experienced and shared by the disciple. Andrew will find his brother Simon and announce, "We have found the Messiah!" (1:41). Here the Old Testament and the Jewish cultural context of the first century illuminate that Jesus is being identified as the expected "Anointed" of David's line who will grace his people with victory and peace. It is a true discovery, but it is a partial one—both because this role has been misconstrued and because it is only one of many aspects of Jesus' identity that will be unveiled in the course of the Gospel.

Many other affirmations in the text of the Gospel will identify Jesus as the fulfillment of hopes and desires already generated in the minds of God's people by ancient as well as contemporary witnesses, from Moses to John the Baptist. Andrew's joy of discovery leads him to share the same with his brother Simon; then either Simon or Jesus himself (for the syntax of 1:43 admits of either interpretation) finds Philip, and Philip finds Nathanael. Whenever one finds a new source of joy, one naturally wishes to find someone with whom to share it. In fact, up to this point the entirety of the disciples' identity is encapsulated in their finding another after having themselves been found by him, and sharing with that other the unexpected treasure that has come to light.[13] Philip's words to Nathanael, as with Andrew's earlier words, underscore that Jesus is the fulfillment of Israel's treasured Scriptures: "We have found the one about whom Moses wrote in the law, and also the prophets, Jesus, son of Joseph, from Nazareth" (1:45).

The combination of the Law and the Prophets in Philip's affirmation seems to signal first of all that Jesus is fulfilling not just one or another of the types with which the Old Testament is replete; rather, he is fulfilling the Old Testament in its entirety, for that is generally what the Jews meant when they referred to "the Law and the Prophets."[14] The English translation given above, however, and indeed all English versions generally, fail to communicate the sense of the Greek text in which that "something greater" is already bursting out of the puzzlingly awkward syntax as a large quantity of gold might burst

13. Culpepper, *The Gospel and Letters of John*, 123.
14. Rudolf Bultmann, *The Gospel of John*, trans. George R. Beasley-Murray (Oxford: Basil Blackwell, 1971), 103n5.

through a sack too small to contain it: *hon egrapsen Môysês en tô nomô kai hoi prophêtai heurêkamen*—literally "the One *whom* Moses [in the Law] and the Prophets wrote, we have found!" Moses and the Prophets had conveyed the word of God to his people in human language, whereas Jesus had now arrived and been encountered as that very Word in person.

In such stories of quest and discovery, the Evangelist reveals a profound respect for the harmony between the orders of creation and redemption (as Painter expressed it). In seeking to satisfy a human need or curiosity, in other words, they are led beyond these earthly realities to supernatural ones. However, this does not mean that the Evangelist is oblivious to the fallenness of the same human nature and therefore to the circuitous route that human nature's natural striving must sometimes take before (and indeed, *if*) the human person will eventually attain the fullness of truth that brings true joy. It is clear that the Samaritan woman in chapter 4, as she comes to recognize Jesus' power to give water that will quench all thirst forever, is concerned at first only with a physical realization of that promise so she can spare herself the difficulty of coming to the well: "Sir, give me this water, so that I may not be thirsty or have to keep coming here to draw water" (4:15). Neither do those in the crowd who respond to Jesus' promise of the bread "which comes down from heaven and gives life to the world" by saying "Sir, give us this bread always" (6:33–34) seem to have moved beyond their initial characterization of this gift made just a few verses earlier: "What sign can you do, that we may see and believe in you? What can you do?" (6:30). And still more pathetic is the poor man, ill for 38 years, who cannot even muster a clear answer to Jesus' inviting question, "Do you want to be well?" (5:6), but can only complain that someone always manages to deprive him of the saving effects of the healing pool by getting there before him (5:7). All of these enter upon the Gospel's stage as seekers, but none is seeking the right object in the right way. Even so, not one of their halting or misguided requests is rebuffed by Jesus; all of them in some way receives from Jesus the grace of transcending their initial quest and attaining gifts they could not have foreseen.

Both Painter and Culpepper point to a recurring pattern in various stories by which Jesus encounters those whose quest is misguided only to redirect it and respond to their deeper, unspoken "request" and elicit their faith. Painter describes the pattern thus:

1) The quester makes an implied or implicit request;
2) The quest dominates the story, and the quester is not simply a foil for Jesus;
3) The quester seeks something essential for human well-being. In

141

John something important at a physical level can become important for well-being at a spiritual level;

4) There is an objection or difficulty to be overcome, and this may redefine the direction of the quest;

5) The pronouncement of Jesus (a word or action) holds the key to the resolution of the quest;

6) The outcome of the quest is of crucial interest and is indicated in the quest story.[15]

This pattern, as one can see in the first Johannine "sign" at the wedding of Cana, sometimes occurs in situations where Jesus encounters seekers in good faith whose requests he answers in unexpected ways. But it also encompasses those who seek wrong-headedly, in which case the pattern might include a rebuke signaling that "some condition must be met or a difficulty overcome for the quest to be successful."[16] Although it is true that a persistently wrong-headed quest will be permanently frustrated in the attainment of its object—indeed, is this not the situation of all those who reject Jesus not because they are not seekers but because they search wrongly?—Jesus repeatedly shows himself willing to redirect the quest to its proper goal.

Unearthing the True Object of the Quest

Some exegetes, however, seem to belittle the connection between the disciples' own act of seeking (including their initial claims of discovery) on the one hand, and the gift Jesus eventually gives them on the other. For example, Francis Moloney offers a reading of the calling of the first disciples that he admits has been "overlooked" by many scholars.

> The claim on the part of the first disciples to have found Jesus and to have come to a decision about his person and role is a blatant untruth. This is seldom noticed by commentators. The theological point that is made by this untruth is that true discipleship flows from the initiative of Jesus. This is the case across both the synoptic and Johannine traditions. For the Johannine Gospel true discipleship involves a correct understanding of who Jesus is. The first disciples fail on both counts.[17]

15. Painter, "The Signs of the Messiah," 240, 245–256, especially 252; Culpepper, *The Gospel and Letters of John*, 155.

16. Painter, "The Signs of the Messiah," 251.

17. Francis J. Moloney, *The Gospel of John*, ed. Daniel Harrington, SaPaSe 4 (Collegeville, MN: Liturgical Press, 1998), 60.

Moloney goes so far as to call it a "lie" when Andrew, and Philip after him, make their affirmations to their fellow seekers saying that they have found the Messiah (1:41), or the one contained in the writings of Moses and the Prophets (1:45). In Moloney's reckoning, such statements are dishonest because Andrew has already received the testimony of John the Baptist and Philip has received it also from another, so that "[t]he initiative for their presence with Jesus and their understanding of him does not belong to them."[18] And as for the latter of the two encounters, he says, "The only person Philip found is Nathanael (1:45a), but he *was found* and called by Jesus."[19]

Moloney likewise points to the deficits of the Samaritan woman's insights and affirmations even after she has run from the encounter with Jesus to spread the word about him. After leaving behind her water jar (4:28) as her apostolic counterparts in discipleship had left behind their nets to follow the same Lord in the Synoptic accounts (Matt 4:20; Mark 1:18) she exhorts the townspeople, "Come see a man who told me everything I have done. Could he possibly be the Messiah?" But Moloney, focusing on the admittedly true fact that her question begins with *mêti*, which signals some doubt as to the likelihood of an affirmative answer, thus seems to side with Teresa Okure's monograph, *The Johannine Approach to Mission*, whom he cites to the effect that "the Samaritan woman in the text is neither a missionary nor a true believer."[20]

Such an analysis, however, seems to dismiss unduly the valid insights into Jesus' identity that these disciples have gained, the real steps toward commitment that they have made, and the unabashed joy that seems to accompany both. In his eagerness to highlight the initiative of Jesus' love, Moloney has discounted the engagement of the ones whom Jesus loves. In order to underscore the truth that it is really Jesus who has found *them*, he overlooks that for the ones thus found by Jesus and called by him, the encounter is also a joyful discovery that they describe as such not in order to take credit for it but out of a sense of wonder and gratitude.

In his concern to point out the limitations of their insight and the halting nature of their newfound faith, Moloney seems to overlook the fact—evident in John far more than in all of the other Gospels—that even those who have come to know Jesus best and to follow him wherever he goes still have much to learn about him. To live in relationship with Jesus is not merely to rest in the memory

---

18. Moloney, *The Gospel of John*, 55.

19. Moloney, *The Gospel of John*, 55, emphasis in the original.

20. Teresa Okure, *The Johannine Approach to Mission*, WUNT Reihe 2, 31 (Tübingen: J.C.B. Mohr, 1988), 169, cited by Moloney in *The Gospel of John*, 135.

of what one has already learned and affirmed about him, but to embark on a perpetual voyage of discovery in which new surprises will yield both new joys and new challenges.

Joy and Mutuality

Where Moloney is clearly correct is in his recognition that the disciples do not really become seekers or finders before they are first sought out and found by Jesus himself. When Andrew and the other disciple who first encounter and are called by Jesus embark on their quest, it is because John has borne before them the witness for which he has been sent (1:36–37). Andrew then *finds* his brother Simon and leads him to Jesus, by whom he is "discovered" in his own way as Jesus bestows on him the name that bespeaks his destiny: *Kêphas*, "which is translated Peter" (1:42). Only when he has been "found" does Philip then *find* Nathanael and bring him to Jesus, before whom his cynical doubt about anything good coming from Nazareth disappears (1:46). More importantly, it is Jesus by whom Nathanael has evidently already been "discovered" in a hidden and mysterious way: "Before Philip called you, I saw you under the fig tree" (1:48).

Nathanael's joy in being thus "found" by Jesus reverberates through his exclamation "Rabbi, you are the Son of God; you are the King of Israel!" Similarly in the case of the Samaritan woman, it is Jesus' knowledge of her past, and therefore also of her interiority, that elicits her exclamation, "Sir, I can see that you are a prophet" (4:19). Granted, this is only the beginning of her own discoveries, which undergo such a dramatic crescendo throughout this passage: from 4:9 where she addresses him by no title ("How can you, a Jew, ask me, a Samaritan woman, for a drink?") to 4:11–12 and 15 where her *kyrie* seems to mean merely "Sir" as she doubts even whether he can claim parity with the Patriarch Jacob, to 4:19 ("I can see that you are a prophet"), then to 4:25 and 29 where she speculates even if haltingly that he may be the "Messiah" or "Christ," and finally to the affirmation that even the recipients of her testimony are able to make at the end in 4:42: "we know that this is truly the savior of the world!"[21]

That it is really the Father and Jesus who "seek" and "find" is made evident in many ways throughout the Gospel. It is the Father who seeks the true worshippers who will "worship the Father in Spirit and truth" (4:23); the Father also seeks the Son's glory (8:50). Even after an initial and momentous encounter with the paralytic in chapter five whom he heals, Jesus "finds him in the

---

21. Moloney, *The Gospel of John*, 143.

temple area" and exhorts him to good living after his having been challenged by the Jews (5:14), and similarly he seeks out the man born blind who has been challenged by the authorities and finds him as well (9:35). Jesus "finds" Lazarus already four days in the tomb but raises him (11:17). So when Jesus exhorts the disciples after his Resurrection, "Cast the net over the right side of the boat and you will find something" (21:6),[22] and when the miraculously enormous catch symbolizes the future success of the mission on which he is sending them, it is really Jesus' own "seeking" that he is placing into their hearts, making them his representatives in the work of evangelization.

Precisely since God alone exists "in the beginning," it is he alone who can *initiate* the whole sequence of joyful discoveries. But in each and every instance of a successful mission, the "finding" of a new disciple by the one who "seeks" in Jesus' name is no less a "finding"—a discovery—on the part of the one who is thus found by Jesus and brought into contact with him. As the Fourth Gospel presents it, the joy of discovery cannot be the terrain of a contest between God and human beings about who gets the credit, any more than Catholic dogma could present justification as a question of the divine initiative *versus* human cooperation. Presented instead is a picture of Christian joy as quintessentially interpersonal—the fruit of an encounter and the seed of further such encounters on an ever-wider scale.

At issue is not merely the joy of the first encounter but moreover the joy that remains as a constitutive element of the relationship begun or fostered by the encounter. This is evident from the fact that Jesus speaks of the communication of his own joy to his disciples as they remain united to him and keep his commandments (15:10). It is the joy of the sheep who follow the voice of their shepherd (10:4). This voice does not merely provide them with a sense of security, for it is the same "bridegroom's voice" (3:29) that brings to the bridegroom's friend a joy so great that in order to hold onto it, this friend wishes to make himself nothing in the bridegroom's presence: "He must increase; I must decrease" (3:30).

This chain of communication begins with the Son's own joy, which he gives to those who become his disciples: "I have told you this so that my joy may be in you and your joy may be complete" (15:11). At issue is not merely the joy of the first encounter but above all the joy that remains as a constitutive element of the relationship that endures. This is evident from the fact that Jesus speaks of the communication of his own joy to his disciples as they remain united to

---

22. The last word, "something," is evidently added for clarity in the English translation, whereas the Greek simply bears the word *heurēsete*—literally, "and you will find."

him and keep his commandments (15:10). Indeed, we can see here that this joy is interpersonal even at its eternal source, since the Son's very personhood is constituted by the eternal "seeking" and "finding" of the Father's begetting. His own seeking and finding of his disciples constitutes the extension to them, even in their brokenness and waywardness, of his own joy in thus being "found," a joy that consists in his own desire to be nothing and do nothing apart from his Father: "A son cannot do anything on his own, but only what he sees his father doing; for what he does, his son will do also. . . . I can do nothing on my own. . . . I do not seek my own will but the will of the one who sent me" (5:19, 30).

Both the interpersonal nature of Gospel joy and its transcendent, eternal provenance are further underscored by the Son's transposition of his evangelical conversation into the key of prayer and therefore of intra-Trinitarian conversation with his Father: "I speak this in the world so that they may share my joy completely" (17:3). And here as well, he goes on to express the features of such joy in ways that protect our understanding of the term from any facile superficiality.

Inextricably bound up with this joy—communicated with it to his disciples as part and parcel of the same reality—is the Father's *word* that he shares with them, a word that clashes so intensely with this world's values that the world hates them because of it (17:14). This word is identified not merely with self-expression but with truth, and it consecrates the disciples for their mission (17:17–19). This joy is closely bound up with the disciples' perception of the Son's *glory* which the Son has now given over to them (1:14; 2:11; 11:4; 17:22, 24). And finally, this joy is the fruit and the seed of the *unity* that he wishes to reign among his disciples, which alone manifests in them the *perfection* of his gifts:

> I pray not only for them, but also for those who will believe in me through their word, so that they may all be one, as you, Father, are in me and I in you, that they also may be in us, that the world may believe that you sent me. And I have given them the glory you gave me, so that they may be one, as we are one, I in them and you in me, that they may be brought *to perfection as one*, that the world may know that you sent me, and that you loved them even as you loved me. (17:21–23, emphasis added)

We have already seen that the joy of discovery in the encounter with Jesus illustrates the dignity of human nature in its longings that stand in openness to such a gift. But perhaps it is here, in the so-called "High Priestly Prayer," that we can see most clearly that the joy of the encounter with Jesus is no merely subjective or superficial datum of human experience but has a divine provenance and a divine ontology. Accordingly, participation in this joy cannot be brought about by any amount of human effort; it can only be accepted freely and in the specific configuration within which it is offered through the encounter. It is Jesus himself who sets himself before the tribunal of human judgment for acceptance or rejection. He does not—in fact, he *cannot!*— offer this joy as a commodity apart from himself, because the joy that he communicates is none other than his own, as an aspect of his own being (15:11; 17:13). One can possess it only by possessing him, in love.

The Refusal or Acceptance of Joy

It is one of the deepest mysteries of the Gospel, but one also corroborated by human experience, that the same encounter with Jesus that elicits wonderment and joy in some, evokes hostility and opposition in others. Precisely when the astounding fact of a man's liberation from thirty-eight years of incapacity towers before their own pusillanimity, some choose instead to see only a Sabbath violation in the man's carrying of the mat by which for so many years he could only be carried helplessly (5:40). The promise of a bread that nourishes eternal life, spoken by one who had just multiplied a tiny amount to feed a multitude, leads some to recoil at the admitted incomprehensibility of Jesus' identification of that bread as his flesh (6:52, 60, 66). Some attribute the wondrous signs that he is accomplishing and his words to the activity of demons (7:20). Moreover, his powerful proclamations during the Feast of Tabernacles to be the source of living water (7:38) and the Light of the world (8:12), although inducing some to recognize him as the Prophet and as the Messiah (7:40–41), leave others cold. They cannot stack together enough vital data to identify him as the one who must be of David's line and come from Bethlehem (7:42), and with bitter irony they fail to recognize that both are true. After Jesus gave the man born blind not only physical sight but also the capacity to recognize the true Light of the world (9:5–7, 35–38), both he and the man who received supernatural vision were opposed by those who were evidently blinder than the man born blind. These were people whose blindness consisted precisely in that they professed to see rightly (9:39–41) without recognizing their Light. Precisely the signs that invited assent and thus stood as invitations to joy became—on the basis of people's differing responses to them—occasions of division (7:43, 9:16; 10:19) and were opposed (11:47–52; 12:37). Instead of opening themselves to joy, the Pharisees responded to Jesus' magnetism with envy (12:19) and Pilate reacted to the cogency and serenity of Jesus' affirmations of truth with fear (19:8).

It is tempting to view the divisions among the hearers of Jesus in purely humanistic terms, as if some simply had temperaments of receptivity whereas others did not. But Jesus makes it clear that belonging to his flock is not merely a matter of finding him, correctly evaluating him, and accepting him. Instead, those who are to be his sheep really must be found by him first, and called. They do not become members of his flock by recognizing his voice; instead, they recognize his voice because they are already members of his flock: "The works I do in my Father's name testify to me. But you do not believe, because you are not among my sheep. My sheep hear my voice; I know them, and they follow me" (10:26–27).

Very telling in any event is the role that joy seems to play in the various stories of individuals called out of their darkness and solitude into the sunlit pastures where the Shepherd feeds his gathered flocks. If we survey those stories we may note the recurring pattern by which the immediate presence of Jesus to his disciples, offering them everything that the Father has given over to him, is received through the testimony of others whose joy became an authentication of their encounter before new recipients of the message. We have seen that this was so in the case of the first disciples. It was so in the case of the Samaritan woman whose wonderment enticed her neighbors to search for Jesus but who subsequently could say to her, "We no longer believe because of your word; for we have heard for ourselves, and we know that this is truly the savior of the world" (4:42). And it continues to be so even as the testimony of the Beloved Disciple passes into the community that endures after his death and as each new generation passes on not a bloodless concept or practical solution but rather the abiding joy of a personal encounter with the Word that "was from the beginning" and has been "made visible"—the One whom "we have seen with our eyes," and "looked upon and touched with our hands" (1 John 1:1).

When we find, then, such an atmosphere of joy surrounding the handing on and the sharing of the Son's gifts as narrated in the Gospel of John, this picture should provide us with material for an examen about whether our own work of evangelization exhibits sufficiently this hallmark of authenticity that is at once the fruit of faith and its seed. After all, we have enough from the Gospel of John to assure us that if the addressee of the Gospel message has not yet caught at least a glimpse of authentic joy within the life of those who bear the message, then he really cannot have either accepted or rejected Jesus definitively, because he has not yet been accorded a real opportunity to meet him.

CHAPTER 9

The Exegete as Seminary Formator

James Keating

The Scripture scholar who possesses a lively faith has had a burden to carry in the last decades because the academic culture has severed the study of Scripture from faith, even calling such severing an advance in knowledge. Paradoxically, the Scripture scholar who possesses a lively faith understands that more is known *in* faith than *apart from* it.[1] In effect, the one who prays to the Living God as he receives His revelation is a more reasonable man and not less. As Maurice Blondel once noted,

> There is in man a life better than man, and it is not man who can sustain life; something divine has to dwell in him. Absolutely impossible and absolutely necessary for man: that is properly the notion of the supernatural. Man's action goes beyond man; and all the effort of his reason is to see that he cannot, that he must not, *restrict himself to it.*[2]

So, to be reasonable is to allow oneself to be affected by the supernatural. In our limited and sinful condition, this truth presents itself as a crucifixion of the mind and the person. To live such a paradox is to be unable to rest, unable to blend in, unable to walk in comfortable shoes in the biblical, religious, philosophical, literary, or even theological academic societies of today. To think out of a lively faith in academia today is to be that man who brings his wife to a bachelor party and feels that it is perfectly natural . . . after all, "This is who I am."

---

1. "[Faith] is recognized as the indispensable means of penetrating into the truth of one's own being." Joseph Ratzinger, *The Nature and Mission of Theology* (San Francisco: Ignatius, 1995), 57.

2. Maurice Blondel, *Action: Essay on a Critique of Life and a Science of Practice*, trans. Oliva Blanchette (South Bend, IN: University of Notre Dame Press, 2003), 357. Emphasis added.

Some scholars may say, "Who you are is not relevant to how or what you come to know," and in some areas of study, this may be true. In Scripture studies, however, one is being engaged at the level *of* the person *by* a Person. Such study is not unmediated mysticism, by any means; rather, it is an encounter between the fullness of one's own powers and the Truth, Who is a Person.

I understand the crucifixion of the mind to be that process wherein who and what the scholar loves confronts the finitude and sinfulness of a biased world. In this confrontation between love and bias or hard-heartedness, the scholar wishes to resist the temptation to fall into disbelief.[3] In resisting the vertigo caused by looking only into this puny space of science, method, or interpretation, he stands ready to receive a message from beyond—a surprise, a shock so substantive that it both brings him into the new and grounds him more deeply in all that has already been given in Christ. This is what happened to Thomas, the Twin.

The doubter is transformed into a theologian only at the open side of Christ, notes Aquinas.[4] Here, at the open side of Christ, is where the Scripture scholar dwells. The scholar, fully aware that bias reigns in culture,[5] desires to penetrate the mystery[6] of the invitation of Christ to enter His wounds. In so entering, the Scripture scholar does not enter the "undisciplined" world of image and poetry, as so defined and disdained by the knowledge class. Rather, he or she is brought into a sharper clarity about the need for intellectual distinctions, sound logic, and deliberate and critical thought.

Christ's invitation to enter into the open side is His invitation for one to use the full powers of man in order to receive revelation, and in so doing, have the mind, will, and affect surge with the energy known by being in communion with the Paschal Mystery. Any reasoning that is born from this communion will be more trustworthy than the sanitized reason of scientism; any images born of this communion with the Paschal Mystery will carry more truth than

---

3. "Hardness of heart is understood as a refusal to yield to God, a stubborn choice to remain 'blind' to God's ways." Mary Healy, *The Gospel of Mark*, CCSSc (Grand Rapids, MI: Baker, 2008), 196.

4. Thomas Aquinas, *Commentum in Matthaeum et Joannem Evangelistas*, chapter 20, lectio 6, in *Opera Omnia*, vol. 10 (Parma: Fiaccadori, 1860), 634.

5. Bias here is understood as whatever blocks insight and the questions that would have arisen if one had not chosen to remain opaque to the supernatural, to the transcendent. See James Connor, SJ, *The Dynamism of Desire: Bernard J.F. Lonergan, S.J., on the Spiritual Exercises of Saint Ignatius of Loyola* (Saint Louis: The Institute of Jesuit Sources, 2006), 87.

6. "Put your finger here and see my hands, and bring your hand and put it into my side, and do not be unbelieving, but believe" (John 20:27 NABRE).

the sterilized snapshots of abstracted history; any decision flowing from this communion will bear with it a devotion born of love of God and not simply a conscience born of the anemic cultural founts now made stagnant by legalism, political correctness, and raw power divorced from truth.[7]

There are, of course, pockets of scholars who desire Divine Love to imbue their reasoning, but many have been indoctrinated away from such a matrix due to the deepest fear of all: intimacy with God. Encountering a cadaver is frightening but not as frightening as encountering a Holy Ghost. The pages of Scripture are in truth more like a fecund habitat than a mediator of sterile ideas. We have chased prayer out of Scripture study in the name of objectivity, but I truly believe that it is in the service of fear. These pages house the real possibility of *encountering a life* and do not simply occasion textual analysis.[8] We fear the raging fire that is Divine encounter; and in an effort to remain in our bias, we banish the vulnerable person who studies Scripture to the retreat house— or worse, to the seminary (!). By cultural decree, these are the only places where the Word can live; and more important still, these are the places that can be safely dismissed by the academy as irrelevant to truth, cultural development, and political power. Such banishment is the scholar's way of narrowing freedom of religion to freedom of worship. Such a one is saying, "You may be affected by God in your powers but you will be so only in private so we may call the fruit of such an encounter idiosyncratic."

---

7. "Today, the dominant philosophy in the university is not western philosophy that claims to be universal, nor is it even science. Rather it is a relativism that professes to begin with the assumptions of multi-culturalism. . . . From this viewpoint, truth is the enemy of culture. Everything is relative to time and place. We are left with what is only the 'practically useful' in our own environment. . . . In the university, we do not much consider the issues that revelation addresses to reason. Revelation is itself directed to reason as such. Its effect is to make reason more reasonable in figuring out how it is meant and how it relates to other truths. The coherence of a university is measured by the scope and source of information that it allows itself and its students to consider in dealing with those fundamental questions about human life and the coherent and incoherent answers to them." James Schall, SJ, "On Graduations, Universities, and What Is 'Practically Useless'," at *Catholic World Report*, May 17, 2015, www.catholicworld report.com/Item/3884/on_graduations_universities_and_what_is_practically_useless.aspx.

8. "A hermeneutical approach to sacred Scripture inevitably brings into play the proper relationship between faith and reason. Indeed, the secularized hermeneutic of sacred Scripture is the product of reason's attempt structurally to exclude any possibility that God might enter into our lives and speak to us in human words. Here too, we need to urge a *broadening of the scope of reason*. In applying methods of historical analysis, no criteria should be adopted *which would rule out in advance God's self-disclosure in human history*" (emphasis in final phrase mine). Pope Benedict XVI, *Verbum Domini* (September 30, 2010) (Boston: Pauline Books and Media, 2010), §36.

The Scripture scholar's classroom is not a chapel or retreat house, of course. The classroom is a space for critical thought, intense analysis of textual meanings, and respect for the origin and intention of the biblical authors. In the service of a more generous definition of reason, however, the classroom is also an arena within which knowledge born of faith, born of the mind's surrender to God as an act of love, can reveal its kind of knowing as well. An "objective" scholarly approach to a text cannot be reduced to being skeptical about the supernatural or miraculous events in Scripture.

Within these realms, knowledge from the Church's relationship with God can assist scholars in pondering revelation's fullest meaning. John Paul II noted this:

> Rationalism is still very widespread in the name of the reductive concept of science, it renders human reason insensitive to an encounter with Divine Revelation and with divine transcendence. . . . There is no longer any reason to fight against God; the individual feels he is simply able to do without Him.[9]

This is the climate that has prevailed for decades now in academia, but in the seminary there is a different culture, which has been deepened by both John Paul II in *Pastores dabo vobis* and Benedict XVI in *Verbum Domini*. It is a culture that is based upon the freedom the truth secures. Therefore, the seminary is the freest academic space on earth, as it welcomes Truth *at the source.* Truth severed from the source is more easily diminished since it exists and is transmitted in culture only by way of its fumes, which escape after bias burns it in a violent conflagration, reducing it to political power and hastening its suppression.

In the midst of this still dominant rationalism in academia, someone of the intellectual stature of Joseph Ratzinger enters center stage as pope. As pope, he begins to promote a way of reading Scripture that appears antithetical to the needs of the academy, *lectio divina*:

> Those aspiring to the ministerial priesthood are called to a profound personal relationship with God's word, particularly in *lectio divina*, so that this relationship will in turn nurture their vocation. . . . Such attention to the prayerful reading of Scripture must not in any way lead to a dichotomy with regard to the exegetical studies which are a part of formation. . . . An authentic life of prayer cannot fail to nurture in the candidate's heart a desire for greater knowledge of the God who has revealed himself in his word as

9. Pope John Paul II, *Pastores dabo vobis* (March 25, 1992), w2.vatican.va/content/john-paul-ii/en/apost_exhortations/documents/hf_jp-ii_exh_25031992_pastores-dabo-vobis.html, §7.

infinite love. Hence, great care should be taken to ensure that seminarians always cultivate this reciprocity between study and prayer in their lives. This end will be served if candidates are introduced to the study of Scripture through methods which favor this integral approach.[10]

If the study of Scripture in the classroom is an extension of the Liturgy of the Word, as I believe it to be, then what method of Scripture study can we learn from the Liturgy of the Word—one that will assist in integrating prayer and knowledge in the future priest's own being? First, we can reverence the fact that because we approach the study of Scripture in faith, Christ still speaks to us in the classroom, albeit in different form, as He does from the ambo.[11] I believe the role of both silence in the classroom and the promotion of a "double notebook" that contains both the lecture material and a recorded notation of any movements of the Spirit that occur during those same lectures best facilitates the integrated approach. Here, in faith, silence, and note-taking from a contemplative stance, a man both achieves competency in scholarship and personal growth in prayer as he shares his prayer with his spiritual director and the fruit of the class's data with his professor.[12] True integration of learning and prayer occurs when knowledge becomes love.[13] As in the liturgy, it is the time of silence that best carries the truth to the heart. Silence in the liturgy and in the classroom is best not as an option but as part of the very fabric of the reality engaged. For it is in silence, as knowledge becomes love, that the integration is achieved.

The seminary is not a place where Scripture is approached simply as words carrying vague vestiges of ancient literature or myth. The seminary is not a place where critical reading is dispensed with in order simply to deepen devotion. No, the seminary is Scripture's home, the place where critical reasoning comes to its fullest powers in a matrix of one's own and the Church's loving response to the Paschal Mystery of Christ. As such, the seminary itself is a community existing in creative tension as it strives to reference in a unified

---

10. Pope Benedict XVI, *Verbum Domini*, §82.

11. "It is not the priest or deacon who proclaims the Gospel. It is Christ who proclaims the Gospel." Paul Turner, *Let Us Pray: A Guide to the Rubrics of Sunday Mass* (Collegeville, MN: Liturgical Press, 2012), 60.

12. See James Keating, *Resting on the Heart of Christ: The Vocation and Spirituality of the Seminary Theologian* (Omaha: IPF, 2009), chapters 3 and 4.

13. See Pope Benedict XVI, Address to the Pontifical Gregorian University (November 3, 2006), www.vatican.va/content/benedict-xvi/en/speeches/2006/november/documents/hf_ben-xvi_spe_20061103_gregoriana.html: "Knowing God is not enough. For a true encounter with him one must also love him. Knowledge must become love."

and integrative manner what sin, finitude, and limit are always grasping to tear. Although frustrating at times, the seminary is in fact, when inhabited by spiritually and affectively mature faculty, a lively scholarly community as it seeks to maintain the reality the universities have already jettisoned as impossible: that study carries one into truth and truth carries one into personal conversion.

In light of the contributions of these collected essays, I would like to meditate upon the importance of promoting questioning as vital to our teaching and at the service of the seminarian's personal integration of truth with spiritual and moral maturation. As Msgr. Magee noted, disciples carry within them a sense of security because they know the voice of Christ.[14] This voice becomes internalized within those whose powers are fully engaged during worship. As the voice is internalized, trust in its nature and content flows into the scriptural classroom to create an environment conducive for receiving questions. The liturgy's environment is one of adoration, praise, wonder, and surrender; and as such, it secures the heart in a sacred exchange between the believer and the mysteries of Christ's own self-surrender to the Father. After worship, the Word of God is further received and contemplated in the classroom in this deepened trust so that students can raise questions out of their spiritually and affectively secure hearts.

Fearful men do not really question; instead, they attack a problem or attempt to master a discipline. These dispositions, born of insecurity, do not augur well for the word of God to dwell within a man securely so as to nourish his life and ministry as a priest. Questions born from faith and the security that tutors one into spiritual freedom, however, are the questions that are able "to draw the honey from the comb," as Fr. Carl has advocated.[15] As Msgr. Magee noted, "To live in relationship with Jesus . . . is to embark on a perpetual voyage of discovery." Secular academics place Scripture on trial or strip it of its life and drain its blood in service of the anemic standards of science and history. Instead, the one who has suffered the coming of Christ within him as an indwelling person sees the Scripture as a home, a place to grow within, and a place to receive life and give life, a true habitat carrying within it the occasion for communion with God. A child who lives with his father is not afraid to ask questions if the father has created an environment of life-giving exchange.

14. "'We Have Found Him!': The Joy of Discovery in the Fourth Gospel," 145.

15. Cf. "Honey in the Comb: Toward a Spiritual Reading of Sacred Scripture in the Twenty-First Century," 118–134.

Granted, there is a role for "fear," in the sense of "respect," for formators. Seminarians and formators are not peers. This has to be emphasized for the sake of those seminarians who suffer from a sense of entitlement toward the vocation. Prescinding from this situation, however, a questioning son to his father would be called healthy in a therapeutic model. It is a questioning noted for its desire to go deep and not necessarily broad. To question is not intrinsically provocative as in a political environment; rather, to question is to seek more intimacy, more communion, more light, more truth, and more freedom within a relationship that is already cherished. Even if a son were to use the question to attack or weaken the bond, the bond itself would be held together by the father as we have seen in the story of the Lost Son in Luke 15. Both the son who questions to deepen communion and the son who questions to break the same will ultimately be "found" by Christ, as Msgr. Magee noted. In this world of sin even to raise a question is to acknowledge we exist in suffering and limit. The question is simply a sign of our lack of union with truth and carries our desire either to welcome and internalize it or weaken it by manipulation for personal gain.

As professors, we do not simply want to invite questions; we want to invite questions that ultimately find their rest in wisdom as Professor Anderson remarked.[16] In her meditation, Anderson highlighted the role of the father as one who "guards."[17] In the context of deepening faith that is secured by worship, the seminary professor can see his time in the classroom as guarding the communion seminarians have with the living Word. His teaching is not idiosyncratic or irresponsibly innovative but fluidly organic, stemming from the faith of the Church which he shares. The theologian seeks nothing more than the deepening of communion between his students and the Trinity within the context of study. In this way, the seminary professor assists the spiritual director as the exegete approaches study in a way that facilitates the training of seminarians to notice when God is emerging from the text.

The Scripture scholar points to the text as place of rendezvous between a man and his God. The scholar stands ready to discuss *the fruits* of such an encounter even as the spiritual director labors to secure the man's consciousness of *actual union* with God. By way of liturgy, spiritual direction, and study, there is a conspiracy of grace that even suffuses the external forum and fills those relationships that are the seminary with a sober delight: God is among us; and healing, insight, love, and truth are expected as a consequence.

16. Cf. "The Father of Proverbs 1–9: A Spiritual Father for Seminary Professors," 103–117.
17. "The Father," 107.

As Professor Anderson said, the seminary professor is to be vulnerable to such intimacy with God as he pores over his beloved texts.[18] Vulnerability to God is a moral duty for the seminary professor, a duty which naturally leads to ongoing professional formation, as well as personal spiritual direction. The latter, I believe, is even more crucial than the former since the Lord can build on possessed theological acumen as this is integrated into spiritual direction.

It is, however, more difficult to become "wise fathers" if we attend only to hermeneutics and neglect our own growth in divine intimacy. To suffer the coming of such vulnerability is a unique burden for the seminary scholar. University scholars simply do not ascribe to this reality. They do not see themselves as "enduring sources of truth" for their students as Professor Anderson asserted.[19] In the university world, all is reduced to outcomes and measurable objectives regarding data and information, and the moral/spiritual development of the professor is seen as a private matter. Certainly, no university administrator expects a professor to become "a father" to students and to pursue holiness as an essential element for teaching. In fact, someone can get a degree today totally online since education has been reduced to the commerce of exchanged data. Fatherhood is expendable. In the seminary, the professor takes his or her place within a set of relationships that exist to facilitate the moral, spiritual, and emotional growth of a man, and so a professor becoming a wisdom figure becomes essential.

The reality of the "question" becomes pervasive: the seminarian is, by his very presence, in formation, one open to being questioned and formulating questions. At his optimum, that is, when he possesses emotional health, he actually delights in being questioned by formators and delights in forming questions in class. The question is also pervasive for us. We are engaged by texts which stir questions in us; and similar to the seminarian, we want to be men and women open to being questioned by God and also by the standards of our discipline, the vision of the dean, and the helpful prodding of our spiritual directors. For both ourselves and our students, the question also carries with it the reality of fear. "I don't want you to question me. What if I don't know the answer? What if I don't like the answer?" In formation, we strive to create an atmosphere that lessens fear and welcomes questions. We can do this because we all reverence truth and are being formed by Truth itself in our liturgical worship. The seminary culture is one that is seeking to be hospitable to Truth. The classroom, human formation, spiritual direction, and pastoral training all

18. Cf. "The Father," 114.
19. Cf. "The Father," 109.

interpenetrate, hoping to be vehicles carrying the truth to a seminarian—the truth about God, about himself, about his intimate communion with the Trinity, and about his competent presence toward those in need. We are to move the men into a dynamic reception of the truth about themselves and God by the power of the indwelling Spirit.

Perhaps, we should think together someday on the need to update the seminary *horarium*—its flow, its content, and its routine as being helpful or harmful to the goal of forming priests. How does the *horarium* allow a seminarian to be more deeply immersed in the Word as his oxygen, as his mental and emotional home, and how does the *horarium* through its sometimes frenetic pace militate against a seminarian being immersed in the Word of God? As Pope Francis reminded us, "It is the task of the exegete to help the judgment of the church mature."[20] Is it not then the task of the exegete to help the seminary mature, to move it from any disproportionate academic imagination to an imagination that truly flows from the liturgy and the mature Christ (Eph 4:13)? If we have a crisis of preaching, does this not mean that seminarians are swimming in a shallow pool as the depths of the Word await? Do we dare ask questions not only about *horarium* but about curriculum and the living Word of God? Each field of study tends to absolutize the importance of its own field. Can we be open to seeing our own field of teaching as simply a part of a larger whole? We teach to further the ends of forming priests, not Scripture scholars. Knowledge of Scripture is essential, but we seminary professors sit within the larger matrix of formation, a formation that is ordered toward the development of dynamic and spiritual priests. If we truly created the seminary around God's Word, would it not be powerful in unexpected ways, possessing a sort of boisterous freedom? Of course, such a paradoxical freedom within structure creates saints not anarchists. What kind of questions do we need to ask about the *horarium* in relation to how effective we are in facilitating the development of a sacred imagination in the seminarian?

An imagination that dwells in communion with God and not simply the values of the current popular and political culture is essential to the development of pastors who preach the Word in power. The exegete can help create a set of relationships that bridge the gap between the scholar and those who inhabit the rush of ordinary parish preoccupations. Exegetes could propose new ways of immersing the seminarians in the key question of Scripture

---

20. Pope Francis, *Evangelii gaudium* (November 24, 2013) (Washington, DC: USCCB, 2013), §40; cf. Second Vatican Council, *Dei verbum* (November 18, 1965), www.vatican.va /archive/hist_councils/ii_vatican_council/documents/vat-ii_const_19651118_dei-verbum_en .html, §12.

studies: "Is the Word living within you?" It is the living Word and sustained communion with it that enables a man to preach a truth that liberates the ordinariness of our days.

We need a hermeneutic of correction for any anemia that might be present in our seminaries regarding knowledge of the Word of God in homiletics. This would include methods like Dr. Smith's "Stand and Deliver"[21] but also ways spontaneous and possibly "eccentric." I would like to propose spontaneous methods where seminarians might gather to "tag-team preach" or preach impromptu. This method is inspired by the film *The Apostle* with Robert Duvall. To do this effectively, however, the seminarians must be deeply immersed in the Word throughout the seminary curriculum.

One suggestion would be for the Scripture scholars to provide verses for the moral theologians, the systematic professors, and so on so that the men might allow the Word to engage them in the midst of lectures on Christ's true nature, the meaning of sin, etc. These Scriptures could be utilized during the silent times within classes as the men ponder the lecture and its ramifications for personal conversion or pastoral ministry.

In the exegete's own classroom, he or she needs to be teaching about the homily and not only that but teaching seminarians how to pray with people in their needs. Not all priests know how to draw upon the depths of Scripture when they are asked to pray spontaneously with a person in the church parking lot or in the food pantry. Some do not even initiate prayer but simply say to their people, "I will pray for you." If Scripture is in the seminarian like his breath, he will more likely breathe forth the Word when he counsels and prays with his people. He will then share his life with his people so naturally and spontaneously that they, too, will be drawn into the life of the Word. What kind of questions do we need to ask about the way we have limited homily preparation to "prepared texts" and public-speaking tenets?

Finally, what does Scripture study look like when we ask the most profound question? Does our knowledge—which has become love—draw non-Catholics into relationship with Christ? How can we arrange the content of priestly formation in such a way that the men we form carry evangelization in their being in the same way a true and good spouse signals to all that he is bound in love to his wife, thus freeing all those around him both to admire and then emulate such a man? Is the Word of God as it is encountered in formation fostering the seminarian's interest in the salvation of souls? Can we question how Scripture

---

21. Steven C. Smith, "Stand and Deliver: Scripture and the Role of the Seminary Professor in Forming Priests for the New Evangelization," 29–41.

studies are not only drawing the seminarian into exegetical competency but also a love of Christ so deep that it is impossible for him not to think of the thirst for souls that inhabited Christ upon the Cross? In a real way, the question of attracting persons who are furthest from Christ, the sinners and the non-Christians, is the crux of seminary Scripture studies. Without such passion for the Word of God, we tend toward the lowest common denominator and place Scripture somewhere on the continuum of liberal arts studies. In the seminary, however, the freest academy on earth, one can be so reasonable as to be open to the supernatural. Let us commit ourselves always to be so reasonable.

APPENDIX

CHAPTER 10

On the Importance of Biblical Hebrew
in Catholic Seminaries and Academic Institutions

André Villeneuve

> In Heaven only shall we be in possession of the clear truth. On earth,
> even in matters of Holy Scripture, our vision is dim. It distresses me to
> see the differences in its translations, and had I been a Priest I would have
> learned Hebrew, so as to read the Word of God as He deigned to utter it in
> human speech.
>
> ST. THÉRÈSE OF LISIEUX[1]

In all her simplicity, the Little Flower and Doctor of the Church St. Thérèse
of Lisieux arrived at a profound insight: When God first deigned to utter His
eternal word to man in human speech, He chose to do so in the Hebrew language. Of all the tongues spoken by man, it is first and foremost in Hebrew that
"the words of God, expressed in human language, have been made like human
discourse."[2]

Hebrew, Aramaic, and Greek studies are the *sine qua non* of biblical and
theological studies in any serious academic institution. The study of sacred
Scripture cannot go far below the surface without at least a basic knowledge of

---

1. "Counsels and Reminiscences of Soeur Therese, The Little Flower of Jesus," in St.
Thérèse of Lisieux, *The Story of a Soul*, trans. T. N. Taylor (London: Burns and Oates, 1912), 249.

2. Second Vatican Council, *Dei verbum* (November 18, 1965), www.vatican.va/archive
/hist_councils/ii_vatican_council/documents/vat-ii_const_19651118_dei-verbum_en.html,
§13.

the biblical languages. This investment in teaching them, however, is not always shared by Catholic seminaries and academic institutions, where language study is often overlooked in favor of other disciplines that are deemed more practical or useful. Moreover, if they give any attention to the Biblical languages at all, a disproportionate emphasis on Latin and Greek in Catholic institutions often comes at the expense of Hebrew.

The study of Latin is rightly privileged in Catholic seminaries of the Latin rite—as mandated by the Second Vatican Council and Canon Law—not only due to its significance for grasping the language of the liturgy and the Vulgate but also so that seminarians are able to "understand and make use of the sources of so many sciences and of the documents of the Church."[3] Likewise, the importance of Greek for the study of the New Testament is obvious. But are these reasons sufficient to justify a neglect of Hebrew, the original language of divine revelation and of the greater part of sacred Scripture?

The present paper argues that the current imbalance in scholarly attention paid to each of the biblical languages cannot be reasonably justified. One may ask why this disparity is so widespread: Is Hebrew deemed less important than Greek for the study of the sacred page? Is it too difficult to learn, so that it is only accessible to scholars and specialists? Is it neglected for theological reasons, because of neo-Marcionist[4] or supersessionist attitudes that tend to depreciate the value of the Old Testament? Is Hebrew perhaps given less attention because of a "classical bias" that has historically dominated Western education,

---

3. Second Vatican Council, *Optatam totius* (October 28, 1965), www.vatican.va/archive /hist_councils/ii_vatican_council/documents/vat-ii_decree_19651028_optatam-totius_en .html, §13, cf. *Code of Canon Law*, c. 249, in *Code of Canon Law: New English Translation* (Washington, DC: Canon Law Society of America, 1998), 76.

4. Marcion (c. 80-c. 155) was one of the most influential heretical Christians of the second century. He advanced the thesis that the Christian Gospel was wholly a Gospel of Love to the absolute exclusion of Law, leading him to completely reject Judaism and the Old Testament. He distinguished the inferior God of the Old Testament (Demiurge) and the superior God of the New Testament as two separate deities: the former was "fickle, capricious, ignorant, despotic, cruel," in sharp contrast to "the Supreme God of Love whom Jesus came to reveal." "Marcion" in F. L. Cross and E. A. Livingstone, eds., *The Oxford Dictionary of the Christian Church*, 3rd ed. rev. (Oxford: Oxford University Press, 2005), 1040; A.G. Padgett, "Marcion," in Ralph P. Martin and Peter H. Davids, eds., *Dictionary of the Later New Testament and Its Developments* (Downers Grove, IL: IVP Academic, 1997), 705–708; *CCC*, §123; Commission for Religious Relations with the Jews, "'The Gifts and the Calling of God Are Irrevocable' (Rom 11:29): A Reflection on Theological Questions Pertaining to Catholic-Jewish Relations" (December 10, 2015), www.ewtn.com/catholicism/library/gifts-of-god-are-irrevocable-2478.

traditionally favoring Latin and Greek over Hebrew and the Semitic languages?[5] Or do the rigors of language study simply clash with a pragmatist, utilitarian mentality that places more value on getting a quick, practical "return on investment" from academic studies geared toward pastoral work, rather than on the theological depth that comes with the knowledge of the sacred languages?

I would like to propose ten reasons why the serious study of Hebrew is essential—and at least as important as Greek and Latin—in Catholic seminaries and theological institutes. In so doing, I do not intend to present any groundbreaking arguments that have not already been made elsewhere. My goal is to contextualize these arguments for Catholics and to make a case as to why learning Hebrew is not an elitist task reserved for experts and biblical scholars (and Protestants!) but an imperative practice for all students of sacred Scripture in biblical and theological schools, including seminaries.

1. The Church Says So

> Seminarians should be provided with the opportunity to learn some elements of biblical Hebrew and Greek, through which they can engage with the original biblical texts. Special attention should also be given to a knowledge of the biblical culture and context, especially the history of the People of Israel, so as to improve the understanding of Sacred Scripture and to come to a proper relationship with the people of the Old Covenant.[6]

In her various documents on biblical studies and on priestly formation, the Church asserts that acquiring knowledge of the biblical languages is a foundational prerequisite to gain a sound understanding of the sacred Scriptures. The Second Vatican Council's *Decree on Priestly Training* emphasizes the priority of this task. Given the fact that seminarians must be prepared "for the ministry of the word: that they might understand ever more perfectly the revealed word of God,"[7] they need to be "formed with particular care in the study of the Bible,

---

5. David M. Green, "Why Study Biblical Hebrew," *Foundations*, no. 57 (Spring 2007): 25. This "classical bias" persists until today, despite a certain revival of Hebrew in the late Middle Ages and Renaissance led by the Christian Hebraists (see Jewish Virtual Library, "Christian Hebraists," www.jewishvirtuallibrary.org/hebraists-christian). Despite this revival, if any languages are taught in seminaries today, Latin is typically prioritized, followed by Greek, with Hebrew invariably in third place.

6. Congregation for Clergy, "The Gift of the Priestly Vocation: *Ratio Fundamentalis Institutionis Sacerdotalis*" (Vatican City: L'Osservatore Romano, December 8, 2016), §166.

7. *Optatam totius*, §4.

which ought to be, as it were, the soul of all theology."[8] For this reason, "a suitable knowledge of the languages of the Bible and of Tradition should be greatly encouraged."[9]

Along the same line, the USCCB's 2006 *Program of Priestly Formation* (PPF) asserts that "the various theological disciplines should recognize Sacred Scripture as foundational and as the point of departure and soul of all theology."[10] Therefore, a knowledge not only of Latin but also of the biblical languages is "foundational and should be given the emphasis that the Church accords it."[11]

The Church's insistence on the importance of learning the biblical languages is evident in two pioneering papal documents on the study of sacred Scripture. In his 1893 encyclical *Providentissimus Deus*, Pope Leo XIII encouraged the study of the biblical tongues, with a special emphasis on the Semitic languages, suggesting:

> It is most proper that Professors of Sacred Scripture and theologians should master those tongues in which the sacred Books were originally written; and it would be well that Church students also should cultivate them, more especially those who aspire to academic degrees. And endeavours should be made to establish in all academic institutions . . . chairs of the other ancient languages, *especially the Semitic*.[12]

Among the "Church students" who "aspire to academic degrees" today are certainly Catholic seminarians who will teach and preach the Word of God for most of their lives. Seminaries should therefore take seriously Leo's recommendation and provide ample opportunities for their students to cultivate the original languages of the sacred Books, "especially the Semitic."

Fifty years later, Pope Pius XII made a similar point, underlining the priority of biblical languages in his 1943 encyclical *Divino afflante Spiritu* on promoting biblical studies:

> In this our time, not only the Greek language . . . is familiar to almost all students of antiquity and letters, but the knowledge of Hebrew also and of [other] oriental languages has spread far and wide among literary men. Moreover there are now such abundant aids to the study of these languages

---

8. *Optatam totius*, §16; cf. *Dei verbum* §24.

9. *Optatam totius*, §13.

10. USCCB, *Program of Priestly Formation*, (Washington, DC: USCCB, 2006), §198.

11. USCCB, *Program of Priestly Formation*, §182.

12. Pope Leo XIII, *Providentissimus Deus* (November 18, 1893), www.vatican.va/content/leo-xiii/en/encyclicals/documents/hf_l-xiii_enc_18111893_providentissimus-deus.html, §17; emphasis added.

that the biblical scholar, who by neglecting them would deprive himself of access to the original texts, could in no wise escape the stigma of levity and sloth. For it is the duty of the exegete to lay hold, so to speak, with the greatest care and reverence of the very least expressions which, under the inspiration of the Divine Spirit, have flowed from the pen of the sacred writer, so as to arrive at a deeper and fuller knowledge of his meaning.[13]

For Pius XII, the knowledge of not only Greek but also Hebrew is so essential to arrive at a "deeper and fuller knowledge" of the meaning of the words communicated by the Holy Spirit to the sacred writer that the biblical scholar is not at liberty to neglect this task, lest he be accused of "levity and sloth"!

The recent magisterial documents of the Catholic Church thus underline the importance of acquiring a familiarity with the biblical languages as a basic prerequisite for the study of sacred Scripture.

2. The Holy Language

When people of different nationalities love each other, they usually learn one another's language. Why do the children of God, especially those who are cultured, not learn the original languages of the Bible?[14]

Hebrew is the principal language of divine inspiration and revelation. As seen in the following table, approximately two-thirds of the Catholic Bible was originally revealed and written in Hebrew (including a few chapters written in its close Semitic cousin, Aramaic):

	NUMBER OF VERSES (NAB)	PERCENT
Hebrew (& Aramaic) OT	23,209 (ca. 269 in Aramaic)	65.3%
Greek OT (LXX additions)	4,362	12.3%
Greek NT	7,956	22.4%
Total	35,527	100%

Yet the significance of Hebrew for the study of sacred Scripture is much more than a quantitative one. For those who hold to a high view of divine inspiration, the Hebrew Old Testament records and transmits to us the actual words God used to reveal Himself to Israel and to the world. By contrast, the sayings

---

13. Pope Pius XII, *Divino afflante spiritu* (September 30, 1943), www.vatican.va/content/pius-xii/en/encyclicals/documents/hf_p-xii_enc_30091943_divino-afflante-spiritu.html, §15.

14. Richard Wurmbrand, *If Prison Walls Could Speak* (London: Hodder & Stoughton, 1974), 95.

of Jesus as recorded in the Greek Gospels and New Testament are, for the most part, not his actual words but a translation. Even though Jesus would likely have been conversant in Greek, in all probability he read and quoted the Scriptures in their original Hebrew and preached and explained them in Aramaic, the commonly spoken language of the Jews in Galilee and Judea at the time.[15]

Because it is the language of sacred texts, the rabbis consider Hebrew itself to be sacred and imbued with a deep mystical meaning. The sacredness of Hebrew even goes back to the origins of the universe. In Jewish tradition, it is the language of creation, the language that God spoke when he uttered the words that brought the world into existence:

> In post-biblical times, [Hebrew] was referred to as *lashon ha-kodesh*, the holy language. Hebrew was often thought to be the language of the angels, and indeed, of God. According to rabbinic tradition, Hebrew was the original language of humanity. It was spoken by all of humankind prior to the dispersion described in the Tower of Babel story in Genesis. In addition, the Hebrew language was thought of as the tool that God used to create the world.[16]

Rabbi Louis Jacobs further comments on the divine origin and cosmic role of Hebrew:

> In [Jewish] mystical texts, Hebrew is the original language of mankind and is God's language, the language in which He "spoke" to Moses and the prophets. For the mystics, Hebrew letters are not mere conventions, as are the letters of other languages, but represent on Earth spiritual, cosmic forces.[17]

Jewish mystics even consider the Hebrew letters to be a sort of divine DNA that when studied could reveal secrets of the cosmos. Consequently, every word and letter of the Hebrew Bible is significant and divinely inspired:

15. Green, "Why Study Biblical Hebrew," 26.

16. 7 Things You Should Know About Hebrew, My Jewish Learning, www.myjewish learning.com/culture/2/Languages/Hebrew.shtml. On the mystical and cosmic role of the Hebrew language, see also "Hebrew: In Ancient Jewish Scriptures," Jewish Virtual Library, www.jewishvirtuallibrary.org/jsource/Judaism/hebscripture.html, and Dan Cohn-Sherbok, "Creation Mysticism: Fashioning the World from Letters," My Jewish Learning, www .myjewishlearning.com/beliefs/Theology/Kabbalah_and_Mysticism/Origins/Creation _Mysticism.shtml.

17. Louis Jacobs, "Hebrew: Its History and Centrality," My Jewish Learning, archived at the Internet Archive, web.archive.org/web/20150303000628/http://www.myjewishlearning .com/culture/2/Languages/Hebrew/History_and_Centrality.shtml.

In traditional Jewish thought, each letter–its name, pictorial form,[18] numerical equivalent, and respective position in the alphabet–is ordained by God. As a corollary of this principle, Jewish law has decreed for millennia that every letter of a Torah scroll must be perfect, or else the entire scroll is forbidden to be used.[19]

Whether or not these religious claims are true, and even if they are dismissed as the product of pious legends, they do reveal the high regard that devout Jews have for the inspired text of the Hebrew Bible. Should Catholics—and especially future priests—not approach the sacred page with at least as much reverence, devotion and love?

One early Catholic pioneer who was convinced of the importance of Hebrew in the Church is St. Jerome. Commissioned by Pope Damasus around AD 382 to revise the Latin translation of the Gospels—which existed in a multiplicity of versions—Jerome eventually set out to correct and improve the Latin text of the Old Testament.[20]

Although Jerome originally worked from the Septuagint, he ultimately became convinced of its inadequacy as a primary source for his work and acknowledged that only a manuscript in the original Hebrew could be a satisfactory source for the production of his Latin translation. Around 390, Jerome decided to start anew and produce his own translation of the "Hebrew verity" (*Hebraica veritas*).[21] Perhaps influenced by the Jewish scholars who taught him Hebrew, Jerome believed in the superiority and even sanctity of the Hebrew text, a position he held despite controversy and opposition.[22] Although he

---

18. The Hebrew alphabet was originally written using a pictographic script. See www .hebrew4christians.com/Grammar/Unit_One/Pictograms/pictograms.html.

19. Edward Hoffman, *The Hebrew Alphabet: A Mystical Journey* (San Francisco: Chronicle, 1998), as quoted in My Jewish Learning, www.myjewishlearning.com/culture/2/Languages /Hebrew/Letters_and_Vocabulary/Mystical_Hebrew/Letters_in_Mysticism.shtml.

20. "Vulgate," in *Catholic Bible Dictionary*, ed. Scott Hahn (New York: Image, 2009), 944.

21. P. R. Ackroyd and C. F. Evans, eds., *The Cambridge History of the Bible: Volume 1, From the Beginnings to Jerome* (Cambridge: Cambridge University Press, 1975), 515; Stefan Rebenich, "Jerome: The 'Vir Trilinguis' and the 'Hebraica Veritas,'" *Vigiliae Christianae* 47, no. 1 (1993): 52; Leslie J. Hoppe, OFM, "St. Jerome: The Perils of a Bible Translator," *St. Anthony Messenger*, September 1997, www.smp.org/resourcecenter/resource/2637/.

22. Some of Jerome's contemporaries, such as Ephiphanius and Rufinus, rejected his approach because they recognized the Septuagint as the only true and legitimate version of the Old Testament. They perceived Jerome's recourse to the *hebraica veritas* as a rejection of the "divinely inspired" Septuagint and a "judaization" of the Old Testament that deviated from Christian tradition! (Rebenich, "Jerome," 53, 63; Ackroyd and Evans, *The Cambridge History of the Bible*, 521).

generally favored a "dynamic equivalency" approach to translation, Jerome held the Scriptures to be in a class apart that required a more precise, word-for-word translation.[23]

Jerome thus concurred with the rabbis: He was convinced that Hebrew, being "God's language," possesses an inherent sanctity and mystical meaning that is conveyed only partially and imperfectly in even the best translation.

3. Bridging the Historical, Geographical, and Cultural Gap

> For what was originally expressed in Hebrew does not have exactly the same sense when translated into another language. Not only this work, but even the law itself, the prophecies, and the rest of the books differ not a little as originally expressed.[24]

The Greek translator of the Book of Sirach, writing only two generations after his grandfather authored the book, expresses dissatisfaction with his own translation, which by his own account "[differs] not a little" from the original Hebrew text. If this is the case for a work that was translated from Hebrew to Greek barely sixty years after it was authored, not too geographically distant from its place of origin,[25] what happens to a text that is read in translation thousands of years after it was written, thousands of miles away from its geographical setting, in a language and culture radically different from its original Semitic context?

To illustrate how a language changes over time, I usually ask a student in my beginner's Hebrew class to read a passage from Chaucer's *Canterbury Tales* (ca. 1386), such as the following:

> O Cupide, out of alle charitee!
> O regne, that wolt no felawe have with thee!
> Ful sooth is seyd that love ne lordshipe
> Wol noght, hir thankes, have no felaweshipe.
> Wel fynden that Arcite and Palamoun.[26]

23. "For I myself not only admit but freely proclaim that in translating from the Greek (except in the case of the holy scriptures where even the order of the words is a mystery) I render sense for sense and not word for word." Jerome, Epistle 57.5, as quoted in Ackroyd and Evans, *The Cambridge History of the Bible*, 523.

24. Sirach, Prologue (RSV2CE).

25. Most scholars agree that Sirach was written in or near Jerusalem and translated in Egypt, probably in Alexandria.

26. Chaucer, *The Knight's Tale, Part II: An Interlinear Translation*, sites.fas.harvard.edu /~chaucer/teachslf/kt-par2.htm, lines 1623–1627.

After I give the students a minute or two to try to decipher the medieval English, I make my point: If a text is barely comprehensible when read *in the same language* some 630 years after it was written, how much more is "lost in translation" in the vast gap of 2,500–3,000 years that stand between the original text of the Hebrew Bible and our modern English translations—not to mention the geographical and cultural gap that exists between the ancient Semitic culture of the Levant and twenty-first century North America. Does this great chasm not justify the study of the language of divine revelation if one is serious about understanding what God has to tell us?

4. Understanding the Old Testament

Reading the Bible in translation is like kissing your new bride through a veil.

The above quote, attributed to the Jewish poet Haim Nachman Bialik (1873–1934), poetically expresses the reality that reading a translation of the Bible is like "listening to God through an interpreter, rather than hearing directly."[27] Indeed, every translation is an interpretation, because every language has nuances, expressions, idioms and ideas that are difficult or impossible to translate accurately.

Semitic languages in particular are quite different from English and other European languages that derive from Greek and Latin—and not just because they are read from right to left. Generally, Biblical Hebrew is less precise than English (and Greek), one reason being that it has no verbal tenses or moods. Although the Hebrew perfect, participle, and imperfect somewhat resemble the English past, present, and future, this is not a perfect equivalence.[28] Moreover, the absence of moods makes it difficult to differentiate between statements of fact, doubtful assertions, wishes, or commands. Statements that may seem clear or precise in Greek or in English can be quite ambiguous in Hebrew, so that words must derive their meaning from context much more than in the classical and European languages.[29]

In other cases, Hebrew is more precise than English. For example, whereas modern English has only one second person pronoun (you), Hebrew has four:

27. Green, "Why Study Biblical Hebrew," 23.

28. For example, although the imperfect tense denotes an incomplete or continuous action that is most commonly rendered as the future tense in English, it sometimes better reflects the present or even past tense (e.g., "a mist [continually] went up from the earth," Gen 2:6). See n. 34 below.

29. Green, "Why Study Biblical Hebrew," 27.

אַתָּה (*atah*, masculine singular), אַתְּ (*at*, feminine singular), אַתֶּם (*atem*, masculine plural), אַתֵּן (*aten*, feminine plural). When reading texts that contain a lot of dialogue such as the Song of Songs, for example, this is crucial. The ambiguity of the English pronoun "you" makes it virtually impossible for an English reader to read the Song and know exactly who is speaking to whom. This is why some translations add superscriptions throughout the text ("HE" and "SHE") in order to identify the speaker.

This element of translation can even cause the obscuring of entire passages of Scripture. A good example is seen in Genesis 18, which narrates the Lord's appearance to Abraham while he is simultaneously visited by three men. The Hebrew text is full of ambiguity that cannot be conveyed in modern translations. Who is speaking to Abraham? Is it the Lord, or the three men? In Genesis 18:3, according to the NAB, Abraham says "Sir, if it please you, do not go on past your servant." According to the RSV, Abraham addresses his visitor(s) as "My lord." Which is it? The Hebrew says *Adonai* (אֲדֹנָי), which could mean "Lord," "my lord," "my lords," or "Sir," but Abraham then goes on to address his guest(s) in the singular. Is Abraham speaking to God or to the three men? An English translation must inevitably decide one way or another, thus dissolving the tension and mystery that is inherent (and likely intentional) in the Hebrew text.

Behind a language stands a whole mentality and worldview. Unlike Greek, which is precise, descriptive, and excellent in communicating abstractions, Hebrew is concrete, action-centered, and lacking in abstract terms. For the Hebrews, "truth was not so much an idea to be contemplated as an experience to be lived, a deed to be done."[30] The active Semitic mentality is reflected in the Hebrew sentence structure, which usually begins with the verb. Hebrew has been called "a language of the senses" in which words primarily expressed "concrete or material things and movements or actions which struck the senses or started the emotions."[31] Hebraisms often communicate abstract thoughts or immaterial conceptions by means of material or physical terminology:

> "Look" is "lift up the eyes" (Gen. 22:4); "be angry" is "burn in one's nostrils" (Exod. 4:14); "disclose something to another" or "reveal" is "unstop someone's ears" (Ruth 4:4); "have no compassion" is "hard-heartedness" (1 Sam. 6:6); "stubborn" is "stiff-necked" (2 Chr. 30:8; cf. Acts 7:51); "get ready" or

---

30. Marvin R. Wilson, *Our Father Abraham: Jewish Roots of the Christian Faith* (Grand Rapids, MI: Eerdmans, 1990), 136.

31. Wilson, *Our Father Abraham*, 137.

"brace oneself" is "gird up the loins" (Jer. 1:17); and "to be determined to go" is "set one's face to go" (Jer. 42:15, 17; cf. Luke 9:51).[32]

Moreover, some Hebrew terms—often theologically significant ones—are virtually untranslatable. A well-known example is the word *hesed*, whose usual translations ("mercy," "loving kindness," or "steadfast love") all lack the essential quality of covenant loyalty.[33]

Other important theological insights are easily missed without knowledge of Hebrew. For example, from the perspective of Christian (Trinitarian) theology, it is significant that the most common word used for God, אֱלֹהִים (*Elohim*) is in the plural. Likewise, the name of the Lord, יְהוָה (YaHWeH), is of little meaning in English, but is pregnant with meaning in Hebrew as a combination of the perfect, participle, and imperfect forms of the verb "to be," which could be loosely rendered as "was" = הָיָה (*hayah*), "is" = הֹוֶה (*howeh*), and "will be" = יִהְיֶה (*yihyeh*).[34] Thus, the very name of the Lord connotes eternity when read in Hebrew.

Moreover, the concept of the "Law" is misunderstood by many Christians due to an ignorance of the Hebrew language. Pious Jews rarely refer to the "Torah" as "law." They simply say "Torah," because the term has a meaning that is not accurately conveyed by "law" (which has the connotation of an undesirable burden of legal obligations). The word Torah (תּוֹרָה) derives from the root יָרָה (*yarah*), which means to throw, to cast, or to shoot (an arrow) and hit the mark. This is also the root of the word "teacher" (מֹורֶה—*moreh*), so Torah really means "instruction" or "teaching" more than "law." This conveys a very different relationship between mankind and God. We are not delinquents, but pupils striving to realize His goal for us, and He is not law enforcer, but tutor providing instruction on how to get there. Thus the Torah is something like an instruction manual that helps man to "hit the mark" and reach the purpose for which he was made, in contrast to "sin," which is to miss the mark of our vocation as children of God, created in His image and likeness.

Also, much is lost in translation in the rich realm of Hebrew names. For the Hebrews, names are not just a label; they express the very identity of the

---

32. Wilson, *Our Father Abraham*, 137.

33. Green, "Why Study Biblical Hebrew," 27.

34. David W. Baker, "God, Names Of," in *Dictionary of the Old Testament: Pentateuch*, ed. T. Desmond Alexander and David W. Baker (Downers Grove, IL: InterVarsity, 2003), 362. The perfect, participle, and imperfect in Biblical Hebrew are not exactly the equivalent of the past, present, and future tense (as in modern Hebrew), but they are usually translated as such because they roughly denote, respectively, a completed, ongoing, and incomplete action.

person. This is seen, for example, in the description of the birth of the sons of Jacob in Genesis 29:31–30:23, where the name of each son is a pun related to the circumstances of his birth. With no knowledge of Hebrew, the entire pericope remains opaque. Some examples:

> Leah conceived and bore a son (בֵּן), and she called his name Reuben (רְאוּבֵן— Reu'ven = "look, a son"). (Gen 29:32)

> "This time will I praise (root ידה—*yadah* = to praise) the LORD;" therefore she called his name Judah (יְהוּדָה—*Yehudah* = "praised"). (Gen 29:35)[35]

Likewise, it is difficult to see the connection in English between the names Joshua, Hosea, Elisha, Isaiah, and Jesus. When read in Hebrew, however,[36] it is immediately evident that these names are all closely related, being all based on the same Hebrew root for "salvation" (יֵשַׁע—*yesha* or יְשׁוּעָה—*yeshuah*).

Often, a name can reveal much about a person's character or mission. Consider, for example, the names of the prophets Ezekiel (יְחֶזְקֵאל = "God strengthens"), Nahum (נַחוּם = comfort, compassion), and Habakkuk (חֲבַקּוּק = embrace, or "hug").

The Hebrew Bible is also full of literary and poetical devices, and puns that are entirely lost in translation. For example:

> The LORD God formed man (הָאָדָם—*ha'adam*) of dust from the ground (הָאֲדָמָה—*ha'adamah*). (Gen 2:7)

> Therefore its name was called Babel (בָּבֶל—*bavel*), because there the LORD confused (בָּלַל—*balal*) the language of all the earth. (Gen 11:9)

Note the alliterations in the following examples, such as the repetition of the sounds "*she*" and "*sha*" in the well-known psalm:

> Pray for the peace of Jerusalem! May they prosper who love you! (שַׁאֲלוּ שְׁלוֹם יְרוּשָׁלָ͏ִם יִשְׁלָיוּ אֹהֲבָיִךְ—*sha'alu sh'lom Yerushalayim, yishlayu ohavayich*). (Ps 122:6)

> . . . and he looked for justice (מִשְׁפָּט—*mishpat*), but behold, bloodshed (מִשְׂפָּח—*mispach*); for righteousness (צְדָקָה—*tsedakah*), but behold, a cry (צְעָקָה—*tse'akah*)! (Isa 5:7)

Acrostics are another literary device that are completely lost in translation, that is, texts where every line or verse begins with the next letter of the Hebrew alphabet (e.g., Pss 34; 111–112; 119; 145; Prov 31; Lamentations).

---

35. Cf. also Gen 49:8: "Judah, your brothers shall praise you" (יוֹדוּךְ—*yodukha*).

36. Respectively: יְהוֹשֻׁעַ—*Yehoshua*, הוֹשֵׁעַ—*Hoshea*, יְשַׁעְיָהוּ—*Yeshayahu*, אֱלִישָׁע—*Elisha*, יֵשׁוּעַ—*Yeshua*.

These few examples suffice to demonstrate the limitations of translations and to raise again the question: Should Catholics—and especially future priests—be content with "listening to God through an interpreter"? God's word is worthy of some investment in time and effort, so that we may understand as accurately as possible what the Lord has to say to His people.

5. Understanding Jesus and the New Testament

> The Hebrew language is the best language of all ... If I were younger I would want to learn this language, because no one can really understand the Scriptures without it. For although the New Testament is written in Greek, it is full of Hebraisms and Hebrew expressions. It has therefore been aptly said that the Hebrews drink from the spring, the Greeks from the stream that flows from it, and the Latins from a downstream pool.[37]

Although the author cited here does not exactly hold the highest authority for Catholics, there is much truth in this particular statement of his. Even though the New Testament is written in Greek, it remains a thoroughly Jewish book, written almost entirely by Jewish authors who spoke Hebrew.[38] This means that a knowledge of Hebrew is essential not only for understanding the Old Testament, but for entering into the mind of the New as well. "Jesus was and always remained a Jew,"[39] an observant, orthodox Jew who knew, spoke, and prayed in Hebrew. We must always keep in mind that "the Son of God is incarnate in a people and a human family"[40]—that is, the eternal Word became flesh as a Jewish, Hebrew-speaking man who was "at home in the Jewish tradition of his time, and was decisively shaped by this religious milieu."[41]

One may ask, then, to what extent it is possible to really know Jesus in his humanity—his *Jewish* humanity—without some understanding of Judaism and the Hebraic mindset. The latest document of the Commission for Religious

37. Martin Luther, *Table Talk*, as quoted in Pinchas E. Lapide, *Hebrew in the Church* (Grand Rapids, MI: Eerdmans, 1984), x.

38. Cf. Acts 21:40; 22:2; 26:14; John 5:2; 20:16. Luke is probably the only NT author who was not Jewish.

39. Commission for Religious Relations with the Jews, "Notes on the Correct Way to Present Jews and Judaism in Preaching and Catechesis in the Roman Catholic Church" (1985), www.ewtn.com/catholicism/library/notes-on-the-correct-way-to-present-the-jews-and-judaism-in-preaching-and-catechesis-in-the-roman--catholic-church-2480/.

40. Commission for Religious Relations with the Jews, "Notes," III.4.

41. Commission for Religious Relations with the Jews, "The Gifts and the Calling," 14.

Relations with the Jews makes the same point: "One cannot understand Jesus' teaching or that of his disciples without situating it within the Jewish horizon in the context of the living tradition of Israel; one would understand his teachings even less so if they were seen in opposition to this tradition."[42]

Green notes that because of the "classical bias," however, New Testament Greek has been historically viewed "through the lens of classical Greek, rather than through the lens of Hebrew or Aramaic, the first language(s) of all but one of the New Testament authors."[43] In their book *Understanding the Difficult Words of Jesus*, Bivin and Blizzard forcefully underline why Hebrew is essential in order to understand Jesus' Semitic and Jewish culture:

> It should be emphasized that the Bible (both Old *and* New Testaments) is, in its entirety, highly Hebraic. In spite of the fact that portions of the New Testament were communicated in Greek, the background is thoroughly Hebrew. The writers are Hebrew, the culture is Hebrew, the religion is Hebrew, the traditions are Hebrew, and the concepts are Hebrew.[44]

Many of Jesus' sayings are Hebrew idioms, so that "many Gospel expressions are not just poor Greek, but actually meaningless in Greek."[45] Difficult or cryptic expressions in Greek, often mistranslated in English, become clear when one discovers the Hebraisms that lie behind them. Take, for example, Jesus' statement in Matthew 6:22-23: "The eye is the lamp of the body. So, if your eye is sound, your whole body will be full of light; but if your eye is not sound, your whole body will be full of darkness." What is the meaning of this? It turns out that the puzzling expression in English (and in Greek) becomes quite clear when approached from a Hebraic perspective, for the expressions "good eye" and "bad eye" are common Hebrew idioms for "generous" and "miserly."[46]

Bivin and Blizzard go as far as to say that the Synoptic Gospels are "not really Greek, but Hebrew words in Greek dress." They argue that there is much evidence pointing to Hebrew sources lying behind the present Greek texts, including hundreds of semitisms in the Gospels and the testimony of several Church Fathers who assert that the Gospel of Matthew was originally written

---

42. Commission for Religious Relations with the Jews, "The Gifts and the Calling," 14.

43. Green, "Why Study Biblical Hebrew," 25.

44. David Bivin and Roy Blizzard, *Understanding the Difficult Words of Jesus: New Insights from a Hebrew Perspective* (Shippensburg, PA: Destiny Image Publishers, 1994), Kindle edition, loc. 81.

45. Bivin and Blizzard, *Understanding the Difficult Words of Jesus*, loc. 151.

46. Bivin and Blizzard, *Understanding the Difficult Words of Jesus*, loc. 153.

in Hebrew.[47] On the basis of this evidence, Bivin and Blizzard state in no uncertain terms:

> It is most unfortunate that our Bible colleges and seminaries focus their attention on Greek and Hellenistic theology, and fail, by and large, to equip their students with the proper tools that would allow them to do serious biblical exegesis. A strong statement, to be sure; but sadly, all too true. *It cannot be overemphasized*, that the key to an understanding of the New Testament is a fluent knowledge of Hebrew and an intimate acquaintance with Jewish history, culture, and Rabbinic Literature.[48]

To take another simple example, consider the angel's instructions to Joseph concerning the naming of Jesus. These do not make much sense either in English or Greek: "She will bear a son, and you shall call his name Jesus ('Ιησοῦς), for he will save (σώσει) his people from their sins" (Matt 1:21). When the verse is translated back into Hebrew, however, the reason for Jesus' name is evident: "She will bear a son, and you shall call his name Jesus (יֵשׁוּעַ—*Yeshua*), for he will save (יוֹשִׁיעַ—*yoshia*) his people from their sins" (Matt 1:21). *Yeshua* and *yoshia* share the same root יָשַׁע—*yasha*, which means to rescue or save.

Hebrew and Aramaic words and idioms are found throughout the Greek New Testament. Some of the better known include *mammon, abba, korban,* and *"Eli Eli lama sabachtani."* When Jesus declares, "You will not see me again, until you say, 'blessed is he who comes (בָּרוּךְ הַבָּא—*baruch haba*) in the name of the Lord.'" (Matt 23:39), the translation fails to convey that the expression *baruch haba* simply means "welcome" in Hebrew. In other words, Jesus says that he will not return until Jerusalem welcomes him as their Messiah.[49] And when he says "peace be with you" (שָׁלוֹם לָכֶם—*shalom lachem*, or *shalom aleichem*) to his disciples, what sounds like a solemn episcopal blessing for

---

47. "Now Matthew collected the oracles in the Hebrew language, and each one interpreted them as he was able" [Papias, quoted in Eusebius of Caesarea, *Ecclesiastical History*, book 3, chapter 39]; "Now Matthew published among the Hebrews in their own language a written Gospel, also" [Irenaeus, quoted in Eusebius, *Eccl. Hist.* 5.8; cf. Irenaeus, *Against Heresies* book 3, chapter 1, paragraph 1]. Eusebius of Caesarea, *Ecclesiastical History, Books 1–5*, ed. and trans. Roy Joseph Deferrari, FaCh 19 (Washington, DC: Catholic University of America Press, 1953), 206, 297. Cf. also Origen in Eusebius, *Eccl. Hist.* 6.25; Epiphanius of Salamis, *Refutation of All Heresies* section 29, part 9, sentence 4; Jerome of Stridon, *De Viris Inlustribus*, chapter 3.

48. Bivin and Blizzard, *Understanding the Difficult Words of Jesus*, loc. 159–62. Emphasis in the original.

49. Daniel Botkin, "The Importance of Studying Hebrew," robt.shepherd.tripod.com /ivrit.html.

Catholics is in fact a common, informal Jewish and Semitic greeting (as is its Arabic equivalent, *assalam aleikum*).

In its 2002 document "The Jewish People and their Sacred Scriptures in the Christian Bible," the Pontifical Biblical Commission notes that Jewish exegetical methods are frequently employed in the New Testament. These include Second Temple methods of interpretation, similarities in how the New Testament and the Qumran community make use of the Hebrew Scriptures, and rabbinic methods of exegesis. The frequent use of rabbinic styles of argumentation thus "undoubtedly attests that the New Testament emerged from the matrix of Judaism and that it is infused with the mentality of Jewish biblical commentators."[50]

In short, as Leslie Allen rightly states, "it is strange but true that knowledge of Hebrew makes one at home in the Greek New Testament."[51] Is it right, then, to deprive Catholic seminarians and future priests of such essential keys to unlock and access the sacred Scriptures? Pawlikowski warns that this deficiency impacts not only exegesis but also Christian spirituality:

> Christians are coming to recognize that without deep immersion into the spirit of the Hebrew Scriptures, they are left with a truncated vision of Jesus' message—which in fact relied heavily on "the Scriptures"—and hence an emaciated version of Christian spirituality.[52]

Hence, we see that the usefulness of Biblical Hebrew is not limited to the Old Testament. It is also essential in order to understand the words of the Jewish Jesus and the message of the New Testament, which is thoroughly immersed in Hebrew thought and culture.

---

50. Pontifical Biblical Commission, *The Jewish People and Their Sacred Scriptures in the Christian Bible* (Vatican City: Libreria Editrice Vaticana, 2002), 12–15.

51. Leslie C. Allen, "Why Not Learn Hebrew?," *TSF Bulletin* 30 (1961): 4.

52. John T. Pawlikowski, "The Re-Judaization of Christianity," *Immanuel* 22/23 (1989): 61. Likewise, Marvin Wilson adds: "The authors of God's Word—virtually every one of them a Jew—have a profoundly Hebraic perspective on life and the world. If we are to interpret the Bible correctly, we must become attuned to this Hebraic setting in the ancient Near East. Thus we must look primarily not to Athens but to Jerusalem for the biblical view of reality. For the prophets and apostles produced a Book that is, without question, Hebraic in composition and orientation.... Our tutors to Christ are Moses and the Prophets, and not Plato and the Academies." Wilson, *Our Father Abraham*, 9.

6. Praying the Psalms

> In the liturgy of the hours the Church in large measure prays through the magnificent songs that the Old Testament authors composed under the inspiration of the Holy Spirit. The origin of these verses gives them great power to raise the mind to God, to inspire devotion, to evoke gratitude in times of favor, and to bring consolation and courage in times of trial.[53]

The psalms are at the heart of the Hebrew Bible, a "microcosm" of the Old Testament that summarizes—albeit in non-systematic fashion—all the great themes of salvation history, from creation to the patriarchs, the Exodus and wilderness wanderings, the Israelite monarchy, the Babylonian exile, and the return to Zion.[54]

Jesus prayed the psalms in Hebrew. He meditated upon them throughout his life and saw himself as their ultimate fulfillment. All four evangelists—with the other writers of the New Testament—apply the psalms to Jesus in order to disclose his identity and mission. Indeed, the Psalter is the most quoted Old Testament book in the New Testament.[55] One thinks, for example, of God's "son" in Psalm 2,[56] of "the LORD said to my Lord" in Psalm 110,[57] or of the use of Psalm 118 in all four Gospels, bringing together themes such as "the stone which the builders rejected has become the cornerstone" (v. 22),[58] Israel's call for the Lord's salvation through the acclamation *Hoshana* (v. 25), and the words "blessed is he who comes in the name of the Lord" (v. 26) that are to welcome Jesus when he returns.[59]

The Psalter is also the beating heart of both the synagogue and the Church—and a potential bridge between them. Both communities of faith have been praying the Psalms with devotion and love since biblical times. Used as "hymnbook" in the Temple until its destruction, they were integrated in the Jewish liturgy that developed after the fall of Jerusalem, becoming the "spiritual girders of the synagogue worship."[60] The Psalms also became part of the

---

53. Congregation for Divine Worship, *General Instruction of the Liturgy of the Hours* (February 2, 1971), www.ewtn.com/catholicism/library/general-instruction-on-the-liturgy-of-the-hours-2175/, §100.

54. C. Hassell Bullock, *Encountering the Book of Psalms: A Literary and Theological Introduction, Encountering Biblical Studies* (Grand Rapids, MI: Baker Academic, 2004), 99–118.

55. Bullock, *Encountering the Book of Psalms*, 89.

56. Cf. Acts 13:33; Heb 1:5; 5:5.

57. Cf. Matt 22:44; Mark 12:36; Luke 20:42; Acts 2:34; Heb 1:13.

58. Cf. Matt 21:42; Mark 12:10–11; Luke 20:17; Acts 4:11; 1 Pet 2:7.

59. Cf. Matt 21:9; Matt 23:39; Mark 11:9–10; Luke 13:35; 19:38; John 12:13.

60. Bullock, *Encountering the Book of Psalms*, 93.

liturgy of the early Church and integral to the writings of the Fathers. St. Athanasius called the Psalter "an epitome of the whole Scriptures," and Basil of Caesarea saw it as "a compendium of all theology."[61] Today, the Psalms are prayed in every Eucharistic liturgy, and they form the core of the Liturgy of the Hours. It may indeed be said that "no collection of poems has ever exercised as much influence on the Western world as the Book of Psalms."[62]

The Psalms are moving when prayed in any language, but they are particularly beautiful and powerful when prayed in the original Hebrew, communicating the raw emotion of their human authors, the nuances and poignant expressions of Hebrew poetry, and the power of their divine inspiration.

What better way to pray the psalms with "new warmth" and to come to a deeper understanding of them, than to learn the original language in which they were composed, prayed and sung?

7. Recovering Our Jewish Roots

> Without her Jewish roots the Church would be in danger of losing its soteriological anchoring in salvation history and would slide into an ultimately unhistorical Gnosis.[63]

The importance of Hebrew in the Church touches upon the broader issue of the Jewish roots of the Christian faith. It is now widely acknowledged that Christianity suffered no small loss as it gradually separated itself from its Hebrew and Jewish heritage in the early centuries of the Church. Kurt Cardinal Koch, president of the Pontifical Council for Promoting Christian Unity and the Pontifical Commission for Religious Relations with the Jews, is one of many scholars and churchmen who are convinced that "the schism between synagogue and church forms the first split in the history of the church."[64] Fr. Raniero Cantalamessa, Preacher to the Papal Household, concurs. He sees the original split between Judaism and Christianity as the "proto-schism" that has historically impoverished Catholicism by the loss of living contact with its Judaic roots. In Cantalamessa's words, "the great original schism afflicting the Church and

---

61. Cf. Tremper Longman III, *How to Read the Psalms* (Downers Grove, IL: IVP Academic, 1988), 52.

62. Bullock, *Encountering the Book of Psalms*, 15.

63. Commission for Religious Relations with the Jews, "The Gifts and the Calling," 13.

64. Kurt Cardinal Koch, "Theological Questions and Perspectives in Jewish-Catholic Dialogue," *Studies in Christian-Jewish Relations* 7, no. 1 (January 5, 2012): 1, ejournals.bc.edu/ojs/index.php/scjr/article/view/2072.

impoverishing it is not so much the schism between East and West or between Catholics and Protestants, as the more radical one between the Church and Israel."[65]

The impoverishment caused by the loss of the Church's Hebrew and Jewish roots has had far-reaching consequences. What began as a shift from Hebrew to Greek thought and culture soon led to the development of supersessionist (or "replacement") theology claiming—contrary to Scripture (see Rom 11:28–29)—that God had rejected Israel as His chosen people and replaced them by the Church.[66] From there, the "primal rift" between Jews and Christians led to the gradual deterioration of the relationship between them so that "the awareness of belonging to the same family was gradually lost."[67] With the historic triumph of Christianity, what began as religious polemics devolved into discriminatory, anti-Jewish legislation and "great strain and hostility which has in many cases unfortunately led to anti-Jewish attitudes involving outbreaks of violence and pogroms against the Jews."[68]

The Church suffered the prolonged hardship of this division for too long—a division that unfortunately tarnished her witness of Christ to the Jewish people. In 1965, the Vatican II declaration *Nostra aetate* sought to amend this by authoritatively and definitively rejecting the heritage of supersessionism and anti-Semitism. *Nostra aetate* set the Church on a new course—or rather, a corrected course—that was more faithful to the biblical and Jewish foundations of the Christian faith. It not only acknowledged the permanence of God's covenant with Israel but also recalled that the Church "draws sustenance from the root of that well-cultivated olive tree"—a well-known

---

65. Raniero Cantalamessa, *The Mystery of Christmas: A Comment on the Magnificat, Gloria, Nunc Dimittis* (Collegeville, MN: Liturgical Press, 1989), quoted in "Christ, the Glory of Israel: A Chapter from *The Mystery of Christmas*," Catholics for Israel, www.catholicsforisrael.com /articles/israel-and-the-church/100-christ-the-glory-of-israel.

66. The Commission for Religious Relations with the Jews describes supersessionism as follows: "The promises and commitments of God would no longer apply to Israel because it had not recognized Jesus as the Messiah and the Son of God, but had been transferred to the Church of Jesus Christ which was now the true 'new Israel', the new chosen people of God." "The Gifts and the Calling," 17.

67. Koch, "Theological Questions," 1.

68. Koch, "Theological Questions," 1. For surveys of the history of Christian anti-Semitism, see James Parkes, *The Conflict of the Church and the Synagogue: A Study in the Origins of Antisemitism* (Cleveland: Meridian, 1961); Edward Flannery, *The Anguish of the Jews: Twenty-Three Centuries of Antisemitism*, 2nd ed. (New York: Paulist, 2004); Michael L. Brown, *Our Hands Are Stained with Blood* (Shippensburg, PA: Destiny Image, 1992); William Nicholls, *Christian Antisemitism: A History of Hate* (Northvale, NJ: Jason Aronson, Inc., 1995).

metaphor for Israel in the Old Testament.[69] This point is repeated even more emphatically in the aptly titled document, "The Gifts and Calling of God are Irrevocable" (§34): The image of the olive tree is "to be taken seriously in the sense that the Church draws nourishment and strength from the root of Israel, and that the grafted branches would wither or even die if they were cut off from the root of Israel." The Church now asserts that "[a] replacement or supersession theology which sets against one another two separate entities, a Church of the Gentiles and the rejected Synagogue whose place it takes, is deprived of its foundations."[70] Therefore, "it should be evident for Christians that the covenant that God concluded with Israel has never been revoked but remains valid on the basis of God's unfailing faithfulness to his people." Moreover, "the Church without Israel would be in danger of losing its locus in the history of salvation."[71]

The recovery of the Church's Hebraic roots thus goes far beyond recognizing the permanent value of the Old Testament as "an indispensable part of Sacred Scripture" because the Old Covenant "has never been revoked" by God.[72] It is a bare minimum to acknowledge that "without the Old Testament, the New Testament would be an unintelligible book, a plant deprived of its roots and destined to dry up and wither."[73] Pope Benedict makes the same point in his 2010 apostolic exhortation *Verbum Domini*:

> Jesus of Nazareth was a Jew and the Holy Land is the motherland of the Church: the roots of Christianity are found in the Old Testament, and *Christianity continually draws nourishment from these roots*. Consequently, sound Christian doctrine has always resisted all new forms of Marcionism, which tend, in different ways, to set the Old Testament in opposition to the New.[74]

Going beyond this basic necessity of gaining a renewed appreciation for the Old Testament, Benedict reminds us that, "the Jewish understanding of the Bible can prove helpful to Christians for their own understanding and study

---

69. Second Vatican Council, *Nostra aetate* (October 28, 1965), pp. 253–260 in *The Sixteen Documents of Vatican II*, trans. National Catholic Welfare Council (Boston: St. Paul Editions, [1967?]), §4; cf. Rom 11:17–24; Jer 11:16; Ps 52:8.

70. Commission for Religious Relations with the Jews, "The Gifts and the Calling," §17.

71. Commission for Religious Relations with the Jews, "The Gifts and the Calling," §33.

72. Pope John Paul II, "Address to Representatives of the West German Jewish Community," (November 17, 1980); *CCC*, §121; Commission for Religious Relations with the Jews, "The Gifts and the Calling," §39.

73. Pontifical Biblical Commission, *The Jewish People*, §84; see also "The Gifts and the Calling," §28.

74. Pope Benedict XVI, *Verbum Domini* (Vatican City: Libreria Editrice Vaticana, 2010), §40; emphasis added. Cf. *CCC*, §123.

of the Scriptures."[75] In other words, the recovery of a genuine biblical world-view—in order to better understand the "Word made flesh"—not only requires giving the Hebrew Scriptures the attention they deserve; it also calls Christians to acquire a broader and deeper knowledge of our Hebraic and Jewish roots. Can we really know the Jesus who "was and always remained a Jew," without knowing much about the Torah he embraced, the Jewish festivals he celebrated, the prayers he prayed, and the language in which he studied, lived, and prayed?[76] Hebrew also helps us to understand our own Christian liturgy by giving us access to the rich blessings, Scriptures, and prayers of the synagogue which Jews have preserved with great devotion for thousands of years.

The Commission for Religious Relations with the Jews views it as "indispensable" that Christians become acquainted with Judaism as it developed over time:

> Christians need to refer to the Judaism of Jesus' time and to a degree also the Judaism that developed from it over the ages for their own self-understanding. Given Jesus' Jewish origins, coming to terms with Judaism in one way or another is indispensable for Christians.[77]

Even though there has been a substantial recovery of the Jewish roots of Christianity in the academic world in the past few decades—some even speak of a "genuine revolution in New Testament scholarship"[78]—encouraged by the popes and the Magisterium of the Church, we may ask whether this recovery has effectively made its way to the seminary classroom, to the pews, and to the average Catholic. Without questioning the positive values of our classical heritage, it is undeniable that Greek and Latin have so dominated the Western Christian tradition that the distancing of the Church from her Jewish, Hebrew, and Semitic roots has not been entirely overcome.

Pawlikowski thinks that the "re-Judaization of Christianity" as a whole is a vital necessity: "The restoration of Jesus and his teachings to a fully Jewish matrix by New Testament scholars will not reach its full potential within

---

75. Pope Benedict XVI, *Verbum Domini*, §41. See also Pontifical Biblical Commission, *The Jewish People*, §22: Christians can "learn much from Jewish exegesis practised for more than two thousand years." See also Commission for Religious Relations with the Jews, "Notes," 1985, I.2.

76. Commission for Religious Relations with the Jews, "Notes," III.1–9.

77. Commission for Religious Relations with the Jews, "The Gifts and the Calling," §14.

78. "We are witnessing a genuine revolution in New Testament scholarship, made possible in part by a much greater understanding of Hebrew and Aramaic and an enhanced reliance on Jewish materials from the Second Temple." Pawlikowski, "The Re-Judaization of Christianity," 67.

Christianity until this vision begins to penetrate other theological disciplines." For now, he believes that these disciplines are still marked by "a fairly widespread, though often subtle, theological anti-Judaism."[79] Thus, for Pawlikowski and Cardinal Martini,

> what is here at stake is not simply the more or less lively continuation of a dialogue. It is the awareness of Christians of their bond with Abraham's stock and of the consequences of this fact, not only for doctrine, discipline, liturgy and spiritual life of the Church, but also for its mission in the world of today.[80]

8. Resurrection of a Language and Nation

> Thus says the LORD: I will return to Zion, and will dwell in the midst of Jerusalem, and Jerusalem shall be called the faithful city. . . . Old men and old women shall again sit in the streets of Jerusalem. . . . And the streets of the city shall be full of boys and girls playing in its streets. . . . Behold, I will save my people from the east country and from the west country; and I will bring them to dwell in the midst of Jerusalem; and they shall be my people and I will be their God, in faithfulness and in righteousness. (Zech 8:3–8)

It is marvelous indeed that Hebrew is the only ancient language that has ever been revived as a modern spoken language—providing the only successful instance in human history of a complete linguistic revival. One hundred and fifty years ago, Hebrew was virtually a dead language, with not a single native Hebrew speaker in the world. Today, the ancient, sacred language of the Bible has come back to life as the living language of a modern nation, spoken by about 9 million people, including over 5 million native speakers.[81]

Although Hebrew continued to be spoken at the time of Jesus, co-existing with Aramaic as the vernacular language of Jews in the land of Israel,[82] it eventually fell into disuse as a spoken language near the end of the Roman period

---

79. Pawlikowski, "The Re-Judaization of Christianity," 68.

80. Martini, "The Relation of the Church to the Jewish People," *From the Martin Buber House* 6 (September 1984), 9, as quoted in Pawlikowski, "The Re-Judaization of Christianity," 60–61.

81. Jeff Kaufman, "The Revival of the Hebrew Language," December 25, 2005, www.jefftk .com/files/revival.pdf, p. 1.

82. "An impressive amount of extra-biblical evidence points to the use of Hebrew in first-century Israel: the testimony of the church fathers, the Dead Sea Scrolls, coins, and inscriptions from the first centuries B.C.-A.D., A.D., the writings of Josephus, and Rabbinic Literature." Bivin and Blizzard, *Understanding the Difficult Words of Jesus*, loc. 200.

(around 200 CE).[83] Hebrew survived as a liturgical and literary language and continued to be spoken by a few Jewish scholars throughout the Middle Ages. But for all intents and purposes, it was a "dead language," no longer spoken as a mother tongue by anyone.

This changed with the birth of the Zionist movement in the late nineteenth century. Centuries of anti-Semitism in Europe led to a renewal of Jewish nationalistic fervor and the increased desire to reestablish a Jewish homeland in Palestine. Among the early Jewish immigrants who settled in Ottoman Palestine was a young Lithuanian Jew by the name of Eliezer Ben-Yehuda (1858–1922). Influenced by nineteenth-century nationalist revivals in Europe, Ben-Yehuda became convinced that the Jews must return to their land and begin anew to speak their ancient language.[84] Helped by the local population and waves of young, idealistic Jewish immigrants who enthusiastically learned Hebrew and passed it on to their children, Ben-Yehuda's project miraculously succeeded:

> Within a biblical generation, in the forty years between 1881–1921, a core of young, fervent Hebrew-language speakers was formed, with Hebrew as the unique symbol of their linguistic nationalism. This fact was acknowledged by the British mandate authorities, who on November 29, 1922, recognized Hebrew as the official language of the Jews in Palestine. The Hebrew revival was now complete, and Ben-Yehuda's lifelong dream had been fulfilled.[85]

As remarkable as this is, the Hebrew language is not the only thing that has been resurrected, for along with it also came the "resurrection" of the nation of Israel. The return of the Jews to the land of Israel in the last century, together with the birth of the modern State of Israel, is in itself an extraordinary event. Until the reestablishment of Israel in 1948, it was unheard of in the annals of human history that a people scattered across the nations—often facing severe persecutions—would not only survive, resist assimilation and maintain their national and religious identity, but eventually return home and re-establish their nation in the land of their forefathers after two millennia of exile. Since the founding of the modern State of Israel, the question of Zionism with all of its theological and moral implications has been a hot topic among Christians, gathering as much ardent support as it has drawn vehement opposition. Nevertheless, it cannot be denied that one of the most repeated prophecies in the

---

83. Angel Sáenz-Badillos, *A History of the Hebrew Language*, trans. John Elwolde (New York: Cambridge University Press, 1996), 171.

84. Jack Fellman, "Eliezer Ben-Yehuda & the Revival of Hebrew," Jewish Virtual Library, www.jewishvirtuallibrary.org/jsource/biography/ben_yehuda.html.

85. Fellman, "Eliezer Ben-Yehuda & the Revival of Hebrew."

Hebrew Scriptures is the promise that God would eventually return His people to the land of Israel[86]—a promise that is never revoked in the New Testament.[87] Could the return of the Jews to the land of Israel in the past century have something to do with the fulfillment of God's ancient promises to His people? This is the question raised by many, including Fr. Raniero Cantalamessa:

> We know that God gave Israel the land but there is no mention of his taking it back again forever. Can we Christians exclude that what is happening in our day, that is, the return of Israel to the land of its fathers, is not connected in some way, still a mystery to us, to this providential order which concerns the chosen people and which is carried out even through human error and excess as happens in the Church itself? [...] The fact that Israel has remained an ethnic unity throughout the centuries and throughout many historical upheavals is, in itself, a sign of a destiny that has not been interrupted but is waiting to be fulfilled. Many peoples have been driven out of their land over the centuries, but not one of them has been able to remain intact as a people in their new situation.[88]

This is also the view of Christoph Cardinal Schönborn and, he claimed, Pope John Paul II:

> "Only once in human history did God take a country as an inheritance and give it to His chosen people," Schönborn said, adding that Pope John Paul II had himself declared the biblical commandment for Jews to live in Israel an everlasting covenant that remained valid today. Christians, Schönborn said, should rejoice in the return of Jews to the Holy Land as the fulfillment of biblical prophecy.[89]

---

86. Cf. Deut 30:1–6; Amos 9:14–15; Isa 11:10–12; 14:1; 43:5–6; 49:8–12; Zeph 3:16–20; Jer 3:16–18; 7:5–7; 16:14–16; 23:7–8; 31:10–11, 17, 35–37; 32:36–44; 33:6–9, 25–26; Ezek 11:16–20; 28:25–26; 36:8–12, 24–28; 37:1–14, 21–27; 39:25–28; Neh 1:8–9; Zech 2:9; 10:6–12.

87. On the contrary, Jesus asserts in the Gospel of Luke that "Jerusalem will be trampled by Gentiles until the times of the Gentiles are fulfilled" (Luke 21:24). These words seem to imply that Jerusalem will return under Jewish sovereignty after the "times of the Gentiles"—i.e., their dominion over the city—comes to an end.

88. Cantalamessa, "Christ, the Glory of Israel."

89. Sam Ser, "Papal Candidate Delivers Staunchly Pro-Zionist Speech," *Jerusalem Post* [Daily Edition], March 31, 2005. As Rabbi David Rosen reports, in an 1994 interview with Tad Szulc, published in *Parade* Magazine shortly after the establishment of relations between the Holy See and the State of Israel, the pontiff stated: "It must be understood that the Jews, who for two thousand years were dispersed among the nations of the world, had decided to return to the land of their ancestors. This is their right. . . . The act of establishing diplomatic relations with Israel is simply an international affirmation of this relationship." David Rosen, "Christian-Jewish Relations—The Legacy of Pope John Paul II," *Jewish-Christian Relations*, February 29, 2004, www.jcrelations.net/Christian-Jewish+Relations+%96+The+Legacy+of+Pope+-

If the modern restoration of Israel is indeed related to the fulfillment of God's promises and designs for His people, then learning Hebrew not only connects us with past salvation history; it also connects us with salvation history as it continues to unfold.

The student who decides to study Hebrew thus sets out to learn a remarkable language—not only that of divine revelation, but also the only ancient language that has ever been successfully "resurrected from the dead" in a "resurrected" nation. Even though the study of Biblical and Modern Hebrew are two distinct disciplines, they are close enough that by learning one, the student can quickly learn and understand the other with little effort. Studying the language of Moses, David, and Jesus, therefore, also gives the student access to centuries of Jewish religious tradition and to the rich world of modern Israeli literature, scholarship, arts, and culture.

9. Resurrection of the Jewish Church

> For I will take you from the nations, and gather you from all the countries, and bring you into your own land. . . . A new heart I will give you, and a new spirit I will put within you; and I will take out of your flesh the heart of stone and give you a heart of flesh. And I will put my spirit within you, and cause you to walk in my statutes and be careful to observe my ordinances. You shall dwell in the land which I gave to your fathers; and you shall be my people, and I will be your God. (Ezek 36:24–28)

The prophets often link the return of the people of Israel to their land with a spiritual resurrection. In the same passage that announces God's ingathering of Israel from the nations, Ezekiel speaks of a great spiritual purification by which the Lord will give His people a "new heart" and put His spirit within them (Ezek 36:22–36). Ezekiel's famous vision of the valley of dry bones makes the same point: the dry bones, which represent "the whole house of Israel" (Ezek 37:11) will come back to life in a two-staged process: first, the Lord will bring His people home into the land of Israel—illustrated by the sinews, flesh and skin covering the dry bones (Ezek 37:8, 12). Second, the people will experience a spiritual resurrection when God pours out His Spirit upon them—portrayed by the prophet breathing life back upon the slain bodies (Ezek 37: 9–10, 14).

The future spiritual resurrection of Israel is also an integral part of the

---

John+Paul+II.2815.0.html. See also John Tagliabue, "Pope Offers Conciliation to Jews and Christians," *The New York Times*, April 3, 1994, www.nytimes.com/1994/04/03/world/pope-offers-conciliation-to-jews-and-christians.html.

message of the New Testament. This belief is most clearly seen in Saint Paul's Epistle to the Romans, where the apostle expresses great hope that "all Israel will be saved" after "the full number of the Gentiles come in" (Rom 11:25–26). The Catholic Church has adopted this view as her own, believing and hoping in the eschatological salvation of Israel in the fullness of time, as expressed in the *Catechism of the Catholic Church*:

> The glorious Messiah's coming is suspended at every moment of history until his recognition by "all Israel," for "a hardening has come upon part of Israel" in their "unbelief" toward Jesus. . . . The "full inclusion" of the Jews in the Messiah's salvation, in the wake of "the full number of the Gentiles," will enable the People of God to achieve "the measure of the stature of the fullness of Christ," in which "God may be all in all."[90]

It is significant that in the midst of the great exodus from religious practice and identity in Gentile Christianity in the twentieth and twenty-first centuries, something else happened that bears momentous theological significance: the rebirth of the Church of the Circumcision. Since the 1967 Six Day War, tens of thousands of Jews across the globe have come to faith in Jesus of Nazareth, in what has become known as the Messianic Jewish movement. Messianic Jews believe that Jesus is the Messiah of Israel, but they wish to preserve their Jewish identity without becoming assimilated into a Christian denomination. Since 1967, Messianic Judaism has grown from a small, fringe group to a large movement with congregations in most countries of the world. It has become theologically significant enough to warrant the establishment of a Catholic-Messianic dialogue group in the year 2000 (even involving cardinals of the Church), which continues until today.[91] In addition, there is also a growing movement of "Hebrew Catholics." Although much smaller than the Messianic Jewish movement, Hebrew Catholics have had their own vicariate in Israel since the 1950s, the "Saint James Vicariate for Hebrew-Speaking Catholics in Israel,"[92] while in the U.S. and other English-speaking countries they are represented by groups such as the Association of Hebrew Catholics.[93]

The recent rise of the Messianic Jewish and Hebrew Catholic movements, following the extensive loss of faith in the Gentile Christian world, raises a pressing—though speculative—question: could the rebirth of the "Church of

---

90. *CCC*, §674.

91. On the Catholic-Messianic dialogue, see Mark S. Kinzer, *Searching Her Own Mystery: Nostra Aetate, the Jewish People, and the Identity of the Church* (Eugene, OR: Cascade, 2015).

92. Saint James Vicariate for Hebrew Speaking Catholics in Israel, catholic.co.il/.

93. Association of Hebrew Catholics, www.hebrewcatholic.net/.

the Circumcision" be a sign of the times? If so, it is worth taking notice, because Saint Paul emphasizes that the salvation of the Jewish people will have a revitalizing effect not only on the Church but also on the whole world: "For if their rejection means the reconciliation of the world, what will their acceptance mean but life from the dead?" (Rom 11:15).

Closely related to the growth of Messianic Judaism and Hebrew Catholicism is the growth of the "Jewish Roots" movement within Christianity. For centuries, a Christianity that appeared to be largely based on Greek and Latin thought, language and culture had little to commend itself to Jews, who perceived it as alien to their own religious and cultural heritage. As Christianity recovers its Hebrew roots and returns to more Semitic and Jewish forms of expression, more and more Jews are realizing that Christianity is in fact not a "Gentile religion" foreign to the spirit of Judaism, but in reality its true fulfillment. This underscores again the importance of having the priests and theologians of the Church formed in the Hebrew language and culture.

10. Will Catholics Join the Hebrew "Renaissance"?

"Fancy the priests of a religion unable to read their own sacred books!" There is a wayward Zeitgeist that is blinding its contemporaries to the plain logic of [this] statement – that is the only way to account for the amazing apathy towards Hebrew. Can one imagine a person who is going to devote his life to appreciating and helping others to appreciate French literature never bothering to learn French? How much less excusable is an ignorance of Hebrew on the part of those who believe the Old Testament to be part of God's vital message to man.[94]

Will Catholics join the renaissance of Hebrew roots that has been taking place across denominational lines in the last generation? This great wave of "Hebraiophilia" is not only a revitalizing influence on the Church, but also a crucial counterweight to the new rise of anti-Semitism that seems to be spreading again in the world. In addition, it is potentially of great significance for the New Evangelization, for the Christian *re*covery of Jesus/Yeshua as *Jewish* Messiah is turning out to be closely linked to the Jewish *dis*covery of the same Yeshua.

Yet it would appear that this Hebrew revival has only slowly trickled down to the Catholic pew. Although an increasing number of Catholics are interested in rediscovering their long-lost Hebrew roots, they often trail behind their evangelical peers in this respect. This is perhaps one of the reasons why the

94. Allen, "Why Not Learn Hebrew?," 2.

Messianic Jewish movement has been experiencing dynamic growth in the past generation, while the Hebrew-Catholic movement remains relatively small. If we are approaching the time in salvation history when the great falling away of the Gentile Church (Rom 11:21–22; 2 Thess 2:3) is to be followed by the "removing of the veil" and salvation of the Jewish people (Rom 11:23–26; 2 Cor 3:14–16), then the best way for the Church to prepare to welcome Jesus' own kin into the household of faith is to lead the way in the recovery of Christianity's Hebrew roots.

Does it make sense in the twenty-first century that Catholic priests who preach the Word of God every day are unable to access the Bible in its original language? Is it right that Protestant pastors sometimes study Hebrew for years while many Catholic priests are unable to read a single word in "God's tongue"? While some may feel hesitant to learn Biblical Hebrew for fear that it is too difficult, in reality the syntax and grammar of Hebrew are far less complex than the inflectional languages of Latin and Greek.[95] Leslie Allen makes a bold observation:

> One suspects that there tends to be a "Hebrew-phobia" abroad. An unfounded rumor that Hebrew is ten times as difficult as Chinese quickly gives rise to the rationalization that, of course, Hebrew is not indispensable and is in fact a luxury which the average theologian may forgo with little loss.[96]

Hebrew is neither excessively difficult, nor is it a dispensable luxury for any serious student of sacred Scripture—let alone for priests. Studying the sacred language of Hebrew follows from our conviction about the importance of the Word of God: It is a fundamental necessity in order to recover the fullness of God's "vital message to man."

Conclusion

The present paper has argued that it is time for Catholic seminaries and academic institutions to restore the Hebrew language to its rightful place in the study of sacred Scripture and sacred theology. As important as the language of Caesar, Augustine, and Aquinas may be, do Catholics not owe at least as much attention, veneration and love to the language of Moses, David, and Jesus?

The Church recommends the study of the Hebrew language, for it is the

---

95. Wilson, *Our Father Abraham*, 145.
96. Allen, "Why Not Learn Hebrew?," 2.

holy language that God spoke when He revealed Himself to the world. Hebrew is vital to bridge the historical, geographical, and cultural gap between the Bible's context and our own. It is an invaluable tool to understand not only the Old Testament but also the New. It is indispensable to understand the words of Jesus, who prayed, read, studied, and spoke in Hebrew. It can greatly enrich our own reading and praying of the Psalms. Hebrew is the essential foundation for the recovery of Christianity's Jewish roots and for overcoming the error of supersessionism and its tragic fruit of anti-Semitism. Moreover, Biblical Hebrew connects together the past, the present, and the future: it provides an excellent foundation for learning modern Hebrew, connecting the student with the remarkable "resurrection" of not only the language, but also the nation of Israel and the nascent Church of the Circumcision. Hebrew thus opens a new door to the mystery of God's ongoing providence for His ancient people and to the continual unfolding of salvation history, as well as paving the way for the future reconciliation of the Jewish people with their Messiah. Simply put: It makes sense to study Hebrew.

Contributors

KELLY ANDERSON, Saint Charles Borromeo Seminary, Wynnewood, PA

SCOTT CARL, Saint Paul Seminary School of Divinity, University of Saint Thomas, Saint Paul, MN

JAMES KEATING, Kenrick-Glennon Seminary, Saint Louis, MO

MICHAEL MAGEE, Saint Charles Borromeo Seminary, Wynnewood, PA

JUANA L. MANZO, Saint Mary's Seminary, University of Saint Thomas, Houston, TX

STEPHEN RYAN, OP, Dominican House of Studies, Washington, DC

STEVEN C. SMITH, Mundelein Seminary, University of Saint Mary of the Lake, Mundelein, IL

ANDRÉ VILLENEUVE, Azusa Pacific University, Azusa, CA

PETER S. WILLIAMSON, Sacred Heart Major Seminary, Detroit, MI

KEVIN ZILVERBERG, Saint Paul Seminary School of Divinity, University of Saint Thomas, Saint Paul, MN

Index of Names and Subjects

Index of Scripture References